the digital person

1 0 1 0 1 0 1 0 1 0 1 0 1 0 1
1 0 1 0 1 0 1 0 1 0 1 0 1
1 0 1 0 1 0 1 0 1 0 1
1 0 1 0 1 0 1 0 1
1 0 1 0 1 0 1
1 0 1
1

Ex Machina: Law, Technology, and Society
General Editors: Jack M. Balkin *and* Beth Simone Noveck

The Digital Person
Technology and Privacy in the Information Age
Daniel J. Solove

the digital person

Technology and Privacy in the Information Age

daniel j. solove

 NEW YORK UNIVERSITY PRESS   *New York and London*

new york university press
New York and London
www.nyupress.org

Library of Congress Cataloging-in-Publication Data
Solove, Daniel J., 1972–
The digital person :
technology and privacy in the information age / Daniel J. Solove.
p. cm.—(Ex machina)
Includes bibliographical references and index.
ISBN 0–8147–9846–2 (cloth : alk. paper)
1. Data protection—Law and legislation—United States.
2. Electronic records—Access control—United States.
3. Public records—Law and legislation—United States.
4. Government information—United States.
5. Privacy, Right of—United States. I. Title. II. Series.
KF1263.C65S668   2004
343.7308'58—dc22   2004010188

New York University Press books are printed on acid-free paper,
and their binding materials are chosen for strength and durability.

Manufactured in the United States of America

10 9 8 7 6 5 4

```
0
1 0
0 1 0
1 0 1 0
0 1 0 1 0
1 0 1 0 1 0
0 1 0 1 0 1 0
1 0 1 0 1 0
0 1 0 1 0
1 0 1 0
0 1 0
1 0
0
```

In loving memory of

my grandma,

Jean

Contents

iii government access

Acknowledgments

It is often said that books are written in solitude, but that wasn't true for this one. The ideas in this book were created in conversation with many wise friends and mentors. I owe them immense gratitude. Michael Sullivan has had an enormous influence on my thinking, and he has continually challenged me to strengthen my philosophical positions. Paul Schwartz has provided countless insights, and his work is foundational for the understanding of privacy law. Both Michael's and Paul's comments on the manuscript have been indispensable. I also must thank Judge Guido Calabresi, Naomi Lebowitz, Judge Stanley Sporkin, and Richard Weisberg, who have had a lasting impact on the way I think about law, literature, and life.

Charlie Sullivan deserves special thanks, although he disagrees with most of what I argue in this book. He has constantly forced me to better articulate and develop my positions. I may never convince him, but this book is much stronger for making the attempt.

So many other people are deserving of special mention, and if I were to thank them all to the extent they deserve, I would more than double the length of this book. Although I only list their names, my gratitude extends much further: Anita Allen, Jack Balkin, Carl Coleman, Howard Erichson, Timothy Glynn, Rachel Godsil, Eric Goldman, Chris Hoofnagle, Ted Janger, Jerry Kang, Orin Kerr, Raymond Ku, Erik Lillquist, Michael Risinger, Marc Rotenberg, Richard St. John, Chris Slobogin, Richard Sobel, Peter Swire, Elliot Turrini, and Benno Weisberg.

I greatly benefited from the comments I received when presenting my ideas, as well as portions of the manuscript, at conferences and symposia at Berkeley Law School, Cornell University, Emory Law School, Minnesota Law School, Seton Hall Law School, Stanford Law School, and Yale Law School.

My research assistants Peter Choy, Romana Kaleem, John Spaccarotella, and Eli Weiss provided excellent assistance throughout the writing of this book. Dean Pat Hobbs and Associate Dean Kathleen Boozang of Seton Hall Law School gave me generous support.

Don Gastwirth, my agent, shepherded me through the book publishing process with great enthusiasm and acumen. With unceasing attention, constant encouragement, and superb advice, he helped me find the perfect publisher. Deborah Gershenowitz at NYU Press believed in this project from the start and provided excellent editing.

Finally, I would like to thank my parents and grandparents. Their love, encouragement, and belief in me have made all the difference.

This book incorporates and builds upon some of my previously published work: *Privacy and Power: Computer Databases and Metaphors for Information Privacy,* 53 Stanford Law Review 1393 (2001); *Access and Aggregation: Privacy, Public Records, and the Constitution,* 86 Minnesota Law Review 1137 (2002); *Digital Dossiers and the Dissipation of Fourth Amendment Privacy,* 75 Southern California Law Review 1083 (2002); and *Identity Theft, Privacy, and the Architecture of Vulnerability,* 54 Hastings Law Journal 1227 (2003). These articles are really part of a larger argument, which I am delighted that I can now present in its entirety. The articles are thoroughly revised, and parts of different articles are now intermingled with each other. The argument can now fully unfold and develop. Privacy issues continue to change at a rapid pace, and even though these articles were written not too long ago, they were in need of updating. The arguments originally made in these articles have been strengthened by many subsequent discussions about the ideas I proposed. I have been forced to think about many issues more carefully and with more nuance. My understanding of privacy is a work in progress, and it has evolved since I began writing about it. This book merely represents another resting place, not the final word.

1 Introduction

We are in the midst of an information revolution, and we are only beginning to understand its implications. The past few decades have witnessed a dramatic transformation in the way we shop, bank, and go about our daily business—changes that have resulted in an unprecedented proliferation of records and data. Small details that were once captured in dim memories or fading scraps of paper are now preserved forever in the digital minds of computers, in vast databases with fertile fields of personal data. Our wallets are stuffed with ATM cards, calling cards, frequent shopper cards, and credit cards—all of which can be used to record where we are and what we do. Every day, rivulets of information stream into electric brains to be sifted, sorted, rearranged, and combined in hundreds of different ways. Digital technology enables the preservation of the minutia of our everyday comings and goings, of our likes and dislikes, of who we are and what we own. It is ever more possible to create an electronic collage that covers much of a person's life—a life captured in records, a digital person composed in the collective computer networks of the world.

We are currently confronting the rise of what I refer to as "digital dossiers." A dossier is a collection of detailed data about an individual. Dossiers are used in European courts to assemble information about a person in order to reach a judgment. Today, through the use of computers, dossiers are being constructed about all of us. Data is digitized into binary numerical form, which enables computers to store and manipulate it with unprecedented efficiency. There are hundreds of companies that are constructing gigantic databases of psychological profiles, amassing data about an individual's race, gender, income, hobbies, and purchases. Shards of data from our daily existence are now being assembled and analyzed—to investigate backgrounds, check credit, market products, and make a wide variety of decisions affecting our lives.

This book is about how we should understand and protect privacy in light of these profound technological developments. Our old conceptions of privacy are not up to the task. Much of the law pertaining to privacy is based on these conceptions, and as a result, it has failed to resolve the emerging privacy problems created by digital dossiers. This book aims to rethink longstanding notions of privacy to grapple with the consequences of living in an Information Age.

The Problems of Digital Dossiers

New Technologies and New Problems. In earlier times, communities were small and intimate. Personal information was preserved in the memories of friends, family, and neighbors, and it was spread by gossip and storytelling. Today, the predominant mode of spreading information is not through the flutter of gossiping tongues but through the language of electricity, where information pulses between massive record systems and databases. On the upside, this development means that individuals can more readily escape from the curious eyes of the community, freeing themselves from stifling social norms inhibiting individuality and creativity. On the downside, an ever-growing series of records is created about almost every facet of a person's life. As businesses and the government increasingly share personal information, digital dossiers about nearly every individual are being assembled. This raises serious concerns. The information gathered about us has become quite extensive, and it is being used in ways that profoundly affect our lives. Yet, we know little about how our personal information is being used, and we lack the power to do much about it.

Digital dossiers are constructed and used through three types of "information flow."[1] Information flow is a way of describing the movement of data. Like water in an elaborate system of plumbing, data flows through information pipelines linking various businesses, organizations, and government entities. First, information often flows between large computer databases of private-sector companies. Second, data flows from government public record systems to a variety of businesses in the private sector. Indeed, many companies construct their databases by culling personal data from public records. Third, information flows from the private sector to government agencies and law enforcement officials. The increase in digital dossiers has thus resulted in an elaborate lattice of information networking, where information is being stored, analyzed, and used in ways that have profound implications for society.

Even if we're not aware of it, the use of digital dossiers is shaping our lives. Companies use digital dossiers to determine how they do business with us; financial institutions use them to determine whether to give us credit; employers turn to them to examine our backgrounds when hiring; law enforcement officials draw on them to investigate us; and identity thieves tap into them to commit fraud.

Computer Databases. Computers and cyberspace have vastly increased our ability to collect, store, and analyze information. Today, it seems as if everyone is collecting information—the media, employers, businesses, and government. Countless companies maintain computerized records of their customers' preferences, purchases, and activities. There are hundreds of records detailing an individual's consumption. Credit card companies maintain information about one's credit card purchases. Video stores keep records about one's video rentals. Online retailers, such as Amazon.com, preserve records of all the books and other items a person buys. And there are hundreds of companies people aren't even aware of that maintain their personal information. For example, Wiland Services maintains a database of about 1,000 different points of information on over 215 million individuals.[2] Acxiom.com collects and sells data on consumers to marketers. In its InfoBase, it provides "[o]ver 50 demographic variables . . . including age, income, real property data, children's data, and others." It also contains data on education levels, occupation, height, weight, political affiliation, ethnicity, race, hobbies, and net worth.[3]

Computers enable marketers to collect detailed dossiers of personal information and to analyze it to predict the consumer's behavior. Through various analytic techniques, marketers construct models of what products particular customers will desire and how to encourage customers to consume. Companies know how we spend our money, what we do for a living, how much we earn, and where we live. They know about our ethnic backgrounds, religion, political views, and health problems. Not only do companies know what we have already purchased, but they also have a good idea about what books we will soon buy or what movies we will want to see.

Public Records. Imagine that the government had the power to compel individuals to reveal a vast amount of personal information about themselves—where they live; their phone numbers; their physical description; their photograph; their age; their medical problems; all of their legal transgressions throughout their lifetimes; the names of their parents, children, and spouses; their political party affiliations; where they work and what they do; the property that they own and its value; and sometimes even their psychotherapists' notes, doctors' records, and financial information.

Then imagine that the government routinely poured this information into the public domain—by posting it on the Internet where it could be accessed from all over the world, by giving it away to any individual or company that asked for it, or even by providing entire databases of personal information upon request. Think about how this information would be available to those who make important decisions about an individual's life and career—such as whether the individual will get a loan or a job. Also consider that, in many cases, the individual would not even know that the information is being used to make these decisions.

Imagine as well that this information would be traded among hundreds of private-sector companies that would combine it with a host of other information such as one's hobbies, purchases, magazines, organizations, credit history, and so on. This expanded profile would then be sold back to the government in order to investigate and monitor individuals more efficiently.

Stop imagining. What I described is a growing reality in the United States, and the threat posed to privacy is rapidly becoming worse. Federal, state, and local governments maintain public records spanning an individual's life from birth to death. These records contain a myriad of personal details. Until recently, public records were difficult to access—finding information about a person often involved a scavenger hunt through local offices to dig up records. But with the Internet, public records are increasingly being posted online, where anybody anywhere can easily obtain and search them.

Government Access. The data in digital dossiers increasingly flows from the private sector to the government, particularly for law enforcement use. Law enforcement agencies have long sought personal information about individuals from various companies and financial institutions to investigate fraud, white-collar crime, drug trafficking, computer crime, child pornography, and other types of criminal activity. In the aftermath of the terrorist attacks of September 11, 2001, the impetus for the government to gather personal information has greatly increased, since this data can be useful to track down terrorists and to profile airline passengers for more thorough searches. Detailed records of an individual's reading materials, purchases, diseases, and website activity enable the government to assemble a profile of an individual's finances, health, psychology, beliefs, politics, interests, and lifestyle. Many people communicate over the Internet using a screen name or pseudonym; the data in digital dossiers can unveil their identities as well as expose all of the people with whom they associate and do business.

The government has recently been exploring ways to develop technology to detect patterns of behavior based on our dossiers. In 2002, it was revealed that the Department of Defense was developing a program called Total Information Awareness (since renamed Terrorism Information Awareness). The program begins with the government amassing personal information from private-sector sources into a massive database of dossiers on individuals. Profiling technology is then used to detect those who are likely to be engaged in criminal activity. When Congress learned of Total Information Awareness, it halted the program because of its threat to privacy. However, the same type of collection and use of data envisioned by those who dreamed up Total Information Awareness is already being carried out by the government. The digital dossiers that continue to grow in the private sector and in public records are now becoming a tool for the government to monitor and investigate people.

What Is the Problem? The growing collection and use of personal information in digital form has long been viewed as problematic—a fear typically raised under the banner of "privacy." The use of personal information certainly presents privacy problems, but what exactly is the nature of these problems? Although the problems of personal information are understood as concerns over privacy, beyond this, they are often not well defined. How much weight should our vague apprehensions be given, especially considering the tremendous utility, profit, and efficiency of using personal information?

The answer to this question depends upon how these privacy problems are conceptualized. Unfortunately, so far, the problems have not been adequately articulated. Many discussions of privacy merely scratch the surface by simply pointing out a series of technological developments with the assumption that people will react with anxiety. Rarely do discussions about privacy delve deeper. We need a better understanding of the problems; we must learn how they developed, how they are connected, what precisely they threaten, and how they can be solved.

This book aims to reconceptualize privacy in today's world of rapidly changing technology. The task of conceptualizing the privacy problems digital dossiers create is of the utmost importance. As John Dewey aptly wrote, "a problem well put is half-solved."⁴ We can't really solve a problem until we know the harm that it causes. A good diagnosis of a problem goes a long way toward finding solutions to it.

The goal of this book extends beyond articulating a new understanding of contemporary privacy problems; the book also aims to demonstrate the ways that the problems can be solved. In particular, this is a book about the law. A relatively robust amount of law has developed to protect privacy, but it has often failed to be effective when confronted by the problems of the Information Age. This book discusses why this has happened and what can be done about it.

Traditional Conceptions of Privacy

Traditionally, privacy violations have been understood in a particular manner. In this book, I contend that these ways of understanding privacy must be rethought in order to fully comprehend the problems with digital dossiers. This doesn't mean that these understandings are incorrect. They arose with earlier privacy problems and can certainly be of help in understanding digital dossiers. But these more traditional ways of understanding privacy don't account for key aspects of the unique problems the digital age has introduced.

Orwell's Big Brother. The dominant metaphor for modern invasions of privacy is Big Brother, the ruthless totalitarian government in George Orwell's novel *1984*. Big Brother oppresses its citizens, purges dissenters, and spies on everyone in their homes. The result is a cold, drab, grey world with hardly any space for love, joy, original thinking, spontaneity, or creativity. It is a society under total control. Although the metaphor has proven quite useful for a number of privacy problems, it only partially captures the problems of digital dossiers. Big Brother envisions a centralized authoritarian power that aims for absolute control, but the digital dossiers constructed by businesses aren't controlled by a central power, and their goal is not to oppress us but to get us to buy new products and services. Even our government is a far cry from Big Brother, for most government officials don't act out of malicious intent or a desire for domination. Moreover, Big Brother achieves its control by brutally punishing people for disobedience and making people fear they are constantly being watched. But businesses don't punish us so long as we keep on buying, and they don't make us feel as though we are being watched. To the contrary, they try to gather information as inconspicuously as possible. Making us feel threatened would undermine rather than advance the goal of unencumbered information collection. Finally, while Big Brother aims to control the most intimate details of a citizen's life, much of the information in digital dossiers is not intimate or unusual.

The Secrecy Paradigm. In another traditional way of understanding privacy that I refer to as the "secrecy paradigm," privacy is invaded by uncovering one's hidden world, by surveillance, and by the disclosure of concealed information. The harm such invasions cause consists of inhibition, self-censorship, embarrassment, and damage to one's reputation. The law is heavily influenced by this paradigm. As a result, if the information isn't secret, then courts often conclude that the information can't be private. However, this conception of privacy is not responsive to life in the modern Information Age, where most personal information exists in the record systems of hundreds of entities. Life today is fueled by information, and it is virtually impossible to live as an Information Age ghost, leaving no trail or residue.

The Invasion Conception. Under the traditional view, privacy is violated by the invasive actions of particular wrongdoers who cause direct injury to victims. Victims experience embarrassment, mental distress, or harm to their reputations. The law responds when a person's deepest secrets are exposed, reputation is tarnished, or home is invaded. This view, which I call the "invasion conception," understands privacy to be a kind of invasion, in which somebody invades and somebody is invaded. However, digital dossiers often do not result in any overt invasion. People frequently don't experience any direct injury when data about them is aggregated or transferred from one company to another. Moreover, many of the problems of digital dossiers emerge from the collaboration of a multitude of different actors with different purposes. Each step along the way is relatively small and innocuous, failing to cause harm that the invasion conception would recognize as substantial.

Rethinking Privacy

Digital dossiers pose significant problems, and for a more complete understanding of these issues, I turn to another metaphor—Franz Kafka's depiction of bureaucracy in *The Trial.* Kafka's novel chronicles the surreal nightmare of a person who is unexpectedly informed that he is under arrest but given no reason why. A bureaucratic court maintains a dossier about him, but he has no access to this information. Throughout the rest of the novel, the protagonist desperately attempts to find out why the Court is interested in his life, but his quest is hopeless—the Court is too clandestine and labyrinthine to be fully understood.

The Trial captures an individual's sense of helplessness, frustration, and vulnerability when a large bureaucratic organization has control over a vast dossier of details about one's life. Bureaucracy often results in a routinized and sometimes careless way of handling information—with little to no accountability. This makes people vulnerable to identity theft, stalking, and other harms. The problem is not simply a loss of control over personal information, nor is there a diabolical motive or plan for domination as with Big Brother. The problem is a bureaucratic process that is uncontrolled. These bureaucratic ways of using our information have palpable effects on our lives because people use our dossiers to make important decisions about us to which we are not always privy.

Thus far, the existing law protecting information privacy has not adequately responded to the emergence of digital dossiers. We need to better articulate what the problems are, what is at stake, and what precisely the law must do to solve the problems. We must rethink privacy for the Information Age.

A Roadmap for This Book

In part I, I explore the digital dossiers about individuals that are being assembled through computer databases and the Internet. I focus primarily on the activities of businesses. Chapter 2 traces the history of the developing privacy problems precipitated by computer databases and cyberspace. In chapter 3, I examine the prevailing ways that these privacy problems have been conceptualized. I discuss the predominance of the Orwell metaphor and why it must be supplemented with the Kafka metaphor. Chapter 4 discusses why the law of information privacy has failed to grapple adequately with the problem of digital dossiers. Chapter 5 responds to those who argue that the market (alone or with some minor tinkering) can appropriately deal with the problem. In chapter 6, I argue that beyond a set of individual rights, protecting privacy requires an architecture that regulates the way information may be collected and used. Consequently, protecting privacy must focus not merely on remedies and penalties for aggrieved individuals but on shaping an architecture to govern the ever-increasing data flows of the Information Age.

Part II turns to the way in which public records contribute to the problems of digital dossiers. Chapter 7 describes the increasing accumulation of personal information in public record systems and the emerging threats to privacy posed by the increased accessibility of this information as records are made available on the Internet. In chapter 8, I argue that the regulation of public records in the United States must be rethought in light of the new technologies in the Information Age, and I advance a theory about how to reconcile the tension between transparency and privacy. I also explore why regulating the access and use of public records will not infringe upon First Amendment rights.

Part III examines the problems created by the increasing government access to digital dossiers. In chapter 9, I explore in detail the numerous ways that the government is accessing personal information held by private-sector businesses and why this is problematic. Chapter 10 discusses how the Supreme Court has improperly interpreted the Fourth Amendment so that it doesn't apply to records maintained by third parties, a result that virtually prevents the Fourth Amendment from dealing with the problem of government access to digital dossiers. In the void left by the inapplicability of the Fourth Amendment, Congress has enacted a series of statutes to address the problem. As I explain, however, the statutes create a regulatory regime that is uneven, overly complex, and filled with gaps and loopholes. In chapter 11, I explore how the law should appropriately regulate government access to personal information maintained by the private sector.

i computer databases

0
1 0
0 1 0
1 0 1 0
0 1 0 1 0
1 0 1 0 1 0
0 1 0 1 0 1 0
1 0 1 0 1 0
0 1 0 1 0
1 0 1 0
0 1 0
1 0
0

2 The Rise of the Digital Dossier

We currently live in a world where extensive dossiers exist about each one of us. These dossiers are in digital format, stored in massive computer databases by a host of government agencies and private-sector companies. The problems caused by these developments are profound. But to understand the problems, we must first understand how they arose.

A History of Public-Sector Databases

Although personal records have been kept for centuries,[1] only in contemporary times has the practice become a serious concern. Prior to the nineteenth century, few public records were collected, and most of them were kept at a very local level, often by institutions associated with churches.[2] The federal government's early endeavors at collecting data consisted mainly in conducting the census. The first census in 1790 asked only four questions.[3] With each proceeding census, the government gathered more personal information. By 1860, 142 questions were asked.[4] When the 1890 census included questions about diseases, disabilities, and finances, it sparked a public outcry, ultimately leading to the passage in the early twentieth century of stricter laws protecting the confidentiality of census data.[5]

Government information collection flourished during the middle of the twentieth century. The creation and growth of government bureaucracy—spawning well over 100 federal agencies within the past century—led to an insatiable thirst for information about individuals. One such agency was the Social Security Administration, created in 1935, which assigned nine-digit numbers to each citizen and required extensive record-keeping of people's earnings.

Technology was a primary factor in the rise of information collection. The 1880 census required almost 1,500 clerks to tally information tediously by hand—and it took seven years to complete.[6] At the rapid rate of population growth, if a faster way could not be found to tabulate the information, the 1890 census wouldn't be completed before the 1900 census began. Fortunately, just in time for the 1890 census, a census official named Herman Hollerith developed an innovative tabulating device—a machine that read holes punched in cards.[7] Hollerith's new machine helped tabulate the 1890 census in under three years.[8] Hollerith left the Census Bureau and founded a small firm that produced punch card machines—a firm that through a series of mergers eventually formed the company that became IBM.[9]

IBM's subsequent rise to prosperity was due, in significant part, to the government's increasing need for data. The Social Security System and other New Deal programs required a vast increase in records that had to be kept about individuals. As a result, the government became one of the largest purchasers of IBM's punch card machines.[10] The Social Security Administration kept most of its records on punch cards, and by 1943 it had more than 100 million cards in storage.[11]

The advent of the mainframe computer in 1946 revolutionized information collection. The computer and magnetic tape enabled the systematic storage of data. As processing speeds accelerated and as memory ballooned, computers provided a vastly increased ability to collect, search, analyze, and transfer records.

Federal and state agencies began to computerize their records. The Census Bureau was one of the earliest purchasers of commercially available computers.[12] Social Security numbers (SSNs)—originally not to be used as identifiers beyond the Social Security System—became immensely useful for computer databases.[13] This is because SSNs enable data to be easily linked to particular individuals. In the 1970s, federal, state, and local governments—as well as the private sector—increasingly began to use them for identification.[14]

Beginning in the 1960s, the growing computerization of records generated a substantial buzz about privacy. Privacy captured the attention of the public, and a number of philosophers, legal scholars, and other commentators turned their attention to the threats to privacy caused by the rise of the computer.[15] Congress began to debate how to respond to these emerging developments.[16] In 1973, the U.S. Department of Health, Education, and Welfare (HEW) issued a report entitled *Records, Computers, and the Rights of Citizens*, which trenchantly articulated the growing concerns over computerized record systems:

> There was a time when information about an individual tended to be elicited in face-to-face contacts involving personal trust and a certain symmetry, or balance, between giver and receiver. Nowadays, an individual must increasingly give information about himself to large and relatively faceless institutions, for handling and use by strangers—unknown, unseen, and, all too frequently, unresponsive. Sometimes the individual does not even know that an organization maintains a record about him. Often he may not see it, much less contest its accuracy, control its dissemination, or challenge its use by others.[17]

These problems continued to escalate throughout the ensuing decades. Computers grew vastly more powerful, and computerized records became ubiquitous. The rise of the Internet in the 1990s added new dimensions to these problems, sparking a revolution in the collection, accessibility, and communication of personal data.

Today, federal agencies and departments maintain almost 2,000 databases,[18] including records pertaining to immigration, bankruptcy, licensing, welfare, and countless other matters. In a recent effort to track down parents who fail to pay child support, the federal government has created a vast database consisting of information about all people who obtain a new job anywhere in the nation. The database contains their SSNs, addresses, and wages.[19]

States maintain public records of arrests, births, criminal proceedings, marriages, divorces, property ownership, voter registration, workers' compensation, and scores of other types of records. State licensing regimes mandate that records be kept on numerous professionals such as doctors, lawyers, engineers, insurance agents, nurses, police, accountants, and teachers.

A History of Private-Sector Databases

Although the government played an integral role in the development of massive dossiers of personal information, especially early on, businesses soon began to play an even greater role. While the public-sector story concerns the quest for regulatory efficiency, the private-sector story involves money and marketing.

Long before the rise of nationwide advertising campaigns there was a personal relationship between merchant and customer. Local merchants lived next door to their customers and learned about their lives from their existence together in the community. To a large extent, marketing was done locally—by the peddler on the street or the shopkeeper on the corner. Mass marketing, which began in the nineteenth century and flourished in the twentieth century, transformed the nature of selling from personal one-to-one persuasion to large-scale advertising campaigns designed for the nameless, faceless American consumer.

Mass marketing consumed vast fortunes, and only a small fraction of the millions of people exposed to the ads would buy the products or services. Soon marketers discovered the power of a new form of marketing—targeted marketing. The idea was to figure out which people were most likely to consume a product and focus the advertising on them.

In the 1920s, the sales department of General Motors Corporation began an early experiment with targeted marketing. GM discovered that owners of Ford vehicles frequently didn't purchase a Ford as their next vehicle—so it targeted owners of two-year-old Fords and sent them a brochure on GM vehicles.[20] GM then began to send out questionnaires asking for consumer input into their products. GM believed that this would be a good marketing device, presenting the image of a big corporation that cared enough to listen to the opinions of everyday people. GM cast itself as a democratic institution, its surveys stating that it was "OF THE PEOPLE, FOR THE PEOPLE, BY THE PEOPLE." One GM print advertisement depicted a delighted child holding up the survey letter exclaiming: "Look dad, a letter from General Motors!" The campaign was quite successful—ironically not because of the data collected but because of GM's image of appearing to be interested in the consumer's ideas.[21]

Today, corporations are desperate for whatever consumer information they can glean, and their quest for information is hardly perceived as democratic. The data collected extends beyond information about consumers' views of the product to information about the consumers themselves, often including lifestyle details and even a full-scale psychological profile.

The turn to targeting was spurred by the proliferation and specialization of mass media throughout the century, enabling marketers to tap into groups of consumers with similar interests and tastes. The most basic form of targeting involved selecting particular television programs, radio shows, or magazines in which to place advertisements. This technique, however, merely amounted to mass marketing on a slightly smaller scale.

The most revolutionary developments in targeted marketing occurred in the direct marketing industry. The practice of sending mail order catalogs directly to consumers began in the late nineteenth century when railroads extended the reach of the mail system.[22] The industry also reached out to people by way of door-to-door salespersons. In the 1970s, marketers began calling people directly on the telephone, and "telemarketing" was born.

Direct marketing remained a fledgling practice for most of the twentieth century. Direct marketers had long accepted the "2 percent" rule—only 2 percent of those contacted would respond.[23] With such a staggering failure rate, direct marketing achieved its successes at great cost. To increase the low response rate, marketers sought to sharpen their targeting techniques, which required more consumer research and an effective way to collect, store, and analyze information about consumers. The advent of the computer database gave marketers this long sought-after ability—and it launched a revolution in targeting technology.

Databases provided an efficient way to store and search for data. Organized into fields of information, the database enabled marketers to sort by various types of information and to rank or select various groups of individuals from its master list of customers—a practice called "modeling." Through this process, fewer mailings or calls needed to be made, resulting in a higher response rate and lower costs. In addition to isolating a company's most profitable customers, marketers studied them, profiled them, and then used that profile to find similar customers.[24] This, of course, required not only information about existing customers, but the collection of data about prospective customers as well.

Originally, marketers sought to locate the best customers by identifying those customers who purchased items most recently and frequently and who spent the most money.[25] In the 1970s, marketers turned to demographic information.[26] Demographics included basic information such as age, income level, race, ethnicity, gender, and geographical location. Marketers could target certain demographic segments of the nation, a practice called "cluster marketing." This approach worked because people with similar incomes and races generally lived together in clusters.

The private sector obtained this demographic information from the federal government. In the 1970s, the United States began selling its census data on magnetic tapes. To protect privacy, the Census Bureau sold the information in clusters of 1,500 households, supplying only addresses—not names. But clever marketing companies such as Donnelley, Metromail, and R. L. Polk reattached the names by matching the addresses with information in telephone books and voter registration lists. Within five years of purchasing the census data, these companies had constructed demographically segmented databases of over half of the households in the nation.[27]

In the 1980s, marketers looked to supplement their data about consumers by compiling "psychographic" information—data about psychological characteristics such as opinions, attitudes, beliefs, and lifestyles.[28] For example, one company established an elaborate taxonomy of people, with category names such as "Blue Blood Estates," "Bohemian Mix," "Young Literati," "Shotguns and Pickups," and "Hispanic Mix."[29] Each cluster had a description of the type of person, their likes, incomes, race and ethnicity, attitudes, and hobbies.[30]

These innovations made targeted marketing—or "database marketing" as it is often referred to today—the hottest form of marketing, growing at twice the rate of America's gross national product.[31] In 2001, direct marketing resulted in almost $2 trillion in sales.[32] On average, over 500 pieces of unsolicited advertisements, catalogs, and marketing mailings arrive every year at each household.[33] Due to targeting, direct mail yields $10 in sales for every $1 in cost—a ratio double that for a television advertisement—and forecasters predict catalog sales will grow faster than retail sales.[34] Telemarketing is a $662 billion a year industry.[35] In a 1996 Gallup poll, 77 percent of U.S. companies used some form of direct mail, targeted email, or telemarketing.[36]

The effectiveness of targeted marketing depends upon data, and the challenge is to obtain as much of it as possible. Marketers discovered that they didn't have to research and collect all the information from scratch, for data is the perspiration of the Information Age. Billions of bytes are released each second as we click, charge, and call. A treasure trove of information already lay untapped within existing databases, retail records, mailing lists, and government records. All that marketers had to do was plunder it as efficiently as possible.

The increasing thirst for personal information spawned the creation of a new industry: the database industry, an Information Age bazaar where personal data collections are bartered and sold. Marketers "rent" lists of names and personal information from database companies, which charge a few cents to a dollar for each name.[37] Over 550 companies compose the personal information industry, with annual revenues in the billions of dollars.[38] The sale of mailing lists alone (not including the sales generated by the use of the lists) generates $3 billion a year.[39] The average consumer is on around 100 mailing lists and is included in at least 50 databases.[40]

An increasing number of companies with databases—magazines, credit card companies, stores, mail order catalog firms, and even telephone companies—are realizing that their databases are becoming one of their most valuable assets and are beginning to sell their data.

A new breed of company is emerging that devotes its primary business to the collection of personal information. Based in Florida, Catalina Marketing Corporation maintains supermarket buying history databases on 30 million households from more than 5,000 stores.[41] This data contains a complete inventory of one's groceries, over-the-counter medications, hygiene supplies, and contraceptive devices, among others. Aristotle, Inc. markets a database of 150 million registered voters. Aristotle's database records voters' names, addresses, phone numbers, party affiliation, and voting frequency. Aristotle combines this data with about 25 other categories of information, such as one's race, income, and employer—even the make and model of one's car. It markets a list of wealthy campaign donors called "Fat Cat." Aristotle boasts: "Hit your opponent in the Wallet! Using Fat Cats, you can ferret out your adversary's contributors and slam them with a mail piece explaining why they shouldn't donate money to the other side."[42] Another company manufactures software called GeoVoter, which combines about 5,000 categories of information about a voter to calculate how that individual will vote.[43]

The most powerful database builders construct information empires, sometimes with information on more than half of the American population. For example, Donnelley Marketing Information Services of New Jersey keeps track of 125 million people. Wiland Services has constructed a database containing over 1,000 elements, from demographic information to behavioral data, on over 215 million people. There are around five database compilers that have data on almost all households in the United States.[44]

Beyond marketers, hundreds of companies keep data about us in their record systems. The complete benefits of the Information Age do not simply come to us—we must "plug in" to join in. In other words, we must establish relationships with Internet Service Providers, cable companies, phone companies, insurance companies, and so on. All of these companies maintain records about us. The Medical Information Bureau, a nonprofit institution, maintains a database of medical information on 15 million individuals, which is available to over 700 insurance companies.[45] Credit card companies have also developed extensive personal information databases. Unlike cash, which often does not involve the creation of personally identifiable records, credit cards result in detailed electronic documentation of our purchases.[46]

Increasingly, we rely on various records and documents to assess financial reputation.[47] According to sociologist Steven Nock, this enables reputations to become portable.[48] In earlier times, a person's financial condition was generally known throughout the community. In modern society, however, people are highly mobile and creditors often lack first-hand experience of the financial condition and trustworthiness of individuals. Therefore, creditors rely upon credit reporting agencies to obtain information about a person's credit history. Credit reports reveal a person's consistency in paying back debts as well as the person's loan defaulting risk. People are assigned a credit score, which impacts whether they will be extended credit, and, if so, what rate of interest will be charged. Credit reports contain a detailed financial history, financial account information, outstanding debts, bankruptcy filings, judgments, liens, and mortgage foreclosures. Today, there are three major credit reporting agencies— Equifax, Experian, and Trans Union. Each agency has compiled extensive dossiers about almost every adult U.S. citizen.[49] Credit reports have become essential to securing a loan, obtaining a job, purchasing a home or a car, applying for a license, or even renting an apartment. Credit reporting agencies also prepare investigative consumer reports, which supplement the credit report with information about an individual's character and lifestyle.[50]

Launched in 2002, Regulatory DataCorp (RDC) has created a massive database to investigate people opening new bank accounts. RDC was created by many of the world's largest financial companies. Its database, named the Global Regulatory Information Database (GRID), gathers information from over 20,000 different sources around the world.[51] RDC's purpose is to help financial companies conduct background checks of potential customers for fraud, money laundering, terrorism, and other criminal activity. Although some people's information in the database may be incorrect, they lack the ability to correct the errors. RDC's CEO and president responds: "There are no guarantees. Is the public information wrong? We don't have enough information to say it's wrong."[52]

Cyberspace and Personal Information

Cyberspace is the new frontier for gathering personal information, and its power has only begun to be exploited. The Internet is rapidly becoming the hub of the personal information market, for it has made the peddling and purchasing of data much easier. Focus USA's website boasts that it has detailed information on 203 million people.[53] Among its over 100 targeted mailing lists are lists of "Affluent Hispanics," "Big-Spending Parents," "First Time Credit Card Holders," "Grown But Still At Home," "Hi-Tech Seniors," "New Homeowners," "Status Spenders," "Big Spending Vitamin Shoppers," and "Waist Watchers."[54] For example, Focus USA states for its list of "New Movers":

> As much as 20% of the population moves every year. . . . New movers have a lot of needs in their first few months. . . . During this lifestyle change period, new movers tend to be more receptive to direct mail and telemarketing offers for a wide variety of products.

The database contains data about age, gender, income, children, Internet connections, and more. There is a list devoted exclusively to "New Movers With Children," which includes data on the ages of the children. A list called "Savvy Single Women" states that "[s]ingle women represent a prime market for travel/vacation, frequent flyer clubs, credit cards, investing, dining out, entertainment, insurance, catalog shopping, and much more."

There's also a list of "Mr. Twenty Somethings" that contains mostly college-educated men who Focus USA believes are eager to spend money on electronic equipment. And there are lists of pet lovers, fitness-conscious people, cat and dog owners, motorcycle enthusiasts, casino gamblers, opportunity seekers, and sub-prime prospects.[55] Dunhill International also markets a variety of lists, including "America's Wealthiest Families," which includes 9.6 million records "appended with demographic and psychographic data."[56] There are also databases of disabled people, consumers who recently applied for a credit card, cruise ship passengers, teachers, and couples who just had a baby. Hippo Direct markets lists of people suffering from "medical maladies" such as constipation, cancer, diabetes, heart disease, impotence, migraines, enlarged prostate, and more.[57] Another company markets a list of 5 million elderly incontinent women.[58] In addition to serving as a marketplace for personal information, cyberspace has provided a revolution for the targeted marketing industry because web pages are not static—they are generated every time the user clicks. Each page contains spaces reserved for advertisements, and specific advertisements are downloaded into those spots. The dynamic nature of web pages makes it possible for a page to download different advertisements for different users.

Targeting is very important for web advertising because a web page is cluttered with information and images all vying for the users' attention. Similar to the response rates of earlier efforts at direct marketing, only a small percentage of viewers (about 2 percent) click the advertisements they view.[59] The Internet's greater targeting potential and the fierce competition for the consumer's attention have given companies an unquenchable thirst for information about web users. This information is useful in developing more targeted advertising as well as in enabling companies to better assess the performance and popularity of various parts of their websites.

Currently, there are two basic ways that websites collect personal information. First, many websites directly solicit data from their users. Numerous websites require users to register and log in, and registration often involves answering a questionnaire. Online merchants amass data from their business transactions with consumers. For example, I shop on Amazon.com, which keeps track of my purchases in books, videos, music, and other items. I can view its records of every item I've ever ordered, and this goes back well over six years. When I click on this option, I get an alphabetized list of everything I bought and the date I bought it. Amazon.com uses its extensive records to recommend new books and videos. With a click, I can see dozens of books that Amazon.com thinks I'll be interested in. It is eerily good, and it can pick out books for me better than my relatives can. It has me pegged.

Websites can also secretly track a customer's websurfing. When a person explores a website, the website can record data about her ISP, computer hardware and software, the website she linked from, and exactly what parts of the website she explored and for how long. This information is referred to as "clickstream data" because it is a trail of how a user navigates throughout the web by clicking on various links. It enables the website to calculate how many times it has been visited and what parts are most popular. With a way to connect this information to particular web users, marketers can open a window into people's minds. This is a unique vision, for while marketers can measure the size of audiences for other media such as television, radio, books, and magazines, they have little ability to measure attention span. Due to the interactive nature of the Internet, marketers can learn how we respond to what we hear and see. A website collects information about the way a user interacts with the site and stores the information in its database. This information will enable the website to learn about the interests of a user so it can better target advertisements to the user. For example, Amazon.com can keep track of every book or item that a customer browses but does not purchase.

To connect this information with particular users, a company can either require a user to log in or it can secretly tag a user to recognize her when she returns. This latter form of identification occurs through what is called a "cookie." A cookie is a small text file of codes that is deployed into the user's computer when she downloads a web page.[60] Websites place a unique identification code into the cookie, and the cookie is saved on the user's hard drive. When the user visits the site again, the site looks for its cookie, recognizes the user, and locates the information it collected about the user's previous surfing activity in its database. Basically, a cookie works as a form of high-tech cattle-branding.

Cookies have certain limits. First, they often are not tagged to particular individuals—just to particular computers. However, if the website requires a user to log in or asks for a name, then the cookies will often contain data identifying the individual. Second, typically, websites can only decipher the cookies that they placed on a user's computer; they cannot use cookies stored by a different website.

To get around these limitations, companies have devised strategies of information sharing with other websites. One of the most popular information sharing techniques is performed by a firm called DoubleClick. When a person visits a website, it often takes a quick detour to DoubleClick. DoubleClick accesses its cookie on the person's computer and looks up its profile about the person. Based on the profile, DoubleClick determines what advertisements that person will be most responsive to, and these ads are then downloaded with the website the person is accessing. All this occurs in milliseconds, without the user's knowledge. Numerous websites subscribe to DoubleClick. This means that if I click on the same website as you at the very same time, we will receive different advertisements calculated by DoubleClick to match our interests. People may not know it, but DoubleClick cookies probably reside on their computer. As of the end of 1999, DoubleClick had amassed 80 million customer profiles.[61]

Another information collection device, known as a "web bug," is embedded into a web page or even an email message. The web bug is a hidden snippet of code that can gather data about a person.[62] For example, a company can send a spam email with a web bug that will report back when the message is opened. The bug can also record when the message is forwarded to others. Web bugs also can collect information about people as they explore a website. Some of the nastier versions of web bugs can even access a person's computer files.[63]

Companies also use what has become known as "spyware," which is software that is often deceptively and secretly installed into people's computers. Spyware can gather information about every move one makes when surfing the Internet. This data is then used by spyware companies to target pop-up ads and other forms of advertising.[64]

Legal scholar Julie Cohen has noted another growing threat to privacy—technologies of digital rights management (DRM), which are used by copyright holders to prevent piracy. Some DRM technologies gather information about individuals as they listen to music, watch videos, or read e-books. DRM technologies thus "create records of intellectual exploration, one of the most personal and private of activities."[65]

Copyright holders are also using computer programs called "bots" (shorthand for "robots"). Also known as "crawlers" or "spiders," bots can automatically prowl around the Internet looking for information. Industry trade groups, such as the Recording Industry Association of America (RIAA) and the Motion Picture Association of America

(MPAA), have unleashed tens of thousands of bots to identify potential illegal users of copyrighted materials.[66] Spammers—the senders of junk email—also employ a legion of bots to copy down email addresses that appear on the web in order to add them to spam lists. Bots also patrol Internet chat rooms, hunting for data.[67]

As we stand at the threshold of an age structured around information, we are only beginning to realize the extent to which our lives can be encompassed within its architecture. "The time will come," predicts one marketer, "when we are well known for our inclinations, our predilections, our proclivities, and our wants. We will be classified, profiled, categorized, and our every click will be watched."[68] As we live more of our lives on the Internet, we are creating a permanent record of unparalleled pervasiveness and depth. Indeed, almost everything on the Internet is being archived. One company has even been systematically sweeping up all the data from the Internet and storing it in a vast electronic warehouse.[69] Our online personas—captured, for instance, in our web pages and online postings—are swept up as well. We are accustomed to information on the web quickly flickering in and out of existence, presenting the illusion that it is ephemeral. But little on the Internet disappears or is forgotten, even when we delete or change the information. The amount of personal information archived will only escalate as our lives are increasingly digitized into the electric world of cyberspace.

These developments certainly suggest a threat to privacy, but what specifically is the problem? The way this question is answered has profound implications for the way the law will grapple with the problem in the future.

3 Kafka and Orwell

Reconceptualizing Information Privacy

The most widely discussed metaphor in the discourse of information privacy is George Orwell's depiction of Big Brother in *1984*. The use of the Big Brother metaphor to understand the database privacy problem is hardly surprising. Big Brother has long been the metaphor of choice to characterize privacy problems, and it has frequently been invoked when discussing police search tactics,[1] wiretapping and video surveillance,[2] and drug testing.[3] It is no surprise, then, that the burgeoning discourse on information privacy has seized upon this metaphor.

With regard to computer databases, however, Big Brother is incomplete as a way to understand the problem. Although the Big Brother metaphor certainly describes particular facets of the problem, it neglects many crucial dimensions. This oversight is far from inconsequential, for the way we conceptualize a problem has important ramifications for law and policy.

The Importance of Metaphor

A metaphor, as legal scholar Steven Winter aptly defines it, "is the imaginative capacity by which we relate one thing to another."[4] In their groundbreaking analysis, linguistics professor George Lakoff and philosopher Mark Johnson observe that metaphors are not mere linguistic embellishments or decorative overlays on experience; they are part of our conceptual systems and affect the way we interpret our experiences.[5] Metaphor is not simply an act of description; it is a way of conceptualization. "The essence of metaphor," write Lakoff and Johnson, "is understanding and experiencing one kind of thing in terms of another."[6]

Much of our thinking about a problem involves the metaphors we use. According to legal philosopher Jack Balkin, "metaphoric models selectively describe a situation, and in so doing help to suppress alternative conceptions." Metaphors do not just distort reality but compose it; the "power [of metaphors] stems precisely from their ability to empower understanding by shaping and hence limiting it."[7]

Winter, as well as Lakoff and Johnson, focus on metaphors embodied in our thought processes, pervading the type of language we use.[8] The metaphors I speak of are not as deeply ingrained. Metaphors are tools of shared cultural understanding.[9] Privacy involves the type of society we are creating, and we often use metaphors to envision different possible worlds, ones that we want to live in and ones that we don't. Orwell's Big Brother is an example of this type of metaphor; it is a shared cultural narrative, one that people can readily comprehend and react to.

Ascribing metaphors is not only a descriptive endeavor but also an act of political theorizing with profound normative implications.[10] According to Judge Richard Posner, however, "it is a mistake to try to mine works of literature for political or economic significance" because works of literature are better treated as aesthetic works rather than "as works of moral or political philosophy."[11] To the contrary, literature supplies the metaphors by which we conceptualize certain problems, and Posner fails to acknowledge the role that metaphor plays in shaping our collective understanding. Metaphors function not to render a precise descriptive representation of the problem; rather, they capture our concerns over privacy in a way that is palpable, potent, and compelling. Metaphors are instructive not for their realism but for the way they direct our focus to certain social and political phenomena.

George Orwell's Big Brother

Orwell's Totalitarian World. Journalists, politicians, and jurists often describe the problem created by databases with the metaphor of Big Brother—the harrowing totalitarian government portrayed in George Orwell's *1984*.[12] Big Brother is an all-knowing, constantly vigilant government that regulates every aspect of one's existence. In every corner are posters of an enormous face, with "eyes [that] follow you about when you move" and the caption "BIG BROTHER IS WATCHING YOU."[13]

Big Brother demands complete obedience from its citizens and controls all aspects of their lives. It constructs the language, rewrites the history, purges its critics, indoctrinates the population, burns books, and obliterates all disagreeable relics from the past. Big Brother's goal is uniformity and complete discipline, and it attempts to police people to an unrelenting degree—even their innermost thoughts. Any trace of individualism is quickly suffocated.

This terrifying totalitarian state achieves its control by targeting the private life, employing various techniques of power to eliminate any sense of privacy. Big Brother views solitude as dangerous. Its techniques of power are predominantly methods of surveillance. Big Brother is constantly monitoring and spying; uniformed patrols linger on street corners; helicopters hover in the skies, poised to peer into windows. The primary surveillance tool is a device called a "telescreen" which is installed into each house and apartment. The telescreen is a bilateral television—individuals can watch it, but it also enables Big Brother to watch them:

> There was of course no way of knowing whether you were being watched at any given moment. How often, or on what system, the Thought Police plugged in on any individual wire was guesswork. It was even conceivable that they watched everybody all the time. . . . You had to live—did live, from habit that became instinct—in the assumption that every sound you made was overheard, and, except in darkness, every movement scrutinized.[14]

In *1984*, citizens have no way of discovering if and when they are being watched. This surveillance, both real and threatened, is

combined with swift and terrifying force: "People simply disappeared, always during the night. Your name was removed from the
registers, every record of everything you had ever done was wiped
out, your one-time existence was denied and then forgotten."[15]

Orwell's narrative brilliantly captures the horror of the world it depicts, and its images continue to be invoked in the legal discourse of
privacy and information. "The ultimate horror in Orwell's imagined
anti-utopia," observes sociologist Dennis Wrong, "is that men are de-
prived of the very capacity for cherishing private thoughts and feel-
ings opposed to the regime, let alone acting on them."[16]

Panoptic Power. The telescreen functions similarly to the Panopticon,
an architectural design for a prison, originally conceived by Jeremy
Bentham in 1791.[17] In *Discipline and Punish,* Michel Foucault provides
a compelling description of this artifice of power:

> [A]t the periphery, an annular building; at the centre, a tower;
> this tower is pierced with wide windows that open onto the inner
> side of the ring; the peripheric building is divided into cells, each
> of which extends the whole width of the building. . . . All that is
> needed, then, is to place a supervisor in a central tower and to
> shut up in each cell a madman, a patient, a condemned man, a
> worker or a schoolboy. By the effect of backlighting, one can ob-
> serve from the tower, standing out precisely against the light, the
> small captive shadows in the cells of the periphery. They are like
> so many cages, so many small theatres, in which each actor is
> alone, perfectly individualized and constantly visible.[18]

The Panopticon is a device of discipline; its goal is to ensure order,
to prevent plots and riots, to mandate total obedience. The Panopticon achieves its power through an ingenious technique of surveillance, one that is ruthlessly efficient. By setting up a central
observation tower from which all prisoners can be observed and by
concealing from them any indication of whether they are being
watched at any given time, "surveillance is permanent in its effects,
even if it is discontinuous in its action."[19] Instead of having hundreds
of patrols and watchpersons, only a few people need to be in the
tower. Those in the tower can watch any inmate but they cannot be

seen. By always being visible, by constantly living under the reality that one could be observed at any time, people assimilate the effects of surveillance into themselves. They obey not because they are monitored but because of their fear that they could be watched. This fear alone is sufficient to achieve control. The Panopticon is so efficient that nobody needs to be in the tower at all.

As Foucault observed, the Panopticon is not merely limited to the prison or to a specific architectural structure—it is a technology of power that can be used in many contexts and in a multitude of ways. In 1984, the telescreen works in a similar way to the Panopticon, serving as a form of one-way surveillance that structures the behavior of those who are observed. The collection of information in cyberspace can be readily analogized to the telescreen. As we surf the Internet, information about us is being collected; we are being watched, but we do not know when or to what extent.

The metaphor of Big Brother understands privacy in terms of power, and it views privacy as an essential dimension of the political structure of society. Big Brother attempts to dominate the private life because it is the key to controlling an individual's entire existence: her thoughts, ideas, and actions.

The Ubiquity of the Metaphor. Big Brother dominates the discourse of information privacy. In 1974, when the use of computer databases was in its infancy, U.S. Supreme Court Justice William Douglas observed that we live in an Orwellian age in which the computer has become "the heart of a surveillance system that will turn society into a transparent world."[20] One state supreme court justice observed that the "acres of files" being assembled about us are leading to an "Orwellian society."[21]

Academics similarly characterize the problem.[22] In *The Culture of Surveillance,* sociologist William Staples observes that we have internalized Big Brother—we have created a Big Brother culture, where we all act as agents of surveillance and voyeurism.[23] "The specter of Big Brother has haunted computerization from the beginning," computer science professor Abbe Mowshowitz observes. "Computerized personal record-keeping systems, in the hands of police and intelligence agencies, clearly extend the surveillance capabilities of the state."[24]

Commentators have adapted the Big Brother metaphor to describe the threat to privacy caused by private-sector databases, often referring to businesses as "Little Brothers."[25] As sociologist David Lyon puts it: "Orwell's dystopic vision was dominated by the central state. He never guessed just how significant a decentralized consumerism might become for social control."[26] Legal scholar Katrin Byford writes: "Life in cyberspace, if left unregulated, thus promises to have distinct Orwellian overtones—with the notable difference that the primary threat to privacy comes not from government, but rather from the corporate world."[27] In *The End of Privacy*, political scientist Reg Whitaker also revises the Big Brother narrative into one of a multitude of Little Brothers.[28]

Internet "surveillance" can be readily compared to Orwell's telescreen. While people surf the web, companies are gathering information about them. As Paul Schwartz, a leading expert on privacy law, observes, the "Internet creates digital surveillance with nearly limitless data storage possibilities and efficient search possibilities." Instead of one Big Brother, today there are a "myriad" of "Big and Little Brothers" collecting personal data.[29]

Even when not directly invoking the metaphor, commentators frequently speak in its language, evoke its images and symbols, and define privacy problems in similar conceptual terms. Commentators view databases as having many of the same purposes (social control, suppression of individuality) and employing many of the same techniques (surveillance and monitoring) as Big Brother. David Flaherty, who served as the first Information and Privacy Commissioner for British Columbia, explains that the "storage of personal data can be used to limit opportunity and to encourage conformity." Dossiers of personal information "can have a limiting effect on behavior."[30] Oscar Gandy, a noted professor of communications and media studies, writes that "panopticism serves as a powerful metaphorical resource for representing the contemporary technology of segmentation and targeting."[31] As legal scholar Jerry Kang observes:

> [D]ata collection in cyberspace produces data that are detailed, computer-processable, indexed to the individual, and perma-

nent. Combine this with the fact that cyberspace makes data collection and analysis exponentially cheaper than in real space, and we have what Roger Clarke has identified as the genuine threat of "dataveillance."[32]

Dataveillance, as information technology expert Roger Clarke defines it, refers to the "systematic use of personal data systems in the investigation or monitoring of the actions or communications of one or more persons."[33] According to political scientist Colin Bennet, "[t]he term *dataveillance* has been coined to describe the surveillance practices that the massive collection and storage of vast quantities of personal data have facilitated."[34] Dataveillance is thus a new form of surveillance, a method of watching not through the eye or the camera, but by collecting facts and data. Kang argues that surveillance is an attack on human dignity, interfering with free choice because it "leads to self-censorship."[35] Likewise, Paul Schwartz claims that data collection "creates a potential for suppressing a capacity for free choice: the more that is known about an individual, the easier it is to force his obedience."[36] According to this view, the problem with databases is that they are a form of surveillance that curtails individual freedom.

The Limits of the Metaphor. Despite the fact that the discourse appropriately conceptualizes privacy through metaphor and that the Big Brother metaphor has proven quite useful for a number of privacy problems, the metaphor has significant limitations for the database privacy problem. As illustrated by the history of record-keeping and databases in chapter 2, developments in record-keeping were not orchestrated according to a grand scheme but were largely ad hoc, arising as technology interacted with the demands of the growing public and private bureaucracies. Additionally, the goals of data collection have often been rather benign—or at least far less malignant than the aims of Big Brother. In fact, personal information has been collected and recorded for a panoply of purposes. The story of record-keeping and database production is, in the end, not a story about the progression toward a world ruled by Big Brother or a multitude of Little

Brothers. Instead, it is a story about a group of different actors with different purposes attempting to thrive in an increasingly information-based society.

The most significant shortcoming of the Big Brother metaphor is that it fails to focus on the appropriate form of power. The metaphor depicts a particular technique of power—surveillance. Certainly, monitoring is an aspect of information collection, and databases may eventually be used in ways that resemble the disciplinary regime of Big Brother. However, most of the existing practices associated with databases are quite different in character. Direct marketers wish to observe behavior so they can tailor goods and advertisements to individual differences. True, they desire consumers to act in a certain way (to purchase their product), but their limited attempts at control are far from the repressive regime of total control exercised by Big Brother. The goal of much data collection by marketers aims not at suppressing individuality but at studying it and exploiting it.

The most insidious aspect of the surveillance of Big Brother is missing in the context of databases: human judgment about the activities being observed (or the fear of that judgment). Surveillance leads to conformity, inhibition, and self-censorship in situations where it is likely to involve human judgment. Being observed by an insect on the wall is not invasive of privacy; rather, privacy is threatened by being subject to *human* observation, which involves judgments that can affect one's life and reputation. Since marketers generally are interested in aggregate data, they do not care about snooping into particular people's private lives. Much personal information is amassed and processed by computers; we are being watched not by other humans, but by machines, which gather information, compute profiles, and generate lists for mailing, emailing, or calling. This impersonality makes the surveillance less invasive.

While having one's actions monitored by computers does not involve immediate perception by a human consciousness, it still exposes people to the possibility of future review and disclosure. In the context of databases, however, this possibility is remote. Even when such data is used for marketing, marketers merely want to make a profit, not uproot a life or soil a reputation.

I do not, however, want to discount the dangerous effects of surveillance through the use of databases. Although the purposes of the users of personal data are generally not malignant, databases can still result in unintended harmful social effects. The mere knowledge that one's behavior is being monitored and recorded certainly can lead to self-censorship and inhibition. Foucault's analysis of surveillance points to a more subtle yet more pervasive effect: surveillance changes the entire landscape in which people act, leading toward an internalization of social norms that soon is not even perceived as repressive.[37] This view of the effects of surveillance raises important questions regarding the amount of normalization that is desirable in society. While our instincts may be to view all normalization as an insidious force, most theories of the good depend upon a significant degree of normalization to hold society together.

Although the effects of surveillance are certainly a part of the database problem, the heavy focus on surveillance miscomprehends the most central and pernicious effects of databases. Understanding the problem as surveillance fails to account for the majority of our activities in the world and web. A large portion of our personal information involves facts that we are not embarrassed about: our financial information, race, marital status, hobbies, occupation, and the like. Most people surf the web without wandering into its dark corners. The vast majority of the information collected about us concerns relatively innocuous details. The surveillance model does not explain why the recording of this non-taboo information poses a problem. The focus of the surveillance model is on the fringes—and often involves things we may indeed want to inhibit such as cult activity, terrorism, and child pornography.

Digital dossiers do cause a serious problem that is overlooked by the Big Brother metaphor, one that poses a threat not just to our freedom to explore the taboo, but to freedom in general. It is a problem that implicates the type of society we are becoming, the way we think, our place in the larger social order, and our ability to exercise meaningful control over our lives.

Franz Kafka's Trial

Kafka's Distopic Vision. Although we cannot arbitrarily adopt new metaphors, we certainly can exercise control over the metaphors we use. Since understanding our current society is an ongoing process, not a once-and-done activity, we are constantly in search of new metaphors to better comprehend our situation.

Franz Kafka's harrowing depiction of bureaucracy in *The Trial* captures dimensions of the digital dossier problem that the Big Brother metaphor does not.[38] *The Trial* opens with the protagonist, Joseph K., awakening one morning to find a group of officials in his apartment, who inform him that he is under arrest. K. is bewildered at why he has been placed under arrest: "I cannot recall the slightest offense that might be charged against me. But even that is of minor importance, the real question is, who accuses me? What authority is conducting these proceedings?" When he asks why the officials have come to arrest him, an official replies: "You are under arrest, certainly, more than that I do not know."[39] Instead of taking him away to a police station, the officials mysteriously leave.

Throughout the rest of the novel, Joseph K. begins a frustrating quest to discover why he has been arrested and how his case will be resolved. A vast bureaucratic court has apparently scrutinized his life and assembled a dossier on him. The Court is clandestine and mysterious, and court records are "inaccessible to the accused."[40] In an effort to learn about this Court and the proceedings against him, Joseph K. scuttles throughout the city, encountering a maze of lawyers, priests, and others, each revealing small scraps of knowledge about the workings of the Court. In a pivotal scene, Joseph K. meets a painter who gleaned much knowledge of the obscure workings of the Court while painting judicial portraits. The painter explains to K.:

> "The whole dossier continues to circulate, as the regular official routine demands, passing on to the highest Courts, being referred to the lower ones again, and then swinging backwards and forwards with greater or smaller oscillations, longer or shorter delays. . . . No document is ever lost, the Court never forgets anything. One day—quite unexpectedly—some Judge will take up

the documents and look at them attentively. . . ." "And the case begins all over again?" asked K. almost incredulously. "Certainly" said the painter.[41]

Ironically, after the initial arrest, it is Joseph K. who takes the initiative in seeking out the Court. He is informed of an interrogation on Sunday, but only if he has no objection to it: "Nevertheless he was hurrying fast, so as if possible to arrive by nine o'clock, although he had not even been required to appear at any specific time."[42] Although the Court has barely imposed any authority, not even specifying when Joseph K. should arrive for his interrogation, he acts as if this Court operates with strict rules and makes every attempt to obey. After the interrogation, the Court seems to lose interest in him. Joseph K., however, becomes obsessed with his case. He wants to be recognized by the Court and to resolve his case; in fact, being ignored by the Court becomes a worse torment than being arrested.

As K. continues his search, he becomes increasingly perplexed by this unusual Court. The higher officials keep themselves hidden; the lawyers claim they have connections to Court officials but never offer any proof or results. Hardly anyone seems to have direct contact with the Court. In addition, its "proceedings were not only kept secret from the general public, but from the accused as well." Yet K. continues to seek an acquittal from a crime he hasn't been informed of and from an authority he cannot seem to find. As Joseph K. scurries through the bureaucratic labyrinth of the law, he can never make any progress toward his acquittal: "Progress had always been made, but the nature of the progress could never be divulged. The Advocate was always working away at the first plea, but it had never reached a conclusion."[43] In the end, Joseph K. is seized by two officials in the middle of the night and executed.

Kafka's *The Trial* best captures the scope, nature, and effects of the type of power relationship created by databases. My point is not that *The Trial* presents a more realistic descriptive account of the database problem than Big Brother. Like *1984*, *The Trial* presents a fictional portrait of a harrowing world, often exaggerating certain elements of society in a way that makes them humorous and absurd. Certainly, in the United States most people are not told that they are inexplicably under arrest, and they do not expect to be executed unexpectedly one evening. *The Trial* is in part a satire, and what is important for the purposes of my argument are the insights the novel provides about society through its exaggerations. In the context of computer databases, Kafka's *The Trial* is the better focal point for the discourse than Big Brother. Kafka depicts an indifferent bureaucracy, where individuals are pawns, not knowing what is happening, having no say or ability to exercise meaningful control over the process. This lack of control allows the trial to completely take over Joseph K.'s life. *The Trial* captures the sense of helplessness, frustration, and vulnerability one experiences when a large bureaucratic organization has control over a vast dossier of details about one's life. At any time, something could happen to Joseph K.; decisions are made based on his data, and Joseph K. has no say, no knowledge, and no ability to fight back. He is completely at the mercy of the bureaucratic process.

As understood in light of the Kafka metaphor, the primary problem with databases stems from the way the bureaucratic process treats individuals and their information.

Bureaucracy. Generally, the term "bureaucracy" refers to large public and private organizations with hierarchical structures and a set of elaborate rules, routines, and processes.[44] I will use the term to refer not to specific institutions but to a particular set of practices—specifically, how bureaucratic processes affect and influence individuals subjected to them. Bureaucratic organization, sociologist Max Weber asserts, consists of a hierarchical chain-of-command, specialized offices to carry out particular functions, and a system of general rules to manage the organization.[45] Bureaucracy is not limited to government administration; it is also a feature of business management. The modern world requires the efficient flow of information in order to communicate, to deliver goods and services, to regulate, and to carry out basic functions. According to Weber, bureaucracy is "capable of attaining the highest degree of efficiency and is in this sense formally the most rational known means of exercising authority over human beings."[46] Bureaucratic processes are highly routinized, striving for increased efficiency, standardization of decisions, and the cultivation of specialization and expertise. As Paul Schwartz notes, bureaucracy depends upon "vast quantities of information" that "relates to identifiable individuals."[47] Much of this information is important and necessary to the smooth functioning of bureaucracies.

Although bureaucratic organization is an essential and beneficial feature of modern society, bureaucracy also presents numerous problems. Weber observes that bureaucracy can become "dehumanized" by striving to eliminate "love, hatred, and all purely personal, irrational, and emotional elements which escape calculation."[48] Bureaucracy often cannot adequately attend to the needs of particular individuals—not because bureaucrats are malicious, but because they must act within strict time constraints, have limited training, and are frequently not able to respond to unusual situations in unique or creative ways. Schwartz contends that because bureaucracy does not adequately protect the dignity of the people it deals with, it can "weaken an individual's capacity for critical reflection and participation in society."[49] Additionally, decisions within public and private bureaucratic organizations are often hidden from public view, decreasing accountability. As Weber notes, "[b]ureaucratic administration always tends to exclude the public, to hide its knowledge and action from criticism as well as it can."[50] Bureaucratic organizations often have hidden pockets of discretion. At lower levels, discretion can enable abuses. Frequently, bureaucracies fail to train employees adequately and may employ subpar security measures over personal data. Bureaucracies are often careless in their uses and handling of personal information.

The problem with databases emerges from subjecting personal information to the bureaucratic process with little intelligent control or limitation, which results in our not having meaningful participation in decisions about our information. Bureaucratic decision-making processes are being exercised ever more frequently over a greater sphere of our lives, and we have little power or say within such a system, which tends to structure our participation along standardized ways that fail to enable us to achieve our goals, wants, and needs.

Bureaucracy and Power. The power effects of this relationship to bureaucracy are profound; however, they cannot adequately be explained by resorting only to the understanding of power in Orwell's

1984. Big Brother employs a coercive power that is designed to dominate and oppress. Power, however, is not merely prohibitive; as illustrated by Aldous Huxley in *Brave New World*, it composes our very lives and culture. Huxley describes a different form of totalitarian society—one controlled not by force, but by entertainment and pleasure. The population is addicted to a drug called Soma, which is administered by the government as a political tool to sedate the people. Huxley presents a narrative about a society controlled not by a despotic coercive government like Big Brother, but by manipulation and consumption, where people participate in their own enslavement. The government achieves obedience through social conditioning, propaganda, and other forms of indoctrination.[51] It does not use the crude coercive techniques of violence and force, but instead employs a more subtle scientific method of control—through genetic engineering, psychology, and drugs. Power works internally—the government actively molds the private life of its citizens, transforming it into a world of vapid pleasure, mindlessness, and numbness.

Despite the differences, power for both Orwell and Huxley operates as an insidious force employed for a particular design. *The Trial* depicts a different form of power. The power employed in *The Trial* has no apparent goal; any purpose remains shrouded in mystery. Nor is the power as direct and manipulative in design as that depicted by Orwell and Huxley. The Court system barely even cares about Joseph K. *The Trial* depicts a world that differs significantly from our traditional notions of a totalitarian state. Joseph K. was not arrested for his political views; nor did the Court manifest any plan to control people. Indeed, Joseph K. was searching for some reason why he was arrested, a reason that he never discovered. One frightening implication is that there was no reason, or if there were, it was absurd or arbitrary. Joseph K. was subjected to a more purposeless process than a trial. Indeed, the Court does not try to exercise much power over Joseph K. His arrest does not even involve his being taken into custody—merely a notification that he is under arrest—and after an initial proceeding, the Court makes no further effort even to contact Joseph K.

What is more discernible than any motive on the part of the Court or any overt exercise of power are the social effects of the power relationship between the bureaucracy and Joseph K. The power depicted in *The Trial* is not so much a force as it is an element of relationships between individuals and society and government. These relationships have balances of power. What *The Trial* illustrates is that power is not merely exercised in totalitarian forms, and that relationships to bureaucracies which are unbalanced in power can have debilitating effects upon individuals—regardless of the bureaucracies' purposes (which may, in fact, turn out to be quite benign).

Under this view, the problem with databases and the practices currently associated with them is that they disempower people. They make people vulnerable by stripping them of control over their personal information. There is no diabolical motive or secret plan for domination; rather, there is a web of thoughtless decisions made by low-level bureaucrats, standardized policies, rigid routines, and a way of relating to individuals and their information that often becomes indifferent to their welfare.

The Interplay of the Metaphors. The Kafka and Orwell metaphors are not mutually exclusive. As I will discuss in more depth in part III of this book, the interplay of the metaphors captures the problems with government access to digital dossiers. In particular, the government is increasingly mining data from private-sector sources to profile individuals. Information about people is observed or recorded and then fed into computer programs that analyze the data looking for certain behavior patterns common to criminal or terrorist activity. This method of investigation and analysis employs secret algorithms to process information and calculate how "dangerous" or "criminal" a person might be. The results of these secret computations have palpable effects on people's lives. People can be denied the right to fly on an airplane without a reason or a hearing; or they can be detained indefinitely without the right to an attorney and without being told the reasons why.

In another example, political scientist John Gilliom's study of the surveillance of welfare recipients chronicles a world of constant observation coupled by an almost pathological bureaucracy.[52] Recipients must fill out mountains of paperwork, answer endless questions, and be routinely monitored. Often, they receive so little financial assistance that they resort to odd jobs to obtain more income, which, if discovered, could make them ineligible for benefits. The system creates a strong incentive for transgression, severe penalties for any breach, and elaborate data systems that attempt to detect any malfeasance through automated investigations. The system combines pervasive surveillance with a bureaucratic process that has little compassion or flexibility.

A quote by noted playwright and author Friedrich Dürrenmatt best captures how surveillance and bureaucracy interrelate in the Information Age:

> [W]hat was even worse was the nature of those who observed and made a fool of him, namely a system of computers, for what he was observing was two cameras connected to two computers observed by two further computers and fed into computers connected to *those* computers in order to be scanned, converted, reconverted, and, after further processing by laboratory computers, developed, enlarged, viewed, and interpreted, by whom and where and whether at any point by human beings he couldn't tell.[53]

Surveillance generates information, which is often stored in record systems and used for new purposes. Being watched and inhibited in one's behavior is only one part of the problem; the other dimension is that the data is warehoused for unknown future uses. This is where Orwell meets Kafka.

Beyond the Secrecy Paradigm

Understanding the database privacy problem in terms of the Kafka metaphor illustrates that the problem with databases concerns the use of information, not merely keeping it secret. Traditionally, privacy problems have been understood as invasions into one's hidden world. Privacy is about concealment, and it is invaded by watching and by public disclosure of confidential information. I refer to this understanding of privacy as the "secrecy paradigm." This paradigm is so embedded in our privacy discourse that privacy is often represented visually by a roving eye, an open keyhole, or a person peeking through Venetian blinds.

Information about an individual, however, is often not secret, but is diffused in the minds of a multitude of people and scattered in various documents and computer files across the country. Few would be embarrassed by the disclosure of much of the material they read, the food they eat, or the products they purchase. Few would view their race, ethnicity, marital status, or religion as confidential. Of course, databases may contain the residue of scandals and skeletons—illicit websites, racy books, stigmatizing diseases—but since information in databases is rarely publicized, few reputations are tarnished. For the most part, the data is processed impersonally by computers without ever being viewed by the human eye. The secrecy paradigm focuses on breached confidentiality, harmed reputation, and unwanted publicity. But since these harms are not really the central problems of databases, privacy law often concludes that the information in databases is not private and is thus not entitled to protection. Indeed, one commentator defended DoubleClick's tracking of web browsing habits by stating:

> Over time, people will realize it's not Big Brother who's going to show up [at] your door in a black ski mask and take your kids away or dig deep into your medical history. This is a situation where you are essentially dropped into a bucket with 40 million people who look and feel a lot like you do to the advertising company.[54]

This commentator, viewing privacy with the Big Brother metaphor, focuses on the wrong types of harms and implicitly views only secret information as private.

The problem with databases pertains to the uses and practices associated with our information, not merely whether that information remains completely secret. Although disclosure can be a violation of privacy, this does not mean that avoiding disclosure is the sum and substance of our interest in privacy. What people want when they demand privacy with regard to their personal information is the ability to ensure that the information about them will be used only for the purposes they desire. Even regarding the confidentiality of information, the understanding of privacy as secrecy fails to recognize that individuals want to keep things private from some people but not others. The fact that an employee criticizes her boss to a co-worker does not mean that she wants her boss to know what she said.

Helen Nissenbaum, a professor of information technology, is quite right to argue that we often expect privacy even when in public.[55] Not all activities are purely private in the sense that they occur in isolation and in hidden corners. When we talk in a restaurant, we do not expect to be listened to. A person may buy condoms or hemorrhoid medication in a store open to the public, but certainly expects these purchases to be private activities. Contrary to the notion that any information in public records cannot be private, there is a considerable loss of privacy by plucking inaccessible facts buried in some obscure document and broadcasting them to the world on the evening news. Privacy can be infringed even if no secrets are revealed and even if nobody is watching us.

The Aggregation Effect

The digital revolution has enabled information to be easily amassed and combined. Even information that is superficial or incomplete can be quite useful in obtaining more data about individuals. Information breeds information. For example, although one's SSN does not in and of itself reveal much about an individual, it provides access to one's financial information, educational records, medical records, and a whole host of other information. As law professor Julie Cohen notes, "[a] comprehensive collection of data about an individual is vastly more than the sum of its parts."[56] I refer to this phenomenon as the "aggregation effect." Similar to a Seurat painting, where a multitude of dots juxtaposed together form a picture, bits of information when aggregated paint a portrait of a person.

In the Information Age, personal data is being combined to create a digital biography about us. Information that appears innocuous can sometimes be the missing link, the critical detail in one's digital biography, or the key necessary to unlock other stores of personal information. But why should we be concerned about a biography that includes details about what type of soap a person buys, whether she prefers Pepsi to Coca-Cola, or whether she likes to shop at Macy's rather than Kmart? As legal scholar Stan Karas points out, the products we consume are expressive of our identities.[57] We have many choices in the products we buy, and even particular brands symbolize certain personality traits and personal characteristics. Karas notes that Pepsi has marketed itself to a younger, more rebellious consumer than Coca-Cola, which emphasizes old-fashioned and traditional images in its advertisements.[58] Whether punk, yuppie, or hippie, people often follow a particular consumption pattern that reflects the subculture with which they identify.[59]

Of course, the products we buy are not wholly reflective of our identities. A scene from Henry James's *Portrait of a Lady* best captures the complexities of the situation. Madame Merle, wise in the ways of the world yet jaded and selfish, is speaking to Isabel Archer, a young American lady in Europe full of great aspirations of living a bold and exceptional life, far beyond convention. Merle declares: "What shall we call our 'self'? Where does it begin? Where does it end? It overflows into everything that belongs to us—and then it flows back again. I know a large part of myself is the clothes I choose to wear. I've a great respect for *things*!" Isabel disagrees: "nothing that belongs to me is any measure of me." "My clothes only express the dressmaker," Isabel says, "but they don't express me. To begin with, it is not my own choice that I wear them; they've been imposed upon me by society."[60]

Merle is obsessed by things, and she views herself as deeply intertwined with her possessions. The objects she owns and purchases are deeply constitutive of her personality. Isabel, in her proud individualism, claims that she is vastly distinct from what she owns and wears. Indeed, for her, things are a tool for conformity; they do not express anything authentic about herself.

Yet Madame Merle has a point—the information is indeed expressive. But Isabel is right, too—this information is somewhat superficial, and it only partially captures who we are. Although the digital biography contains a host of details about a person, it captures a distorted persona, one who is constructed by a variety of external details.[61] Although the information marketers glean about us can be quite revealing, it still cannot penetrate into our thoughts and often only partially captures who we are.[62] Information about our property, our professions, our purchases, our finances, and our medical history does not tell the whole story. We are more than the bits of data we give off as we go about our lives. Our digital biography is revealing of ourselves but in a rather standardized way. It consists of bits of information pre-defined based on the judgment of some entity about what categories of information are relevant or important. We are partially captured by details such as our age, race, gender, net worth, property owned, and so on, but only in a manner that standardizes us into types or categories. Indeed, database marketers frequently classify consumers into certain categories based on stereotypes about their values, lifestyle, and purchasing habits. As Julie Cohen observes, people are not simply "reducible to the sum of their transactions, genetic markers, and other measurable attributes."[63]

Our digital biography is thus an unauthorized one, only partially true and very reductive. We must all live with these unauthorized biographies about us, the complete contents of which we often do not get to see. Although a more extensive dossier might be less reductive in capturing our personalities, it would have greater controlling effects on an individual's life.

Not only are our digital biographies reductive, but they are often inaccurate. In today's bureaucratized world, one of the growing threats is that we will be subject to the inadvertence, carelessness, and mindlessness of bureaucracy. A scene from the darkly humorous movie *Brazil* illustrates this problem.[64] The movie opens with an exhausted bureaucrat swatting a fly, which inconspicuously drops into a typewriter, causes a jam, and results in him mistyping a letter in a person's name on a form. The form authorizes the arrest and interrogation of suspected rebels. In the next scene, an innocent man peacefully sits in his home with his family when suddenly scores of armor-clad police storm inside and haul him away.

These dangers are not merely the imaginary stuff of movies. The burgeoning use of databases of public record information by the private sector in screening job applicants and investigating existing employees demonstrates how errors can potentially destroy a person's career. For example, a Maryland woman wrongly arrested for a burglary was not cleared from the state's criminal databases. Her name and SSN also migrated to a Baltimore County database relating to child protective services cases. She was fired from her job as a substitute teacher, and only after she could establish that the information was in error was she rehired. When she later left that job to run a day care center for the U.S. military, she was subjected to questioning about the erroneous arrest. Later on, when employed as a child care director at a YMCA, she was terminated when her arrest record surfaced in a background clearance check. Since she could not have the error expunged in sufficient time, the job was given to another person. Only after several years was the error finally cleared from the public records.[65] As our digital biographies are increasingly relied upon to make important decisions, the problems that errors can cause will only escalate in frequency and magnitude.

To the extent that the digital biography is accurate, our lives are not only revealed and recorded, but also can be analyzed and investigated. Our digital biographies are being assembled by companies which are amassing personal information in public records along with other data. Collectively, millions of biographies can be searched, sorted, and analyzed in a matter of seconds. This enables automated investigations of individuals on a nationwide scale by both the government and the private sector. Increasingly, companies are conducting investigations which can have profound consequences on people's lives—such as their employment and financial condition. Employers are resorting to information brokers of public record information to assist in screening job applicants and existing employees. For example, the firm HireCheck serves over 4,000 employers to conduct background checks for new hires or current employees.[66] It conducts a national search of outstanding arrest warrants; a SSN search to locate the person's age, past and current employers, and former addresses; a driver record search; a search of worker's compensation claims "to avoid habitual claimants or to properly channel assignments"; a check of civil lawsuit records; and searches for many other types of information.[67] These investigations occur without any external oversight, and individuals often do not have an opportunity to challenge the results.

Forms of Dehumanization: Databases and the Kafka Metaphor

Expounding on the Kafka metaphor, certain uses of databases foster a state of powerlessness and vulnerability created by people's lack of any meaningful form of participation in the collection and use of their personal information. Bureaucracy and power is certainly not a new problem. Databases do not cause the disempowering effects of bureaucracy; they exacerbate them—not merely by magnifying existing power imbalances but by transforming these relationships in profound ways that implicate our freedom. The problem is thus old and new, and its additional dimensions within the Information Age require extensive explication.

Impoverished Judgments. One of the great dangers of using information that we generally regard as private is that we often make judgments based on this private information about the person. As legal scholar Kenneth Karst warned in the 1960s, one danger of "a centralized, standardized data processing system" is that the facts stored about an individual "will become the only significant facts about the subject of the inquiry."[68] Legal scholar Jeffrey Rosen aptly observes, "Privacy protects us from being misdefined and judged out of context in a world of short attention spans, a world in which information can easily be confused with knowledge. True knowledge of another person is the culmination of a slow process of mutual revelation."[69]

Increased reliance upon the easily quantifiable and classifiable information available from databases is having profound social effects. The nature and volume of information affects the way people analyze, use, and react to information. Currently, we rely quite heavily on quantifiable data: statistics, polls, numbers, and figures. In the law alone, there is a trend to rank schools; to measure the influence of famous jurists by counting citations to their judicial opinions;[70] to assess the importance of law review articles by tabulating citations to them;[71] to rank law journals with an elaborate system of establishing point values for authors of articles;[72] and to determine the influence of academic movements by checking citations.[73] The goal of this use of empirical data is to eliminate the ambiguity and incommensurability of many aspects of life and try to categorize them into neat, tidy categories. The computer has exacerbated this tendency, for the increase in information and the way computers operate furthers this type of categorization and lack of judgment.[74] Indeed, in legal scholarship, much of this tendency is due to the advent of computer research databases, which can easily check for citations and specific terms.

In our increasingly bureaucratic and impersonal world, we are relying more heavily on records and profiles to assess reputation. As H. Jeff Smith, a professor of management and information technology, contends:

> [D]ecisions that were formerly based on judgment and human factors are instead decided according to prescribed formulas. In today's world, this response is often characterized by reliance on a rigid, unyielding process in which computerized information is given great weight. Facts that actually require substantial evaluation could instead be reduced to discrete entries in preassigned categories.[75]

Certainly, quantifiable information can be accurate and serve as the best way for making particular decisions. Even when quantifiable information is not exact, it is useful for making decisions because of administrative feasibility. Considering all the variables and a multitude of incommensurate factors might simply be impossible or too costly.

Nevertheless, the information in databases often fails to capture the texture of our lives. Rather than provide a nuanced portrait of our personalities, compilations of data capture the brute facts of what we do without the reasons. For example, a record of an arrest without the story or reason is misleading. The arrest could have been for civil disobedience in the 1960s—but it is still recorded as an arrest with some vague label, such as "disorderly conduct." It appears no differently from the arrest of a vandal. In short, we are reconstituted in databases as a digital person composed of data. The privacy problem stems paradoxically from the pervasiveness of this data—the fact that it encompasses much of our lives—as well as from its limitations—how it fails to capture us, how it distorts who we are.

Powerlessness and Lack of Participation. Privacy concerns an individual's power in the elaborate web of social relationships that encompasses her life. Today, a significant number of these relationships involve interaction with public and private institutions. In addition to the myriad of public agencies that regulate the products we purchase, the environment, and the like, we depend upon private institutions such as telephone companies, utility companies, Internet service providers, cable service providers, and health insurance companies. We also depend upon companies that provide the products we believe are essential to our daily lives: hygiene, transportation, entertainment, news, and so on. Our lives are ensconced in these institutions, which have power over our day-to-day activities (through what we consume, read, and watch), our culture, politics, education, and economic well-being. We are engaged in relationships with these institutions, even if on the surface our interactions with them are as rudimentary and distant as signing up for services, paying bills, and requesting repairs. With many firms—such as credit reporting agencies—we do not even take affirmative steps to establish a relationship.

Companies are beginning to use personal information to identify what business experts call "angel" and "demon" customers.[76] Certain customers—the angels—are very profitable, but others—the demons—are not. Angel customers account for a large amount of a company's business whereas demon customers purchase only a small amount of goods and services and are likely to cost the company money. For example, a demon customer is one who uses up a company's resources by frequently calling customer service. Some business experts thus recommend that companies identify these types of customers through the use of personal information and treat them differently. For example, businesses might serve the angels first and leave the demons waiting; or they might offer the angels cheaper prices; or perhaps, they might even try to turn the demons away entirely.[77] The result of companies moving in this direction is that people will be treated differently and may never know why. Even before the concept of angel and demon customers was articulated, one bank routinely denied credit card applications from college students majoring in literature, history, and art, based on the assumption that they would not be able to repay their debts. The bank's practice remained a secret until the media ran a story about it.[78]

We are increasingly not being treated as equals in our relationships with many private-sector institutions. Things are done to us; decisions are made about us; and we are often completely excluded from the process. With considerably greater frequency, we are ending up frustrated with the outcome. For example, complaints about credit reporting agencies to the Federal Trade Commission have been rapidly escalating, with 8,000 in 2001 and over 14,000 in 2002.[79]

Privacy involves the ability to avoid the powerlessness of having others control information that can affect whether an individual gets a job, becomes licensed to practice in a profession, or obtains a critical loan. It involves the ability to avoid the collection and circulation of such powerful information in one's life without having any say in the process, without knowing who has what information, what purposes or motives those entities have, or what will be done with that information in the future. Privacy involves the power to refuse to be treated with bureaucratic indifference when one complains about errors or when one wants certain data expunged. It is not merely the collection of data that is the problem—it is our complete lack of control over the ways it is used or may be used in the future.

Problematic Information Gathering Techniques. This powerlessness is compounded by the fact that the process of information collection in America is clandestine, duplicitous, and unfair. The choices given to people over their information are hardly choices at all. People must relinquish personal data to gain employment, procure insurance, obtain a credit card, or otherwise participate like a normal citizen in today's economy. Consent is virtually meaningless in many contexts. When people give consent, they must often consent to a total surrender of control over their information.

Collection of information is often done by misleading the consumer. General Electric sent a supposedly anonymous survey to shareholders asking them to rate various aspects of the company. Unbeknownst to those surveyed, the survey's return envelope was coded so that the responses could be matched to names in the company's shareholder database.[80]

Some information is directly solicited via registration questionnaires or other means such as competitions and sweepstakes. The warranty registration cards of many products—which ask a host of lifestyle questions—are often sent not to the company that makes the product but to National Demographics and Lifestyles Company at a Denver post office box. This company has compiled information on over 20 million people and markets it to other companies.[81] Often, there is an implicit misleading notion that consumers must fill out a registration questionnaire in order to be covered by the warranty.

Frequent shopper programs and discount cards—which involve filling out a questionnaire and then carrying a special card that provides discounts—enable the scanner data to be matched to data about individual consumers.[82] This technique involves offering savings in return for personal information and the ability to track a person's grocery purchases.[83] However, there are scant disclosures that such an exchange is taking place, and there are virtually no limits on the use of the data.

Conde Nast Publications Inc. (which publishes the *New Yorker, Vanity Fair, Vogue,* and other magazines) recently sent out a booklet of 700 questions asking detailed information about an individual's hobbies, shopping preferences, health (including medications used, acne problems, and vaginal/yeast infections), and much more. Almost 400,000 people responded. In return for the data, the survey said: "Just answer the questions below to start the conversation and become part of this select group of subscribers to whom marketers listen first." Conde Nast maintains a database of information on 15 million people. Stephen Jacoby, the vice president for marketing and databases, said: "What we're trying to do is enhance the relationship between the subscriber and their magazine. In a sense, it's a benefit to the subscriber."[84]

There is no "conversation" created by supplying the data. Conde Nast does not indicate how the information will be used. It basically tries to entice people to give information for a vague promise of little or no value. While the company insists that it will not share information with "outsiders," it does not explain who constitutes an "outsider." The information remains in the control of the company, with no limitations on use. Merely informing the consumer that data may be sold to others is an inadequate form of disclosure. The consumer does not know how many times the data will be resold, to whom it will be sold, or for what purposes it will be used.

Irresponsibility and Carelessness. A person's lack of control is exacerbated by the often thoughtless and irresponsible ways that bureaucracies use personal information and their lack of accountability in using and protecting the data. In other words, the problem is not simply a lack of individual control over information, but a situation where *nobody* is exercising meaningful control over the information.

In bureaucratic settings, privacy policy tends to fall into drift and be reactionary. In a detailed study of organizations such as banks, insurance companies, and credit reporting agencies, H. Jeff Smith concluded that all of the organizations "exhibited a remarkably similar approach: the policy-making process, which occurred over time, was a wandering and reactive one." According to a senior executive at a health insurance company, "We've been lazy on the privacy [issues] for several years now, because we haven't had anybody beating us over the head about them." According to Smith, most executives in the survey were followers rather than leaders: "[M]ost executives wait until an external threat forces them to consider their privacy policies."[85]

Furthermore, there have been several highly publicized instances where companies violated their own privacy policies. Although promising its users that their information would remain confidential, the website GeoCities collected and sold information about children who played games on the site.[86] RealNetworks, Inc. secretly collected personal information about its users in direct violation of its privacy policy. And a website for young investors promised that the data it collected about people's finances would remain anonymous, but instead it was kept in identifiable form.[87]

More insidious than drifting and reactionary privacy policies are irresponsible and careless uses of personal information. For example, Metromail Corporation, a seller of direct marketing information, hired inmates to enter the information into databases. This came to light when an inmate began sending harassing letters that were sexually explicit and filled with intimate details of people's lives.[88] A television reporter once paid $277 to obtain from Metromail a list of over

5,000 children living in Pasadena, California. The reporter gave the name of a well-known child molester and murderer as the buyer.[89] These cases illustrate the lack of care and accountability by the corporations collecting the data.

McVeigh v. Cohen[90] best illustrates this problem. A highly decorated 17-year veteran of the Navy sought to enjoin the Navy from discharging him under the statutory policy known as "Don't Ask, Don't Tell, Don't Pursue."[91] When responding to a toy drive for the crew of his ship, Tim McVeigh (no relation to the Oklahoma City bomber) accidentally used the wrong email account, sending a message under the alias "boysrch." He signed the email "Tim" but included no other information. The person conducting the toy drive searched through the member profile directory of America Online (AOL), where she learned that "boysrch" was an AOL subscriber named Tim who lived in Hawaii and worked in the military. Under marital status, he had identified himself as "gay." The ship's legal adviser began to investigate, suspecting that "Tim" was McVeigh. Before speaking to McVeigh, and without a warrant, the legal adviser had a paralegal contact AOL for more information. The paralegal called AOL's toll-free customer service number and, without identifying himself as a Navy serviceman, concocted a story that he had received a fax from an AOL customer and wanted to confirm who it belonged to. Despite a policy of not giving out personal information, the AOL representative told him that the customer was McVeigh. As a result, the Navy sought to discharge McVeigh.

In *Remsburg v. Docusearch, Inc.,*[92] a man named Liam Youens began purchasing information about Amy Lynn Boyer from a company called Docusearch. He requested Boyer's SSN, and Docusearch obtained it from a credit reporting agency and provided it to him. Youens then requested Boyer's employment address, so Docusearch hired a subcontractor, who obtained it by making a "pretext" phone call to Boyer. By lying about her identity and the reason for the call, the subcontractor obtained the address from Boyer. Docusearch then gave the address to Youens, who went to Boyer's workplace and shot and killed her. Docusearch supplied the information without ever asking who Youens was or why he was seeking the information.

Within the past few years, explicit details of 90 psychotherapy patients' sex lives, as well as their names, addresses, telephone numbers, and credit card numbers, were inadvertently posted on the Internet.[93] A banker in Maryland who sat on a state's public health commission checked his list of bank loans with records of people with cancer in order to cancel the loans of the cancer sufferers.[94] A hacker illegally downloaded thousands of patients' medical files along with their SSNs from a university medical center.[95] Due to a mix-up, a retirement plan mailed financial statements to the wrong people at the same firm.[96] Extensive psychological records describing the conditions of over 60 children were inadvertently posted on the University of Montana's website.[97] An employee of a company obtained 30,000 credit reports from a credit reporting agency and peddled them to others for use in fraud and identity theft.[98] Health information and SSNs of military personnel and their families were stolen from a military contractor's database.[99]

In sum, the privacy problem created by the use of databases stems from an often careless and unconcerned bureaucratic process—one that has little judgment or accountability—and is driven by ends other than the protection of people's dignity. We are not just heading toward a world of Big Brother or one composed of Little Brothers, but also toward a more mindless process—of bureaucratic indifference, arbitrary errors, and dehumanization—a world that is beginning to resemble Kafka's vision in *The Trial.*

4 The Problems of Information Privacy Law

A distinctive domain of law relating to information privacy has been developing throughout the twentieth century. Although the law has made great strides in dealing with privacy problems, the law of information privacy has been severely hampered by the difficulties in formulating a compelling theory of privacy. The story of privacy law is a tale of changing technology and the law's struggle to respond in effective ways.

Information privacy law consists of a mosaic of various types of law: tort law, constitutional law, federal and state statutory law, evidentiary privileges, property law, and contract law. Much of privacy law is interrelated, and as legal scholar Ken Gormley observes, "various offshoots of privacy are deeply intertwined at the roots, owing their origins to the same soil."[1]

Information privacy law has made great strides toward protecting privacy. Nevertheless, there are systematic deficiencies across the spectrum of privacy law in addressing the special nature of the problem of digital dossiers.

The Privacy Torts

Warren and Brandeis. Privacy law owes its greatest debt to Samuel Warren and Louis Brandeis. Warren and Brandeis practiced law together in a Boston law firm. Brandeis later went on to become a Supreme Court justice.[2] In 1890, they wrote their profoundly influential article, *The Right to Privacy*,[3] considered by many to be one of the primary foundations of privacy law in the United States.[4] In the article, Warren and Brandeis raised alarm at the intersection of yellow journalism,[5] with its increasing hunger for sensational human interest stories, and the development of new technologies in photography. During the latter half of the nineteenth century, newspapers were the most rapidly growing form of media, with circulation increasing about 1,000 percent from 1850 to 1890. In 1850, there were approximately 100 newspapers with 800,000 readers. By 1890, there were 900 papers with over 8 million readers. This massive growth was due, in part, to yellow journalism, a form of sensationalistic reporting that focused on scandals and petty crimes. Reaping the successes of yellow journalism, Joseph Pulitzer and William Randolph Hearst became the barons of the newspaper business. According to Warren and Brandeis: "The press is overstepping in every direction the obvious bounds of propriety and decency. Gossip is no longer the resource of the idle and of the vicious, but has become a trade, which is pursued with industry as well as effrontery."[6]

Warren and Brandeis also expressed concern over what they called "instantaneous" photography. Although photography had been around before 1890, recent developments made photography much cheaper and easier. Cameras had been large, expensive, and not readily portable. In 1884, the Eastman Kodak Company came out with the "snap camera," a hand-held camera for the general public. For the first time, people could take candid photographs. Warren and Brandeis feared the intersection of this new photographic technology with the gossip-hungry press: "Instantaneous photographs and newspaper enterprise have invaded the sacred precincts of private and domestic life; and numerous mechanical devices threaten to make good the prediction that 'what is whispered in the closet shall be proclaimed from the house-tops.'"[7]

On the surface, observed Warren and Brandeis, the existing common law failed to afford a remedy for privacy invasions. But it contained the seeds to develop the proper protection of privacy. The authors looked to existing legal rights and concluded that they were manifestations of a deeper principle lodged in the common law—"the more general right of the individual to be let alone."[8] From this principle, new remedies to protect privacy could be derived. Warren and Brandeis suggested that the primary way to safeguard privacy was through tort actions to allow people to sue others for privacy invasions.

What Warren and Brandeis achieved was nothing short of magnificent. By pulling together various isolated strands of the common law, the authors demonstrated that creating remedies for privacy invasions wouldn't radically change the law but would merely be an expansion of what was already germinating.

As early as 1903, courts and legislatures responded to the Warren and Brandeis article by creating a number of privacy torts to redress the harms that Warren and Brandeis had noted.[9] These torts permit people to sue others for privacy violations. In 1960, William Prosser, one of the most renowned experts on tort law, surveyed over 300 privacy cases in the 70 years since the publication of the Warren and Brandeis article.[10] He concluded that the cases could be classified as involving four distinct torts.[11] These torts are: (1) intrusion upon seclusion; (2) public disclosure of private facts; (3) false light; and (4) appropriation. Today, whether by statute or common law, most states recognize some or all of the privacy torts.[12]

The privacy torts emerged in response to the privacy problems raised by Warren and Brandeis—namely, the incursions into privacy by the burgeoning print media. Today, we are experiencing the rapid rise of a new form of media—the Internet. Although the press still poses a threat to privacy, and photography has become an indispensable tool of journalism (as Warren and Brandeis accurately predicted), there are now many additional threats to privacy other than the press. The privacy torts are capable of redressing specific harms done to individuals—such as when the press discloses a deeply embarrassing secret about a private figure—but are not well adapted to regulating the flow of personal information in computer databases and cyberspace.

Intrusion upon Seclusion. The tort of intrusion upon seclusion protects against the intentional intrusion into one's "solitude or seclusion" or "private affairs or concerns" that "would be highly offensive to a reasonable person."[13] Although this tort could be applied to the information collection techniques of databases, most of the information collection is not "highly offensive to a reasonable person." Each particular instance of collection is often small and innocuous; the danger is created by the aggregation of information, a state of affairs typically created by hundreds of actors over a long period of time. Indeed, courts have thrown out cases for intrusion involving the type of information that would likely be collected in databases. For example, courts have rejected intrusion actions based on obtaining a person's unlisted phone number, selling the names of magazine subscribers to direct mail companies, and collecting and disclosing an individual's past insurance history.[14] Further, intrusion must involve an invasion of "seclusion," and courts have dismissed intrusion suits when plaintiffs have been in public places. With regard to databases, much information collection and use occurs in public, and indeed, many parts of cyberspace may well be considered public places. Therefore, the tort of intrusion cannot provide an adequate safeguard against the gathering of personal information for databases.

Public Disclosure of Private Facts. The tort of public disclosure of private facts creates a cause of action when one makes public "a matter concerning the private life of another" in a way that "(a) would be highly offensive to a reasonable person, and (b) is not of legitimate concern to the public."[15] Courts have sustained public disclosure suits for printing a photograph of a woman whose dress was blown up involuntarily by air jets; for publishing an article describing an individual's unusual disease; and for posting a large sign in a window stating that a person owed a debt.[16]

Although this tort could conceivably be applied to certain uses of databases, such as the sale of personal information by the database industry, the tort of private facts appears to be designed to redress excesses of the press, and is accordingly focused on the widespread dissemination of personal information in ways that become known to the plaintiff. In contrast, databases of personal information are often transferred between specific companies, not broadcast on the evening news. Even if marketers disclosed information widely to the public, the tort is limited to "highly offensive" facts, and most facts in databases would not be highly offensive if made public. Moreover, some marketing data may already be in a public record, or by furnishing data in the first place, an individual may be deemed to have assented to its dissemination.

Additionally, the disclosure of personal information through the use and sale of databases is often done in secret. The trade in information is done behind closed doors in a kind of underworld that most people know little about. This secret trading of data is often completely legal. Thus, it would be difficult for a plaintiff to discover that such sales or disclosures have been made. Even if people are generally aware that their data is being transferred, they will often not be able to find out the specifics—what companies are receiving it and what these companies plan to do with it. As a result, the public disclosure tort is not well-adapted to combating the flow of personal information between various companies.

False Light. The tort of false light is primarily a variation on the defamation torts of libel and slander, protecting against the giving of "publicity to a matter concerning another that places the other before the public in a false light" that is "highly offensive to a reasonable person."[17] Like defamation, this tort has limited applicability to the types of privacy harms created by the collection and use of personal information by way of computer databases. Both defamation and false light protect one's reputation, but the type of information collected in databases often is not harmful to one's reputation.

Appropriation. The tort of appropriation occurs when one "appropriates to his own use or benefit the name or likeness of another."[18] In the courts, this tort has developed into a form of intellectual property right in aspects of one's personhood. The interest protected is the individual's right to "the exclusive use of his own identity, in so far as it is represented by his name or likeness."[19] For example, people can sue under this tort when their names or images are used to promote a product without their consent.[20]

Appropriation could be applied to database marketing, which can be viewed as the use of personal information for profit. However, the tort's focus on protecting the commercial value of personal information has often prevented it from being an effective tool in grappling with the database privacy problem. In *Dwyer v. American Express Co.*, a court held there was no appropriation when American Express sold its cardholders' names to merchants because "an individual name has value only when it is associated with one of defendants' lists. Defendants create value by categorizing and aggregating these names. Furthermore, defendants' practices do not deprive any of the cardholders of any value their individual names may possess."[21] In *Shibley v. Time, Inc.*, a court held that there was no action for appropriation when magazines sold subscription lists to direct mail companies because the plaintiff was not being used to endorse any product.[22] The appropriation tort often aims at protecting one's economic interest in a form of property, and it is most effective at protecting celebrities who have created value in their personalities. This is not the same interest involved with privacy, which can be implicated regardless of the economic value accorded to one's name or likeness.

An Overarching Problem. Even if it were possible to eliminate the above difficulties with some minor adjustments to the privacy torts, the privacy problem with databases transcends the specific injuries and harms that the privacy torts are designed to redress. By its nature, tort law looks to isolated acts, to particular infringements and wrongs. The problem with databases does not stem from any specific act, but is a systemic issue of power caused by the combination of relatively small actions, each of which when viewed in isolation would appear quite innocuous. Many modern privacy problems are the product of information flows, which occur between a variety of different entities. There is often no single wrongdoer; responsibility is spread among a multitude of actors, with a vast array of motives and aims, each doing different things at different times. For example, when a person unwittingly finds herself embroiled in a public news story, the invasiveness of the media is often not the product of one particular reporter. Rather, the collective actions of numerous reporters camping outside a person's home and following her wherever she goes severely disrupt her life. The difficulty in obtaining a legal remedy for this disruption is that no one reporter's actions may be all that invasive or objectionable. The harm is created by the totality of privacy invasions, but the tort of intrusion upon seclusion only focuses on each particular actor.[23]

In sum, tort law often views privacy invasions separately and individually; but the problems of digital dossiers emerge from the collective effects of information transactions, combinations, lapses in security, disclosures, and abusive uses. Therefore, solutions involving the retooling of tort law will be severely limited in redressing the problem.

Constitutional Law

The U.S. Constitution protects privacy in a number of ways even though the word "privacy" does not appear in the document. Although the Constitution does not explicitly provide for a right to privacy, a number of its provisions protect certain dimensions of privacy, and the Supreme Court has sculpted a right to privacy by molding together a variety of constitutional protections. Beyond the U.S. Constitution, many states protect privacy in their own constitutions—some with an explicit right to privacy.[24]

The U.S. Constitution only protects against state action, and many databases belong to the private sector. However, since the government is often a supplier of information to the private sector and is a major source of databases, constitutional protection could serve as a good potential tool for grappling with the problem.

The First Amendment. In addition to protecting free speech, the First Amendment safeguards the right of people to associate with one another. Freedom of association restricts the government's ability to demand organizations to disclose the names and addresses of their members or to compel people to list the organizations to which they belong.[25] As the Supreme Court reasoned, privacy is essential to the freedom to associate, for it enables people to join together without having to fear loss of employment, community shunning, and other social reprisals.[26] However, privacy of associations is becoming more difficult in a world where online postings are archived, where a list of the people a person contacts can easily be generated from telephone and email records, and where records reveal where a person travels, what websites she visits, and so on. The Supreme Court has repeatedly held that the First Amendment protects anonymous speech, and it can restrict the government from requiring the disclosure of information that reveals a speaker's identity.[27] However, the First Amendment only applies when the government plays a role in the compulsion of the information,[28] and most of the gathering of personal information by companies isn't done under the pressure of any law.

The Fourth and Fifth Amendments. The Fourth Amendment restricts the government from conducting "unreasonable searches and seizures."[29] It typically requires that government officials first obtain judicial authorization before conducting a search. According to the Supreme Court, "[t]he overriding function of the Fourth Amendment is to protect personal privacy and dignity against unwarranted intrusion by the State."[30] The Fifth Amendment provides for a privilege against self-incrimination.[31] The government cannot compel individuals to disclose incriminating information about themselves. In 1886, the Court articulated how the Fourth and Fifth Amendments worked in tandem to protect privacy. The case was *Boyd v. United States.*[32] The government sought to compel a merchant to produce documents for use in a civil forfeiture proceeding. The Court held that the government could not require the disclosure of the documents because "any forcible and compulsory extortion of a man's own testimony or of his private papers to be used as evidence to convict him of crime or to forfeit his goods" is an "invasion of his indefeasible right to personal security, personal liberty and private property."[33]

As the administrative state blossomed throughout the twentieth century, the Court sidestepped the broad implications of *Boyd.* The administrative state spawned hundreds of agencies and a vast bureaucracy that maintained records of personal information. As William Stuntz notes, "[g]overnment regulation required lots of information, and *Boyd* came dangerously close to giving regulated actors a blanket entitlement to nondisclosure. It is hard to see how modern health, safety, environmental, or economic regulation would be possible in such a regime."[34] Therefore, the Court abandoned *Boyd*, and it increasingly curtailed the Fourth and Fifth Amendments from regulating the burgeoning government record systems.[35]

The Fourth and Fifth Amendments protect only against government infringements, and do nothing to control the collection and use of information by private bureaucracies. Although it does not apply to the private sector, the Fourth Amendment does have the potential to protect against one problem with digital dossiers. The rise of digital dossiers in the private sector is becoming of increasing interest to law enforcement officials. I will discuss this issue in great depth in part III of this book. As I will demonstrate, the secrecy paradigm has made the Fourth Amendment practically inapplicable when the government seeks to tap into private-sector dossiers. In *Smith v. Maryland*,[36] the Court held that there was no reasonable expectation of privacy in the phone numbers one dials. The Court reasoned that such phone numbers were not secret because they were turned over to third parties (phone companies).[37] Similarly, in *United States v. Miller*, the Court held that financial records possessed by third parties are not private under the Fourth Amendment.[38] The Court's focus—which stems from the paradigm that privacy is about protecting one's hidden world—leads it to the view that when a third party has access to one's personal information, there can be no expectation of privacy in that information.

The Right to Privacy. Beyond specific constitutional provisions, the Supreme Court has held that the Constitution implicitly protects privacy. In 1965, in *Griswold v. Connecticut*, the Court held that a state could not ban the use of or counseling about contraceptives because it invaded the "zone of privacy" protected by the Constitution.[39] Although there is no part of the Bill of Rights that directly establishes a right to privacy, such a right is created by the "penumbras" of many of the 10 amendments that form the Bill of

Rights. In *Roe v. Wade*, the Court held that the right to privacy "is broad enough to encompass a woman's decision whether or not to terminate her pregnancy."[40]

In the 1977 decision, *Whalen v. Roe*, the Supreme Court extended substantive due process privacy protection to information privacy. New York passed a law requiring that records be kept of people who obtained prescriptions for certain addictive medications. Plaintiffs argued that the statute infringed upon their right to privacy. The Court held that the constitutionally protected "zone of privacy" extends to two distinct types of interests: (1) "independence in making certain kinds of important decisions"; and (2) the "individual interest in avoiding disclosure of personal matters."[41] The former interest referred to the line of cases beginning with *Griswold* which protected people's right to make decisions about their health, bodies, and procreation. The latter interest, however, was one that the Court had not previously defined.

The plaintiffs argued that they feared the greater accessibility of their personal information and the potential for its disclosure. As a result of this fear, they argued, many patients did not get the prescriptions they needed and this interfered with their independence in making decisions with regard to their health. The Court, however, held that the constitutional right to information privacy required only a duty to avoid unreasonable disclosure, and that the state had taken adequate security measures.[42]

The plaintiffs' argument, however, was not that disclosure was the real privacy problem. Rather, the plaintiffs were concerned that the collection of and greater access to their information made them lose control over their information. A part of themselves—a very important part of their lives—was placed in the distant hands of the state and completely outside their control. This is similar to the notion of a chilling effect on free speech, which is not caused by the actual enforcement of a particular law but by the fear created by the very existence of the law. The Court acknowledged that the court record supported the plaintiffs' contention that some people were so distraught over the law that they were not getting the drugs they needed. However, the Court rejected this argument by noting that because over 100,000 prescriptions had been filled before the law had been enjoined, the public was not denied access to the drugs.[43] The problem with the Court's response is that the Court failed to indicate how many prescriptions had been filled before the law had been passed. Without this data, there is no way to measure the extent of the deterrence. And even if there were only a few who were deterred, the anxiety caused by living under such a regime must also be taken into account.

The famous case of *Doe v. Southeastern Pennsylvania Transportation Authority (SEPTA)* best illustrates how the constitutional right to information privacy fails to comprehend the privacy problem of databases.[44] The plaintiff Doe was HIV positive and told two doctors (Dr. Press and Dr. Van de Beek) at his work about his condition but nobody else. He strove to keep it a secret. His employer, SEPTA, a self-insured government agency, maintained a prescription drug program with Rite-Aid as the drug supplier. SEPTA monitored the costs of its program. Doe was taking a drug used exclusively in the treatment of HIV, and he asked Dr. Press whether the SEPTA officials who reviewed the records would see the names for the various prescriptions. Dr. Press said no, and Doe had his prescription filled under the plan. Unfortunately, even though SEPTA never asked for the names, Rite-Aid mistakenly supplied the names corresponding to prescriptions when it sent SEPTA the reports. Pierce, the SEPTA official reviewing the records, became interested in Doe's use of the drug and began to investigate. She asked Dr. Van de Beek about the drug, and he told her what the drug was used for but would not answer any questions about the person using the drugs. Pierce also asked questions of Dr. Press, who informed Doe of Pierce's inquiry.

This devastated Doe. Doe began to fear that other people at work had found out. He began to perceive that people were treating him differently. However, he was not fired, and in fact, he was given a promotion. The court of appeals held that the constitutional right to information privacy had not been violated because there had not been any disclosure of confidential information.[45] Pierce had merely informed doctors who knew already. Doe offered no proof that anybody else knew, and accordingly, the court weighed his privacy invasion as minimal.

However, this missed the crux of Doe's complaint. Regardless of whether he was imagining how his co-workers were treating him, he was indeed suffering a real, palpable fear. His injury was the powerlessness of having no idea who else knew he had HIV, what his employer thought of him, or how the information could be used against him. This feeling of unease changed the way he perceived everything at his place of employment. The privacy problem wasn't merely the fact that Pierce divulged his secret or that Doe himself had lost control over his information, but rather that the information appeared to be entirely out of anyone's control. Doe was in a situation similar to that of Kafka's Joseph K.—waiting endlessly for the final verdict. He was informed that information about him had been collected; he knew that his employer had been investigating; but the process seemed to be taking place out of his sight. To some extent, he experienced the desperation that Joseph K. experienced—he knew that information about him was out there in the hands of others and that these people were in fact doing something with that information, but he had no participation in the process.

Statutory Law

Since the early 1970s, Congress has passed over 20 laws pertaining to privacy. Unlike the European Union, which adopted a general directive providing for comprehensive privacy protection,[46] the United States has not enacted measures of similar scope. Instead, Congress has passed a series of statutes narrowly tailored to specific privacy problems.

The Fair Credit Reporting Act (FCRA) of 1970, which regulates credit reporting agencies, fails to adequately restrict secondary uses and disclosures of that information.[47] Although inspired by allegations of abuse and lack of responsiveness of credit agencies, the FCRA was severely weakened due to the effective lobbying of the credit reporting industry.[48] The Act permits credit reporting companies to sell the "credit header" portion of credit histories (which contains names, addresses, former addresses, telephone number, SSN, employment information, and birthdate) to marketers.[49] The FCRA does little to equalize the unbalanced power relationship between individuals and credit reporting companies.

Congress's most significant piece of privacy legislation in the 1970s—the Privacy Act of 1974—regulates the collection and use of records by federal agencies, giving individuals the right to access and correct information in these records.[50] The Privacy Act is a good beginning, but it remains incomplete. In particular, it applies only to agencies of the federal government, and has no applicability to the use of databases by businesses and marketers.

The Family Educational Rights and Privacy Act of 1974 (FERPA), also known as the Buckley Amendment, regulates the accessibility of student records. The FERPA remains quite narrow, only applying to a subset of records in one limited context (education). Excluded are campus security records and health and psychological records.[51]

The Cable Communications Policy Act (CCPA) of 1984 requires cable operators to inform subscribers about the nature and uses of personal information collected.[52] The law prohibits any disclosure that reveals the subscriber's viewing habits, and it is enforced with a private cause of action. The statute, however, applies only to cable operators and it has a broad exception where personal data can be disclosed for a "legitimate business activity." Nevertheless, the CCPA is an important first step in giving consumers control over their cable records.

In 1986, Congress modernized electronic surveillance laws when it passed the Electronic Communications Privacy Act (ECPA).[53] The ECPA extends the protections of the federal wiretap law of 1968 to new forms of voice, data, and video communications, including cellular phones and email. The ECPA restricts the interception of transmitted communications and the searching of stored communications. The focus of the law is on regulating surveillance. The difficulties of the ECPA in responding to the challenges of computer databases is illustrated by the case *In re DoubleClick, Inc. Privacy Litigation*.[54] A group of plaintiffs profiled by DoubleClick contended that DoubleClick's placing and accessing cookies on their hard drives constituted unauthorized access in violation of ECPA. The court concluded that the ECPA didn't apply to DoubleClick because its cookies were permanent and ECPA restricted unauthorized access only to communications in "temporary, intermediate storage." Additionally, DoubleClick didn't illegally intercept a communication in violation of the ECPA because DoubleClick was authorized to access the cookies by the websites that people visited. The *DoubleClick* case illustrates that the ECPA is not well-tailored to addressing a large portion of private-sector information gathering in cyberspace.

After reporters obtained Supreme Court Justice nominee Robert Bork's videocassette rental data, Congress passed the Video Privacy Protection Act (VPPA) of 1988,[55] which has become known as the Bork Bill. The VPPA prohibits videotape service providers from disclosing the titles of the videos a person rents or buys. People are authorized to sue if the statute is violated.[56] However, the Act only applies to video stores, and no similar restrictions are placed on bookstores, record stores, or any other type of retailer, magazine producer, or catalog company.

The Telephone Consumer Protection Act (TCPA) of 1991 permits individuals to sue a telemarketer for damages up to $500 for each call received after requesting not to be called again.[57] If the telemarketer knowingly breaks the law, then the penalty is trebled. The TCPA, however, aims at redressing the aggravation of disruptive phone calls, and it does not govern the collection, use, or sale of personal data.

In 1994, Congress finally addressed the longstanding practice of many states of selling personal information in their motor vehicle records to marketers. The Driver's Privacy Protection Act of 1994 (DPPA) limits this practice, forcing states to acquire a driver's consent before disclosing personal information to marketers.[58] Although the DPPA is an important step in controlling government disclosures of personal information to the private sector, it applies only in the context of motor vehicle records. States are not limited in disclosing information contained in the numerous other forms of records they maintain.

In 1996, Congress passed the Health Insurance Portability and Accountability Act (HIPAA) to help standardize medical information so it could be transferred more easily between different databases.[59] Since this raised privacy concerns, Congress ordered the Department of Health and Human Services (HHS) to regulate the privacy of medical records. HHS's regulations, among other things, require authorization for all uses and disclosures beyond those for treatment, payment, or health care operation (such as for marketing purposes).[60] The HIPAA regulations have apparently pleased nobody. Doctors and hospitals complain that the regulations are too complicated, cumbersome, and expensive to follow. Advocates for privacy find the regulations weak and ineffective.

The first federal law directly addressing privacy in cyberspace, the Children's Online Privacy Protection Act (COPPA) of 1998, regulates the collection of children's personal information on the Internet.[61] Websites targeted at children must post privacy policies and must obtain parental consent in order to use children's personal information. But the law's reach is limited. It applies only to children's websites or when the website operator "has actual knowledge that it is collecting personal information from a child."[62] Only children under age 13 are covered. Additionally, as privacy law expert Anita Allen argues, the law forces parents to become involved in their children's Internet activities when some parents "may want their children to have free access to the Internet for moral or political reasons." Allen concludes that "COPPA is among the most paternalistic and authoritarian of the federal privacy statutes thus far."[63]

The Gramm-Leach-Bliley (GLB) Act of 1999 permits any financial institution to share "nonpublic personal information" with affiliated companies.[64] However, people can opt-out when a company discloses personal information to third parties.[65] In practice, the GLB Act greatly facilitates the disclosure of people's information. Given the large conglomerates of today's corporate world, affiliate sharing is significant. For example, Experian, one of the three largest credit reporting agencies, was purchased by Great Universal Stores, a British retail corporation, which also acquired Metromail, Inc., a direct-marketing company.[66] The Act applies only to "nonpublic" information, and much of the information aggregated in databases (such as one's name, address, and the like) is often considered to be public. Additionally, the Act's opt-out right is ineffective. As legal scholars Ted Janger and Paul Schwartz argue, the financial institution has "superior knowledge" and the GLB "leaves the burden of bargaining on the less informed party, the individual consumer."[67] They conclude that "[a]n opt-out default creates incentives for privacy notices that lead to *inaction* by the consumer."[68]

In sum, the federal laws are a start, but they often give people only a very limited form of control over only some of their information and frequently impose no system of default control on other holders of such information.[69] Although the statutes help in containing the spread of information, they often fail to adequately address the underlying power relationships and contain broad exceptions and loopholes that limit their effectiveness.

Furthermore, the federal statutes cover only a small geography of the database problem. As privacy law expert Joel Reidenberg has pointed out, the laws are "sectoral" in nature, dealing with privacy in certain contexts but leaving gaping holes in others.[70] "This mosaic approach," he observes, "derives from the traditional American fear of government intervention in private activities and the reluctance to broadly regulate industry. The result of the mosaic is a rather haphazard and unsatisfactory response to each of the privacy concerns."[71]

Thus, the federal privacy statutes form a complicated patchwork of regulation with significant gaps and omissions. For example, federal regulation covers federal agency records, educational records, cable television records, video rental records, and state motor vehicle records, but it does not cover most records maintained by state and local officials, as well as a host of other records held by libraries, charities, and merchants (i.e., supermarkets, department stores, mail order catalogs, bookstores, and the like). The COPPA protects the privacy of children under 13 on the Internet, but there is no protection for adults. As political scientist Colin Bennett observes, "[t]he approach to making privacy policy in the United States is reactive rather than anticipatory, incremental rather than comprehensive, and fragmented rather than coherent. There may be a lot of laws, but there is not much protection."[72]

Second, many of Congress's privacy statutes are hard to enforce. It is often difficult, if not impossible, for an individual to find out if information has been disclosed. A person who begins receiving unsolicited marketing mail and email may have a clue that some entity has disclosed her personal information, but that person often will not be able to discover which entity was the culprit. Indeed, the trade in personal information is a clandestine underworld, one that is not exposed sufficiently by federal privacy regulation to enable effective enforcement.

The Kafka metaphor illustrates that the problem with digital dossiers involves the fact that our personal information is not only out of our control but also is often placed within a bureaucratic process that lacks control and discipline in handling and using such information. The federal statutes have certainly made advances in protecting against this problem, and they demonstrate that Congress's resolve to protect privacy has remained strong for over 30 years. But much more work remains to be done.

The FTC and Unfair and Deceptive Practices

Since 1998, the Federal Trade Commission (FTC) has been bringing actions against companies that violate their own privacy policies. The FTC has interpreted the FTC Act, which prohibits "unfair or deceptive acts or practices in or affecting commerce,"[73] to be infringed when a company breaks a promise it made in its privacy policy. The FTC can bring civil actions and seek injunctive remedies. Since it began enforcing the Act in this manner, the FTC has brought several high-profile cases, almost all of which have resulted in settlements.[74]

Yet, the FTC has been rather weak and reactive in its enforcement of privacy policies.[75] In a number of cases involving companies engaging in blatant breaches of their own privacy policies, the FTC has settled, simply requiring companies to sin no more.[76] A recent case involving Microsoft, however, suggests that the FTC might become more proactive. Microsoft's Passport maintains the personal information of Internet users to allow them to use a single username and password to access many different websites without having to sign on to each separately. Although Microsoft promised in its privacy policy that it protected Passport information with "powerful online security technology," the FTC concluded that Microsoft did not provide adequate security. Microsoft and the FTC agreed on a settlement where Microsoft must create a better system of security.[77] Unlike most cases before the FTC, the security problems of Microsoft's Passport had not yet resulted in a major security breach.

In the end, however, the FTC is limited in its reach. It only ensures that companies keep their promises. As Paul Schwartz notes, if a website doesn't make a promise about privacy, then it will "fall outside of the FTC's jurisdiction."[78] Unfortunately, the FTC has only limited time and resources, and its "privacy protection activities already are dwarfed by its more aggressive investigations of fraud and deceptive marketing practices on the Internet."[79]

A World of Radical Transparency: Freedom of Information Law

Some commentators suggest that there is little the law can do to protect privacy in the Information Age. In *The Transparent Society,* technology commentator David Brin argues that privacy is dead:

> [I]t is already far too late to prevent the invasion of cameras and databases. The *djinn* cannot be crammed back into its bottle. No matter how many laws are passed, it will prove quite impossible to legislate away the new surveillance tools and databases. They are here to stay. Light *is* going to shine into every corner of our lives.[80]

Brin suggests that we abandon privacy in favor of a transparent society, one where everything is out in the open, where we watch the watchers, where we have the ability to monitor the elites—the politicians and the corporate leaders—just as much as they have the ability to monitor us. "[W]e may not be able to eliminate the intrusive glare shining on citizens of the [twenty-first century]," Brin observes, "but the glare just might be rendered harmless through the application of more light aimed in the other direction."[81] We should thus regulate in favor of mandating free access to information. According to Brin, a truly transparent society would hold accountable those who would violate our privacy.[82]

Brin fails to realize that affording mutuality of access to information will do little to empower ordinary individuals. The reason is that information is much more of an effective tool in the hands of a large bureaucracy. Information is not the key to power in the Information Age—knowledge is. Information consists of raw facts. Knowledge is information that has been sifted, sorted, and analyzed. The mere possession of information does not give one power; it is the ability to process that information and the capability to use the data that matter. In order to solve the problem, a transparent society would have to make each individual as competent as bureaucratic organizations in processing information into knowledge.

The Law of Information Privacy and Its Shortcomings

As this chapter has demonstrated, the law of information privacy is quite extensive. It developed in response to certain vexing privacy problems, often created by new technologies. The Warren and Brandeis privacy torts were inspired by new photographic technology and a rapidly growing media that was becoming very sensationalistic. The types of injuries Warren and Brandeis had in mind were those caused by intrusive newsgathering techniques and by publishing private information in the newspapers. In the mid-twentieth century, during the Cold War, the law focused heavily on surveillance, which had become one the central threats to privacy. These times witnessed the growth of electronic communication along with new means of electronic espionage such as wiretapping, bugging devices, and video cameras. Americans feared the terrible totalitarian regimes of Nazi Germany, the Soviet Union, and Eastern Europe, all of which employed extensive monitoring of their citizens' private lives as well as secret police and spies to maintain strict control. Law enforcement officials in the United States also increasingly resorted to the use of surveillance, with the rapidly growing FBI leading the way. It is therefore certainly not surprising that the privacy law forged during these times was devoted to ameliorating the kinds of harms so perfectly captured in Orwell's *1984*.

However, the advent of the computer, the proliferation of databases, and the birth of the Internet have created a new breed of privacy problems. The Orwellian dangers have certainly not disappeared; nor have the harms created by the sensationalistic media. But the rise of digital dossiers has created new and different problems. New privacy laws have been created in response. The constitutional right to information privacy has emerged in the courts as a spinoff of the regular constitutional right to privacy. Congress and the states have passed numerous statutes to regulate the collection and use of personal information. The FTC has started to bring enforcement actions against companies that fail to live up to their privacy promises. All of these developments have been promising, but as I have shown throughout this chapter, the law of privacy has not dealt effectively with the new problems created by digital dossiers. The reason is that the law still harbors conceptions of privacy that are not responsive to the realities of the Information Age. These new privacy problems are not isolated infringements, but are systematic and diffuse. They are often not created by a single perpetrator, but by a combination of actors often without sinister purposes. The problems caused by digital dossiers are quite broad, and they apply to the entire information economy, making the narrow federal statutes inapplicable to a large portion of the flow of personal information. Enforcing rights and remedies against the collection and use of personal information is very difficult since much information flow occurs without people even knowing about it.

So what can be done? I have demonstrated some of the law's shortcomings. Can the law adequately respond to these problems? This question will be the focus of the next chapter and beyond.

5 The Limits of Market-Based Solutions

Many solutions to the problems of privacy and information are market-based, relying on property rights or contractual default rules to regulate the flow of information. Does the market already adequately protect privacy? Or can the market, with minor tinkering, develop effective privacy protection? Or must a more radical reconstruction of the market be undertaken?

Market-Based Solutions

Property Rights and Contract. The notion of "control of personal information" is one of the most dominant conceptions of privacy. As privacy expert Alan Westin declares: "Privacy is the claim of individuals, groups, or institutions to determine for themselves when, how, and to what extent information about them is communicated to others."[1] Numerous other scholars embrace this definition.[2]

Theorists who view privacy as control over information frequently understand it within the framework of property and contract concepts. This is not the only way control can be understood, but the leading commentators often define it in terms of ownership—as a property right in information.[3] Understood in such terms, control over something entails a bundle of legal rights of ownership, such as rights of possession, alienability, exclusion of others, commercial exploitation, and so on.[4] This is what leads Westin to conclude: "[P]ersonal information, thought of as the right of decision over one's private personality, should be defined as a property right."[5] The market discourse focuses the debate around who should own certain kinds of information as well as what the appropriate contractual rules should be for trading personal information.

Therefore, in addition to property rights, contract law plays an important role in regulating privacy. Parties can make contractual agreements about privacy at the outset of forming a relationship. In certain instances, courts have held that even though the contract did not specifically mention privacy, it is an implied term in the contract. The common law tort of breach of confidentiality embodies this view. It enables people to sue for damages when a party breaches a contractual obligation (often implied rather than express) to maintain confidentiality. This tort primarily protects the privacy of the patient-physician relationship.[6] The tort also has been used to protect against banks breaching the confidences of their customers.[7]

Implied contractual terms are a form of default rule in the contract. Contractual default rules are the initial set of rules that regulate market transactions. These rules are merely a starting point; they govern only when the parties to a transaction do not negotiate for a different set of rules. As legal scholar Ian Ayres and economist Robert Gertner explain, "default rules" are rules "that parties can contract around by prior agreement" while "immutable rules" (or inalienability rules) are rules that "parties cannot change by contractual agreement."[8] Most market proponents favor default rules that can be bargained around. Market solution proponents, however, are certainly not in agreement over the types of property entitlements and contractual default rules that should be required. But once these are established, then the market can do the rest. People and companies can buy and sell personal information and make contracts about the protection of privacy. For example, a number of commentators recommend contractual solutions to safeguard privacy, such as where consumers license the use of their data to businesses.[9]

Although some might argue that personal information is owned by the individual to whom it pertains based on a natural rights theory or some form of inherent connection, many commentators who approach privacy in terms of property rights assign initial entitlements instrumentally. They claim that the market will achieve the ideal amount of privacy by balancing the value of personal information to a company (i.e., its commercial value in the marketplace) against the value of the information to the individual and the larger social value of having the information within the individual's control.[10] The role of law is to assign the initial entitlements. Thus, the debate in this discourse centers around who should own certain kinds of information.

So who should own personal information when people transact with businesses? The individuals to whom the information pertains? Or the companies that collect it?

Judge Richard Posner suggests that the law should often favor the companies over the individuals. Posner translates control of information into property concepts. Society should provide individuals a property right in true information about themselves when it will foster more efficient transactions.[11] With regard to the sale of customer lists, Posner argues that "the costs of obtaining subscriber approval would be high relative to the value of the list." He concludes: "If, therefore, we believe that these lists are generally worth more to the purchasers than being shielded from possible unwanted solicitations is worth to subscribers, we should assign the property right to the [companies]; and the law does this."[12]

In contrast, law professor Richard Murphy concludes that in many instances, contractual default rules mandating confidentiality of personal information are more efficient than default rules permitting disclosure.[13] For Murphy, privacy has "substantial economic benefits" because "[u]nless a person can investigate without risk of reproach what his own preferences are, he will not be able to maximize his own happiness."[14]

Likewise, Jerry Kang views personal information as a form of property and advocates for a market solution. He recognizes that there are compelling non-market perceptions of privacy that view privacy as a human value and that this way of understanding privacy is "poorly translated, if at all, into efficiency terms." Nevertheless, he favors the market approach. Kang recognizes that merely assigning a default rule as to the ownership of information will be ineffective because individuals lack convenient ways to find out what information about them is collected and how it is used. Thus, he advocates a contractual default rule that "personal information may be processed in only functionally necessary ways" and that parties are "free to contract around the default rule." Kang claims that inalienability rules would be too paternalistic because individuals should be able to sell or disclose their information if they desire. Inalienability rules will risk "surrendering control over information privacy to the state."[15]

Internet law expert Lawrence Lessig also recommends a market-based approach. He argues that a property regime permits each individual to decide for herself what information to give out and "protects both those who value their privacy more than others and those who value it less." Lessig notes that our existing system of posting privacy policies and enabling consumers to opt in or out has high transaction costs because people do not have "the time or patience to read through cumbersome documents describing obscure rules for controlling data." Therefore, Lessig recommends that computer software be crafted to act akin to an "electronic butler," negotiating our privacy concerns: "The user sets her preferences once—specifies how she would negotiate privacy and what she is willing to give up—and from that moment on, when she enters a site, the site and her machine negotiate. Only if the machines can agree will the site be able to obtain her personal data."[16] In other words, Lessig suggests a technological implementation for a market system where people have property rights in their information.

Self-Regulation. Some commentators—especially people in the database industry—argue that the market is functioning optimally and is already adequately accounting for privacy concerns.[17] The market, they argue, is already treating personal information as a property right owned by individuals. Companies have increasingly been adopting privacy policies, which can operate as a form of contractual promise limiting the future uses of the information. The exchange of personal information for something of value is already beginning to take place. Many websites require people to supply personal information in order to gain access to information on the website. Under the market approach, this practice can be justified as an information trade.[18] In order to receive such services as book recommendations, software upgrades, free email, and personal web pages, users must relinquish personal information not knowing its potential uses. In short, useful information and services are being exchanged for personal information, and this represents the going "price" of privacy.

Moreover, there are market incentives for companies to keep their data secret and to be honest about their data collection. There have been a number of instances where companies have canceled various initiatives due to public outcry over privacy. For example, in response to privacy concerns, Yahoo! eliminated the reverse telephone number search from its People Search site.[19] In the early 1990s, in response to a public outcry, Lotus Corporation scrapped plans to sell a database containing the names, addresses, income brackets, and lifestyle data of 120 million citizens.[20] In 1996, Lexis-Nexis announced its P-TRAK Personal Locator, which would provide addresses, maiden names, and SSNs of millions of people. After an intensive 10-day outcry by Internet users, Lexis-Nexis canceled P-TRAK.[21] In 1997, AOL halted its plans to sell customers' phone numbers to direct marketing firms.[22]

Furthermore, proponents of self-regulation argue that information flow has many beneficial uses. Legal scholar Fred Cate contends that information flow makes the consumer credit system cheaper and faster, "enhances customer convenience and service," and enables businesses "to ascertain customer needs accurately and meet those needs rapidly and efficiently."[23] Many people want some targeted marketing and enjoy receiving information about products more tailored to their tastes.

Cate points out that self-regulation is "more flexible and more sensitive to specific contexts and therefore allow[s] individuals to determine a more tailored balance between information uses and privacy than privacy laws do." The most effective way for people to protect their privacy, Cate contends, is to take actions themselves.[24]

Law professor Eric Goldman argues that "consumers' stated privacy concerns diverge from what consumers do." People are quick to say in the abstract that they want privacy, but when offered money or discounts in return for their personal information, they readily relinquish it. "[P]eople won't take even minimal steps to protect themselves," Goldman asserts, "[so] why should government regulation do it for them?" Finally, Goldman argues, "online businesses will invest in privacy when it's profitable."[25]

Thus, the self-regulation proponents conclude that to the extent that consumers want their privacy protected, the market will respond to this demand and appropriately balance it against other interests. The fact that privacy is not afforded much protection demonstrates that people value other things more than privacy—such as efficient and convenient transactions.

Misgivings of the Market

Understanding the privacy problem of databases in terms of the Kafka metaphor—our helplessness and vulnerability in the face of the powerful bureaucracies that handle our personal data—reveals that there are several deficiencies in market solutions.

The Limitations of Contract Law. Although contract law can protect privacy within relationships formed between parties, it does not redress privacy invasions by third parties outside of the contractual bonds. Warren and Brandeis recognized this problem back in 1890 when they spoke of new photographic technologies. Cameras had been quite large, and people had to pose to have their picture taken. This would likely require people to establish some sort of contractual relationship with the photographer. But the development of cheaper portable cameras in the 1880s enabled strangers to take pictures without the subject ever knowing.[26]

Today, our personal information is increasingly obtained by people and organizations that have never established any relationship with us. For example, as public health law expert Lawrence Gostin notes, the law of patient-physician confidentiality "is premised on the existence of a relationship between a physician and a patient, although most health information is not generated within this relationship."[27] Information is often maintained not just by one's physician, but one's health plan, government agencies, health care clearinghouse organizations, and many others.

Problems with Bargaining Power. There are great inequalities in bargaining power in many situations involving privacy, such as employment contracts or contracts between big corporations and individuals. How many people are able to bargain effectively over their contracts with their Internet Service Providers, cable providers, telephone companies, and the like? Oscar Gandy observes that "individuals are largely 'contract term takers' in the bulk of their economic relations with organizations."[28] People frequently accede to standardized contract terms without putting up much of a fight.[29]

Nor does it appear that market competition is producing a wide menu of privacy protections. Companies only rarely compete on the basis of the amount of privacy they offer. People often do not weigh privacy policies heavily when choosing companies. For example, people rarely choose phone companies based on their privacy policies.

Self-regulatory proponents would respond that this fact indicates that privacy isn't very important to most people. If people really cared about privacy, the self-regulators argue, then they would refuse to deal with companies offering inadequate levels of privacy. But as Paul Schwartz contends, there are coordination problems because "individuals may have difficulty finding effective ways to express collectively their relative preferences for privacy."[30]

Although more companies that routinely collect and use personal information are posting privacy policies, these policies have several difficulties. Privacy policies are often written in obtuse prose and crammed with extraneous information.[31] But market proponents—especially those favoring self-regulation—counter that many people don't bother to read privacy policies. This may not necessarily stem from their turgid prose, but from the fact that consumers don't want to take the time to read them. Perhaps people just don't care.

However, perhaps the lack of interest in privacy policies may stem from the fact that the policies hardly amount to a meaningful contract, where the parties bargain over the terms. Privacy policies are little more than "notices" about a company's policies rather than a contract. Privacy policies tend to be self-indulgent, making vague promises such as the fact that a company will be careful with data; that it will respect privacy; that privacy is its number one concern. These public relations statements are far from reliable and are often phrased in a vague, self-aggrandizing manner to make the corporation look good. What consumers do not receive is a frank and detailed description of what will and will not be done with their information, what specific information security measures are being taken, and what specific rights of recourse they have. People must rely on the good graces of companies that possess their data to keep it secure and to prevent its abuse. They have no say in how much money and effort will be allocated to security; no say in which employees get access; and no say in what steps are taken to ensure that unscrupulous employees do not steal or misuse their information. Instead, privacy policies only vaguely state that the company will treat information securely. Particular measures are not described, and individuals have no control over those measures.

Most privacy policies provide no way for customers to prevent changes in the policy, and they lack a binding enforcement mechanism. Frequently, companies revise their privacy policies, making it even more difficult for an individual to keep track. Yahoo!'s privacy policy indicates that it "may change from time to time, so please check back periodically."[32] AOL once told its subscribers that their privacy preferences had expired and that if they did not fill out a new opt-out form, then their personal information would be distributed to marketers.[33] Further, personal information databases can be sold to other businesses with less protective privacy policies, especially when a company goes bankrupt. For example, in 2000, Internet toy retailer Toysmart.com filed for bankruptcy and attempted to auction off its personal information database of over 200,000 customers.[34] Dot-com bankruptcies create a breakdown in the relationship between companies and consumers, resulting in little incentive for the bankrupt company to take measures to protect consumer data. Personal information databases are often a company's most valuable asset and could be sold to third parties at bankruptcy to pay off creditors.[35]

Second, to the extent that privacy policies do provide individuals with privacy protection, it is often provided with an opt-out system, in which personal data can be collected and used unless the individual expressly says no. Opt-out systems require individuals to check a box, send a letter, make a telephone call, or take other proactive steps to indicate their preferences. However, these steps are often time-consuming. There are too many collectors of information for a right of opt-out to be effective. Without a centralized mechanism for individuals to opt-out, individuals would have to spend much of their time guarding their privacy like a hawk.

The Direct Marketing Association (DMA) has established a system where consumers can be placed on a no-solicitation list. This is essentially a database of people who do not want to be in databases. The service records their preference, but does not remove their name from any list.[36] The database is then sent to the subscribing companies so that they can stop mailings to those names.[37] However, many people are unaware of this option, numerous companies are not members of the DMA, and many members fail to comply with DMA guidelines. As legal scholar Jeff Sovern argues, opt-out systems provide little incentive to companies to make opting-out easy; "companies will incur transaction costs in notifying consumers of the existence of the opt-out option and in responding to consumers who opt out."[38] Since companies want to use personal information, their incentive in an opt-out system is to make opting-out more difficult.[39]

These problems arise because people often lack sufficient bargaining power over their privacy. As privacy law expert Peter Swire observes, it is difficult for consumers to bargain with large corporations about their privacy because they lack expertise in privacy issues and because it takes substantial time and effort.[40] Information collection is duplicitous, clandestine, and often coerced. The law currently does not provide meaningful ability to refuse to consent to relinquish information. The FCRA, for example, mandates that individuals consent before an employer can obtain their credit report. According to Joel Reidenberg: "Frequently, individuals will be asked to sign blanket consent statements authorizing inquiry into credit reporting agency files and disclosures of information for any purpose. These consents rarely identify the credit reporting agencies or all the uses to which the personal information will be put."[41] This consent is virtually meaningless. When people seek medical care, among the forms they sign are general consent forms which permit the disclosure of one's medical records to anyone with a need to see them. Giving people property rights or default contract rules is not sufficient to remedy the problem because it does not address the underlying power inequalities that govern information transactions. Unless these are addressed, any privacy protections will merely be "contracted" around, in ways not meaningful either to the problem or to the contract notions supposedly justifying such a solution. People will be given consent forms with vague fine-print discussions of the contractual default privacy rules that they are waiving, and they will sign them without thought. As Julie Cohen correctly contends, "[f]reedom of choice in markets requires accurate information about choices and other consequences, and enough power—in terms of wealth, numbers, or control over resources—to have choices."[42] The bargaining process must be made easier. The way things currently stand, most people don't know even know where to begin if they want to assert their preference for privacy.

The One-Size-Fits-All Problem. Even assuming these problems could be dealt with, a number of additional difficulties remain that prevent individuals from exercising their preferences to protect their privacy. Affording individuals a right to control their personal data improperly assumes that individuals have the ability to exercise meaningful control over their information.[43] Paul Schwartz notes how consent screens on a website asking users to relinquish control over information often do so on a "take-it-or-leave-it basis" resulting in the "fiction" that people have "expressed informed consent to [the website's] data processing practices."[44] Individuals are often presented with an all-or-nothing choice: either agree to all forms of information collection and use or to none whatsoever. Such a limited set of choices does not permit individuals to express their preferences accurately. Individuals frequently desire to consent to certain uses of their personal information, but they do not want to relinquish their information for all possible future uses.

For example, a person may want to purchase books from an online bookseller. Suppose that the person's privacy preferences consist of the information being kept very secure, not being disclosed to the government, and not being traded or disclosed to other companies (even in the event that the company goes bankrupt). But the online bookseller's privacy policy is standardized and often does not address these points with any reasonable degree of specificity. And since privacy policies are remarkably similar among many companies, many other online bookstores offer comparable terms. If the person decides to purchase the book in a bricks-and-mortar bookstore, she faces the same difficulties if she pays by credit card. There, the privacy policies are not even readily available to the purchaser.

This state of affairs exists partly because not many choices are available to people regarding their privacy and partly because people are often not aware of the problems, risks, and dangers about how their information is handled. Even if they were, it is doubtful whether a person could create a special deal with a company to provide greater protections for her privacy.[45] Therefore, with regard to the level of privacy protection offered by companies, a person must simply take it or leave it. People are not afforded enough choices to exercise their privacy preferences. A more complete range of choices must permit individuals to express their preferences for how information will be protected, how it will be used in the future, and with whom it will be shared. Moreover, because companies controlling personal information are secretive about its uses and vague about their privacy policies, people lack adequate knowledge to make meaningful choices.

Market proponents might respond that it is not economically feasible for companies to offer customized privacy policies. This would require companies to keep track of each particular customer's privacy preferences, which could be cumbersome and expensive. However, companies maintain very complex databases, able to handle countless fields of data and multiple variables. Why can't various privacy preferences be recorded along with various pieces of information?

Inequalities in Knowledge. The argument that the market is already providing the optimal level of privacy protection fails because there are vast inequalities in knowledge and much data collection is clandestine. Despite the few instances where information collection initiatives were canceled due to public complaints over privacy, many new, ambitious information gathering endeavors occur outside of the public eye. At any given time, one of thousands of companies or government agencies could decide on a new use of information or on a new form of collection. People should not always have to be ready to mount a large campaign anytime such an eruption could occur. Many of the activities of the database industry are not well known to the public, and will remain that way under default notions of corporate privacy and trade secrets unless something is changed. Ironically, corporate bureaucracies sometimes have more privacy rights than individuals.

The Value of Personal Information

A key aspect of property rights, observes information law scholar Pamela Samuelson, is that property is alienable—people can readily trade it away.[46] Market solutions, which view information as property that can be traded in the market, depend upon the ability of people to accurately assess the value of information. As legal scholar Katrin Byford aptly notes, assigning property rights in information "values privacy only to the extent it is considered to be of personal worth by the individual who claims it."[47] The value of personal information is determined by how much it takes for a person to relinquish it. Since people routinely give out their personal information for shopping discount cards, for access to websites, and even for free, some market proponents (especially the self-regulators) argue that the value of the data is very low to the individuals. The market is thus already adequately compensating individuals for the use of their information.

In a well-functioning market, assuming no market failure, the market might work quite well in valuing personal information. But the market in privacy is not a well-functioning market, and thus its valuation determinations are suspect.

The Aggregation Effect. The aggregation effect severely complicates the individual's ability to ascribe a value to personal information. An individual may give out bits of information in different contexts, each transfer appearing innocuous. However, when aggregated, the information becomes much more revealing. As law professor Julie Cohen observes, each instance in which we give out personal information may seem "trivial and incremental," which "tends to minimize its ultimate effect."[48] It is the totality of information about a person and how it is used that poses the greatest threat to privacy. From the standpoint of each particular information transaction, individuals will not have enough facts to make a truly informed decision.

Uncertain Future Uses. The potential future uses of personal information are too vast and unknown to enable individuals to make the appropriate valuation. The value of much personal information, such as one's SSN, does not stem from its intimacy, its immediate revelations of selfhood, or the fact that the individual has authored it. Rather, the value is in the ability to prevent others from gaining power and control over an individual; from revealing an individual's private life; and from making the individual vulnerable to fraud, identity theft, prying, snooping, and the like. Because this value is linked to uncertain future uses, it is difficult, if not impossible, for an individual to adequately value her information. Since the ownership model involves individuals relinquishing full title to the information, they have little idea how such information will be used when in the hands of others.

For example, a person who signs up for a discount supermarket shopper card might have some vague knowledge that her personal information will be collected. In the abstract, this knowledge may not be all that disconcerting. But what if the person were told that information about the contraceptives and over-the-counter medications she buys would be made available to her employer? Or given to the government? Or used to send her advertisements or spam? Without being informed about how the information will be used, the individual lacks the necessary knowledge to assess the implications of surrendering her personal data.

Is Privacy a Property Right? When personal information is understood as a property right, the value of privacy often is translated into the combined monetary value of particular pieces of personal information. Privacy becomes the right to profit from one's personal data, and the harm to privacy becomes understood as not being adequately paid for the use of this "property." But is this really the harm? Can privacy be translated into property concepts without losing some of its meaning?[49]

An initial difficulty with understanding personal information as a form of property is that it is unclear who really creates the information. Some pro-privacy commentators quickly assume that because information pertains to a person, the person should have a right to own it. However, information is often not created by the individual alone. We often develop personal information through our relationships with others. When a person purchases a product, information is created through the interaction of seller and buyer.

Consider the case of *Dwyer v. American Express Co.* American Express cardholders sued American Express for renting their names to merchants under both invasion of privacy and appropriation. The court held that by using the credit card, "a cardholder is voluntarily, and necessarily, giving information to defendants that, if analyzed, will reveal a cardholder's spending habits and shopping preferences." Thus, there was no invasion of privacy. As for appropriation, the court reasoned:

> Undeniably, each cardholder's name is valuable to defendants. The more names included on a list, the more that list will be worth. However, a single, random cardholder's name has little or no intrinsic value to defendants (or a merchant). Rather, an individual name has value only when it is associated with one of the defendants' lists. Defendants create value by categorizing and aggregating these names. Furthermore, defendants' practices do not deprive any of the cardholders of any value their individual names may possess.[50]

This case indicates what is omitted when information privacy is reduced to property rights in information. The court only focused on the value of the information to each individual, not on the systemic harms to which American Express's practices contributed—namely, the powerlessness of the individuals to have any meaningful control over information pertaining to their personal lives. The problem with databases is not that information collectors fail to compensate people for the proper value of personal information. The problem is people's lack of control, their lack of knowledge about how data will be used in the future, and their lack of participation in the process. It is not merely sufficient to allow people to sell their information, relinquish all title to it, and allow companies to use it as they see fit. This provides people with an all-or-nothing type of exchange, which they are likely to take when they are unaware of how information can or might be used in the future. Nor is it enough to attach some default contractual rights to information transactions such as nondisclosure obligations or a requirement of notification when a future use of information is employed. These solutions cannot work effectively in a situation where the power relationship between individuals and public and private bureaucracies is so greatly unbalanced. In other words, the problem with market solutions is not merely that it is difficult to com- modify information (which it is), but also that a regime of default rules alone (consisting of property rights in information and contrac- tual defaults) will not enable fair and equitable market transactions in personal information. As Julie Cohen warns, giving people property rights in a defective market runs the risk of leading to more trade in personal information, not less.[51]

Due to the problems with ascribing a value to personal informa- tion and because privacy is an issue about societal structure involving our relationships with public and private bureaucracies, some form of regulation is necessary that exceeds the narrow measures pro- posed by proponents of a market solution. There are certain rights we cannot bargain away because they are not mere individual posses- sions but are important for the structure of society as a whole.

Too Much Paternalism?

Market proponents are wary of government regulation because it threatens to usurp individual choice. They argue that people should be free to contract as they see fit. If people want to give up their pri- vacy, the government shouldn't paternalistically say that it knows best. Market proponents contend that people are capable of making rational decisions about their personal information and that the law shouldn't interfere.

This argument is quite compelling, for not all individuals want privacy. For example, people may want their names sold to other companies because they like receiving catalogs. Market proponents thus aim to preserve individual choice.

The problem, however, is that the market currently fails to provide mechanisms to enable individuals to exercise informed meaningful choices. Even market approaches favoring a more pro-privacy regime of contractual default rules neglect to account for the core of the database problem as illustrated by the Kafka metaphor—the power inequalities that pervade the world of information transfers between individuals and bureaucracies.

As a result of these problems, there is little economic incentive for companies to adopt strong privacy protection in the absence of legal regulation. Although the Direct Marketing Association (DMA) maintains standards for self-regulation, polls suggest that less than 25 percent of DMA members adhere to self-regulatory practices.[52] The individual's lack of knowledge about the use of personal information also makes companies less responsive to privacy concerns. One employee at a bank stated: "We joke about it all the time because we officially say that we don't reveal information and we treat it with the utmost respect. What a crock. I hear people laughing in the elevator about credit reports they've pulled!"[53] Unless people have greater knowledge about the uses of their information and practices within a company, they won't be able even to raise an outcry.

I am not arguing that the market can't protect privacy. The market can work well, but not in the absence of structural legal protections. A set of laws and rights is necessary to govern our relationship with bureaucracies. These laws must consist of more than default rules that can be contracted around or property entitlements that can be bartered away. Market-based solutions work within the existing market; the problem with databases is the very way that the market deals with personal information—a problem in the nature of the market itself that prevents fair and voluntary information transactions.

Inalienability rules do not necessarily have to limit a person's ability to disclose or sell certain information; nor must they limit many forms of information collection. If the problem is understood with the Kafka metaphor, the solution to regulating information flow is not to radically curtail the collection of information but to regulate uses. For example, Amazon.com's book recommendation service collects extensive information about a customer's taste in books. If the problem is surveillance, then the most obvious solution would be to provide strict limits on Amazon.com's collection of information. This solution, however, would curtail much data gathering that is necessary for business in today's society and that is put to beneficial uses. Indeed, many Amazon.com customers, myself included, find Amazon.com's book recommendation service to be very helpful. In contrast, if the problem is understood as I have depicted it, then the problem is not that Amazon is spying on its users or that it can use personal data to induce its customers to buy more books. What is troubling is the unfettered ability of Amazon.com to do whatever it wants with this information. This problem was underscored when Amazon.com abruptly changed its privacy policy to allow the transfer of personal information to third parties in the event Amazon.com sold any of its assets or went bankrupt.[54] As a customer, I had no say in this change of policy; no ability to change it or bargain for additional privacy protection; and no sense about whether it would apply retroactively to the purchases I already made. And what's to prevent Amazon.com in the future from changing its policy once again, perhaps retroactively?

Therefore, privacy regulations should focus on our relationships with bureaucracies, for unless these relationships are restructured, markets in information will not consist of fair, voluntary, and informed information transactions. Markets can certainly work to protect privacy, but a precondition of a successful market is establishing rules governing our relationships with bureaucracies.

6 Architecture and the Protection of Privacy

Although information privacy law has taken some important steps to protect privacy, it has thus far suffered numerous failures and difficulties in addressing the privacy problems we are currently facing with digital dossiers. Why has such a diverse body of law failed to be effective? In a world constantly being transformed by technology, how can we erect a robust and effective law of privacy when the ground is constantly shifting?

Two Models for the Protection of Privacy

The Invasion Conception. The question of how to protect privacy was of paramount importance to Samuel Warren and Louis Brandeis in 1890 when they wrote their profoundly influential article, *The Right to Privacy.* The primary remedy for privacy invasions, they suggested, should be a tort action for damages, and to a limited extent, injunctions and criminal penalties.[1]

Warren and Brandeis's conception of privacy problems has been highly influential in the development of privacy law, and I will refer to this understanding as the "invasion conception." Under this conception, privacy is understood as a series of discrete wrongs—invasions—to specific individuals. These wrongs occur through the actions of particular wrongdoers. The injury is experienced by the individuals who are wronged. For example, a privacy violation that would fit well into the invasion conception is a newspaper publishing a photograph of a person in the nude without that person's consent. There is a particular wrongdoer (the newspaper) that engages in a particular action (publishing the photograph) which causes harm to a particular individual. This harm consists of mental distress and any consequent physical or mental impairment.

Under the invasion conception, privacy protections safeguard against these wrongs to individuals. Protection consists of rights and remedies for each instance of harm, and in certain cases, criminal punishments for the wrongdoers. Thus, the invasion conception is reactive. It waits for harms to materialize in concrete form and then reacts. The invasion conception works to prevent future harms through the deterrent effects of civil liability and criminal penalties.

Another aspect of the invasion conception is that it often views privacy protections in the form of rights possessed and remedied at the initiative of the individuals whose privacy has been invaded. The value of protecting privacy is measured in terms of the value of preventing harm to the individual. In the words of one court, "[p]rivacy is inherently personal. The right to privacy recognizes the sovereignty of the *individual*."[2] According to the Restatement of Torts: "The right protected by the action for invasion of privacy is a personal right, peculiar to the individual whose privacy is invaded."[3] Under this view, privacy is enforced by allowing individuals to seek remedies for privacy invasions.

The privacy torts are designed to redress specific harms. In many cases, however, damages are likely to be small, thus creating little incentive to sue. The result is that privacy is most protected in situations where damages can be defined palpably, such as where skeletons in the closet are revealed, where nudity is publicly disclosed, or where the press sneaks into a person's home to obtain personal information.

Like tort law, criminal law focuses on punishing specific wrongdo-ers. It aims to deter crime by establishing penalties for privacy inva-sions. Criminal law is often reactive, responding to crime with punishments after its occurrence. Frequently, criminal law fails to be proactive in preventing crime. Although criminal law certainly works to deter crime, some crimes are difficult to deter. Criminal law can only reach a certain level of deterrence, which can be limited by diffi-culties in catching and prosecuting the perpetrators. Crimes involv-ing the use and dissemination of personal information present complicated enforcement problems, since these crimes can occur from anywhere in the world, are easy to conceal, and take a long time to detect.

Although the invasion conception works for a number of privacy problems, not all privacy problems are the same, and many do not fit well into this model. In particular, the invasion conception does not adequately account for many of the privacy problems arising to-day. The problems of digital dossiers do not consist merely of a se-ries of isolated and discrete invasions or harms, but are systemic in nature, caused by a particular social or legal structure. Moreover, as I explained earlier, the aggregation effect complicates the applica-tion of tort law in specific cases. In isolation, a particular piece of information may not be very invasive of one's privacy. But when pieces of information are combined, they may form a detailed ac-count of an individual. The whole may be greater than the sum of the parts.

Further, the exchange of personal information between businesses cannot be readily analogized to the widespread disclosure of infor-mation by the media. When companies buy and sell information, they disclose it to only a few other entities. How are damages to be as-sessed? These harms do not translate well to tort law or criminal law, which focus on isolated actors and address harms individually rather than collectively.

The traditional view of privacy harms pervades much of the law of information privacy. Courts often look for specific injuries. For example, in *U.S. West, Inc. v. Federal Communications Commission,* the court of appeals struck down FCC regulations requiring that consumers opt-in (by affirmatively giving their consent) before telecommunications carriers could use or disclose their personal information. The court reasoned that the governmental interest in protecting privacy wasn't "substantial" because the government failed to "show that the dissemination of the information desired to be kept private would inflict specific and significant harm on individuals, such as undue embarrassment or ridicule, intimidation or harassment, or misappropriation of sensitive personal information for the purposes of assuming another's identity."[4] First Amendment scholar Eugene Volokh epitomizes this view when he writes:

> [M]any of the proposals to restrict communication of consumer transactional data would apply far beyond a narrow core of highly private information, and would cover all transactional information, such as the car, house, food, or clothes one buys. I don't deny that many people may find such speech vaguely ominous and would rather that it not take place, and I acknowledge that some people get extremely upset about it. . . . If such relatively modest offense or annoyance is enough to justify speech restrictions, then the compelling interest bar has fallen quite low.[5]

This way of viewing the harm to privacy fails to acknowledge the larger systemic problems involved with information flow. As I have argued in chapter 3, the growing use and dissemination of personal information creates a Kafkaesque world of bureaucracy, where we are increasingly powerless and vulnerable, where personal information is not only outside our control but also is subjected to a bureaucratic process that is itself not adequately controlled. This generalized harm already exists; we need not wait for specific abuses to occur.

Enforcement at the initiative of the individual also creates difficulties. Arguing from the invasion conception, Fred Cate contends that although people claim they desire more privacy, their actions illustrate that they do not want to sacrifice much time or energy in obtaining it.[6] The goal of the law, says Cate, should be to assist those who want to protect their privacy rather than to thrust a uniform wall of privacy around everyone: "The law should serve as a gap-filler, facilitating individual action in those situations in which the lack of competition has interfered with private privacy protection."[7] Furthermore, according to Cate, the purpose of privacy rights is to "facilitate . . . the development of private mechanisms and individual choice as a means of valuing and protecting privacy."[8]

However, enforcement mechanisms that rely upon individual initiative often fail because individuals lack the knowledge and resources to use them. Individual remedies are only effective to the extent that individuals have power to exercise them. In the face of forces created by social structure, individual remedies are often powerless. A person may have the legal opportunity to bargain to modify a contract, lease, or employment agreement or to sue for redress if wronged. But unless that person has the knowledge and ability to bargain or to sue, the opportunities are often not very empowering. Rights to consent to the collection of data lack much meaning if people can be readily pressured, misled, or coerced into relinquishing their information.[9]

Additionally, the invasion conception's focus on privacy invasions as harms to specific individuals often overlooks the fact that certain privacy problems are structural—they affect not only particular individuals but society as a whole. Privacy cannot merely be enforced at the initiative of particular individuals. Privacy, as Paul Schwartz contends, should be viewed as a "constitutive value" because "access to personal information and limits on it help form the society in which we live and shape our individual identities."[10] Since certain privacy problems are structural in nature, they affect more than specific aggrieved individuals. As data privacy expert Spiros Simitis aptly observes, "privacy considerations no longer arise out of particular individual problems; rather, they express conflicts affecting everyone."[11]

Architecture. If we look at privacy more as an aspect of social and legal structure, then we begin to see that certain types of privacy harms are systemic and structural in nature, and we need to protect against them differently.

The concept of "architecture" is useful for understanding how certain privacy problems should be understood and dealt with. The term "architecture" typically refers to the design of spaces—of buildings or cities. I use the term architecture in a broader way, similar to Lawrence Lessig and Joel Reidenberg, who contend that architecture does not merely describe the design of physical structures, but can be constructed through computer code.[12] Our environment is not only shaped spatially by the architecture of buildings and the layout of cities, but by the design of information systems. This architecture has similar effects as spatial design on our behavior, attitudes, norms, social interaction, sense of freedom, and security. Both computer hardware and software have architectures. Hardware is built with certain capabilities and limitations; it only has so much memory, a limited processing speed, and so on. Likewise, software has certain constraints—some that exist because programmers have reached the range of their capabilities, but others that exist because they are created by design. The Internet itself has a design, one that affects the way people communicate, the way data is transferred, and the extent to which people can be anonymous.

Architecture creates certain psychological and social effects.[13] According to Neal Katyal, physical architecture affects human conduct.[14] Architecture can structure spaces to "facilitate unplanned social interaction" by positioning door entrances so they face each other.[15] Architecture also alters perception by its aesthetic design, by what it expresses. Frank Lloyd Wright observed that architecture involves "making structure express ideas."[16] By influencing human behavior, attitudes, thoughts, and interactions, architecture plays a profound role in the structuring of society.

One of the ways in which architecture affects society is by enhancing or diminishing privacy. Recall from chapter 3 Jeremy Bentham's design for a prison, the Panopticon. The Panopticon demonstrates how architecture can shape the very constitution of society by affecting privacy. Through its design with a central observation tower, the Panopticon creates a constant fear of observation, resulting in increased obedience and discipline. As Michel Foucault observes, "without any physical instrument other than architecture and geometry, [the Panopticon] acts directly on individuals."[17] Unlike dungeons, which served "to enclose, to deprive of light and to hide," the Panopticon achieves control through visibility.[18] The Panopticon is a form of architecture that inhibits freedom; it is an architecture of social control and discipline. For Foucault, the Panopticon is not merely consigned to physical structures such as prisons; it is an architecture that is increasingly built into the entire social structure.[19] Panoptic architecture is increasingly employed in modern society, in both physical and non-physical forms. Surveillance cameras are a prime example. Since 1994, Britain has overseen city streets through the use of about 2.5 million surveillance cameras monitored by closed circuit television (CCTV).[20] It is virtually impossible to walk the streets of London without being captured on camera numerous times throughout the day. Such a surveillance system replicates Panoptic architecture.

Panoptic architecture, and the architecture Lessig and Reidenberg discuss, are "architectures of control,"[21] for they function to exercise greater dominion over individuals. Lessig observes that "[c]yberspace does not guarantee its own freedom but instead carries an extraordinary potential for control."[22] Lessig is responding to the early buzz about the Internet, which was hailed as a place of unprecedented freedom, a freewheeling and uninhibited world. Although the Internet certainly has the potential to be a realm of liberty, Lessig demonstrates that it can be regulated—through law and computer code. People can be traced; speech can be censored; access to information can be limited; anonymity can be restricted. Therefore, the Internet has the potential to become a realm of comprehensive control.

But beyond control, architecture can function in other problematic ways. In addition to architectures of control, we are seeing the development of what I call "architectures of vulnerability." Architecture can create a world where people are vulnerable to significant harm and are helpless to do anything about it. Architectures of vulnerability function differently than architectures of control. Architectures of control are ways in which people are limited in their actions and their freedom, where they are pressed into conformity to another's will. In contrast, architectures of vulnerability make people weaker, expose them to a host of dangers, and take away their power. Whereas architectures of control are central to Big Brother, architectures of vulnerability pervade the world depicted by Kafka. As I will discuss later, the rapid rise in identity theft is caused by architectures of vulnerability.

For problems that are architectural, the solutions should also be architectural. Privacy must be protected by reforming the architecture, which involves restructuring our relationships with businesses and the government. In other words, the law should *regulate the relationships.* As I discussed earlier in this book, our relationships with businesses and the government are becoming more bureaucratic in nature, and it is this general development that must be addressed. Thus, an architectural solution goes beyond treating the troublesome symptoms that materialize from the use of digital dossiers. The law often works at the surface of the problems, dealing with the overt abuses and injuries that may arise in specific instances. But thus far the law does not do enough to redefine the underlying relationships that cause these symptoms. Unless people's relationships with bureaucracies are placed on more equal footing, affording people default property rights in information or other forms of information control will not adequately protect privacy.

Architecture protects privacy differently than individual remedies. It is more proactive than reactive; it involves creating structures to prevent harms from arising rather than merely providing remedies when harms occur. The invasion conception enforces privacy through legal remedies employed at the initiative of individuals and penalties to specific wrongdoers. Architectural remedies are more systemic in nature, and they work by altering social structure to make it harder for torts and crimes to occur. As Neal Katyal persuasively argues, architecture deals with crime differently than criminal penalties; it can prevent crime, facilitate the capture of criminals, and can even "shape individuals' attitudes toward lawbreaking."[23]

I am not contending that affording individuals with a cause of action or a remedy for privacy invasions is completely ineffective. Indeed, individual remedies must be a component of any architecture. However, individual remedies alone are often not sufficient, for their viability and effectiveness depends upon the architecture in which they are embedded.

I am also not arguing that the invasion conception is incorrect and should be abandoned. The invasion conception was designed for the privacy problems experienced when Warren and Brandeis wrote their article. Although it still works for a number of privacy problems today, it does not work for all privacy problems. In fact, understanding privacy problems with the notion of architecture is not in conflict with the view of privacy articulated by Warren and Brandeis. A critical part of Warren and Brandeis's argument was the importance of the law's ability to respond to new problems. Today, we face a host of different privacy problems. We need to recognize their differences and adapt the law to grapple with them rather than continue to view them through old lenses and attempt to resolve them in the same manner as other problems.

Warren and Brandeis wrote long before the rise of massive record systems and information networks. The problems created by the growing accumulation, dissemination, and networking of personal information are better understood architecturally than under the invasion conception. Viewing these problems through architecture reveals that the problems are caused in a different manner than we might have originally supposed. It recognizes harm within design and structure. And it alters the strategies by which we seek to adapt law to solve the problems.

Thus, the viable protection of privacy must consist of more than a set of protections for a series of isolated injuries. Rather, the protection of privacy depends upon an architecture that structures power, a regulatory framework that governs how information is disseminated, collected, and networked. We need to focus on controlling power. Often, new technology is introduced without adequate controls, and as a result, it creates vulnerability and engenders troublesome shifts in power, even if the proposed uses of the technology do not seem immediately troubling and even if the threat of abuse is not imminent. The protection of privacy does not mean an all-or-nothing tradeoff between the total restriction of information gathering versus the complete absence of regulation. Many privacy problems can be ameliorated if information uses are carefully and thoughtfully controlled.

Toward an Architecture for Privacy and the Private Sector

What should an architecture that regulates the relationships look like? I propose an architecture that establishes controls over the data networking practices of institutions and that affords people greater participation in the uses of their information.

The first step is to redefine the nature of our relationships to businesses and government entities that maintain and use our personal information. At present, the collectors and users of our data are often not accountable to us. A company can collect a person's data without ever contacting that person, without that person ever finding out about it. The relationship is akin to the relationship between strangers—with one very important difference: One of the strangers knows a lot about the other and often has the power to use this information to affect the other's life. But the stranger with the knowledge doesn't have many obligations to the other. At other times, we establish a relationship with a company, a bank, or another institution. We might buy a product online or open up an account and invest money. We are no longer strangers, but the quality of our relationship is often not dramatically improved. Companies collect and maintain our information; they often use it for a myriad of new purposes; and they are frequently careless about the security of our data. As discussed earlier, the law often doesn't afford people the ability to do much to change the situation.

Our relationships with the collectors and users of our personal information thus need to be redefined. Consider another set of relationships—those between us and our doctors and lawyers. Here, the law imposes a number of obligations on doctors and lawyers to focus on our welfare. Indeed, the patient-physician relationship has been likened by courts to a fiduciary one.[24] A fiduciary relationship is a central facet of the law of trusts. Trustees stand in a fiduciary relationship to beneficiaries of the trust. The trustee has been entrusted with the beneficiary's money, and because of this position of special trust, the trustee owes certain special duties to the beneficiary.[25] Justice Benjamin Cardozo, then writing for the Court of Appeals of New York, described fiduciary duties in a famous passage:

> Many forms of conduct permissible in a workaday world for those acting at arm's length, are forbidden to those bound by fiduciary ties. A trustee is held to something stricter than the

morals of the market place. Not honesty alone, but the punctilio of an honor the most sensitive, is then the standard of behavior.[26]

The types of relationships that qualify as fiduciary ones are not fixed in stone. As one court has noted, courts "have carefully refrained from defining instances of fiduciary relations in such a manner that other and perhaps new cases might be excluded."[27] Examples of recognized fiduciary relationships include those between stockbrokers and clients, lawyers and clients, physicians and patients, parents and children, corporate officers and shareholders, and insurance companies and their customers.[28]

Fiduciaries have a duty to disclose personal interests that could affect their professional judgment as well as a duty of confidentiality.[29] For example, doctors who disclose a patient's confidential medical information have been successfully sued by patients for breach of confidentiality.[30] Likewise, banks and schools have been held to be obliged to keep personal information confidential.[31]

I posit that the law should hold that companies collecting and using our personal information stand in a fiduciary relationship with us. This is a radical proposal. Although the concept of a fiduciary relationship is an open-ended and developing one, the concept has not been extended nearly as far as I propose. Generally, courts examine a number of factors to determine the existence of a fiduciary relationship: "[T]he degree of kinship of the parties; the disparity in age, health, and mental condition; education and business experience between the parties; and the extent to which the allegedly subservient party entrusted the handling of . . . business affairs to the other and reposed faith and confidence in [that person or entity]."[32] Most of the factors look at disparities in power and knowledge, and these lean in favor of finding a fiduciary relationship between us and the collectors and users of our data. The last factor, however, understands the relationship as one in which something has been explicitly entrusted to the trustee. This will work in the context of companies that we do business with, for we entrust them with our personal data. But it will be a significant expansion of the concept of fiduciary relationships to extend it to third-party companies that gather our information without having done business with us. We don't entrust anything to these companies; they often take our data surreptitiously, without our consent. Nevertheless, the law is flexible and in the past has responded to new situations. The law should grow to respond here, since all of the other factors for recognizing a fiduciary relationship seem to counsel so strongly for the need to impose fiduciary obligations for the collectors and users of our personal information.

If our relationships with the collectors and users of our personal data are redefined as fiduciary ones, then this would be the start of a significant shift in the way the law understands their obligations to us. The law would require them to treat us in a different way—at a minimum, with more care and respect. By redefining relationships, the law would make a significant change to the architecture of the information economy.

More specifically, how should these relationships be reconstructed? What duties and obligations should the collectors and users of our personal information have? The foundations should be formed by the Fair Information Practices, which, as privacy expert Marc Rotenberg aptly observes, create an architecture for the handling and use of personal information.[33] The Fair Information Practices originate with a 1973 report by the U.S. Department of Housing, Education, and Welfare. The report recommended the passage of a code of Fair Information Practices:

> ▸ There must be no personal-data record-keeping systems whose very existence is secret.
> ▸ There must be a way for an individual to find out what information about him is in a record and how it is used.
> ▸ There must be a way for an individual to prevent information about him obtained for one purpose from being used or made available for other purposes without his consent.
> ▸ There must be a way for an individual to correct or amend a record of identifiable information about him.
> ▸ Any organization creating, maintaining, using, or disseminating records of identifiable personal data must assure the reliability of the data for their intended use and must take reasonable precautions to prevent misuse of the data.[34]

Subsequently, in 1980, the Organization for Economic Cooperation and Development (OECD) established guidelines for the protection of privacy based in large part on the Fair Information Practices.[35] Paul Schwartz, Marc Rotenberg, Joel Reidenberg, and others have long contended that the Fair Information Practices represent the most effective foundation for the protection of privacy in the Information Age.[36]

The Fair Information Practices embody a particular understanding of privacy and its protection. Understood broadly, the Fair Information Practices establish an architecture that alters the power dynamic between individuals and the various bureaucracies that process their personal information. The Fair Information Practices focus on two general concerns: participation and responsibility. They aim to structure the information economy so that people can participate meaningfully in the collection and use of their personal information. This does not necessarily mean that people are afforded dominion over their personal information; rather, people are to be kept informed about the information gathered about them and the purposes of its use; and people must have some say in the way their information is processed. In other words, the Fair Information Practices aim to increase individual involvement in personal information systems.

Additionally, the Fair Information Practices bring information processing under better control. Currently, information processing is out of control. Companies collecting and using personal information are often doing so in careless ways with little concern for the welfare of the individuals to whom the information pertains. The Fair Information Practices recognize that personal data users have special responsibilities and that they must be regulated in order to ensure that they maintain accurate and secure records and use and disseminate information responsibly.

Unfortunately, in the United States the Fair Information Practices have only been selectively incorporated into various statutes in a limited number of contexts. A more comprehensive incorporation of the Fair Information Practices would go far toward addressing the privacy problem as I have characterized it.

Participation: Opting-Out versus Opting-In. The current self-regulatory and legislative solution of enabling people to opt-out of having their data collected or disseminated is ineffectual. When people have to opt-out, the default is that they relinquish significant control over their information unless they take steps (often time-consuming and cumbersome) to indicate that they do not want a company to use or disseminate their data. Providing people with opt-out rights and privacy policies does little to give individuals much control over their information. Regulation mandating that consumers opt-in rather than opt-out will more effectively control the flow of information between unequal parties. Under a system where individuals opt-in, the default rule is that personal information cannot be collected or used about an individual unless the individual provides consent. As Jeff Sovern contends, an opt-in system will place the incentive on entities that use personal information to "make it as easy as possible for consumers to consent to the use of their personal information."[37] Therefore, the law should require companies to adopt an opt-in system rather than an opt-out system.

Even with an opt-in system, steps must be taken to ensure that consent amounts to more than a "notice and choice" system, which, as Marc Rotenberg argues, "imagines the creation of perfect market conditions where consumers are suddenly negotiating over a range of uses for personal information."[38] Thus, effective privacy regulation must legally require an opt-in system which contains a meaningful range of choices as well as addresses inequalities in knowledge and power and other impediments to voluntary and informed consent. For example, inequalities in knowledge—the fact that companies know how they might use data whereas people have little awareness of these plans—could be addressed by limiting such future uses of personal data without first obtaining people's consent.

Limits on the Use of Data. A critical step toward addressing the problems of digital dossiers is providing limits on the use of data. Internationally, the OECD Guidelines provide that "[p]ersonal data should be relevant to the purposes for which they are to be used, and, to the extent necessary for those purposes, should be accurate, complete, and kept up-to-date."[39] In 1996, the European Union issued the *European Community Directive on Data Protection,* which outlines the basic principles for privacy legislation for European Union member countries. The Directive provides for a comprehensive protection of personal information maintained by a broad range of entities. This omnibus approach exists in stark contrast to the United States' approach, which regulates privacy "sectorally" in various narrow contexts.[40]

Although the Directive is far from perfect, it recognizes some of the dimensions of the problem that are neglected by U.S. privacy law. For example, Article 15 provides:

> Member States shall grant the right to every person not to be subject to a decision which produces legal effects concerning him or significantly affects him and which is based solely on automated processing of data intended to evaluate certain personal aspects relating to him, such as his performance at work, creditworthiness, reliability, conduct, etc.[41]

Further, Article 8 prohibits, subject to a number of necessary exceptions, "the processing of personal data revealing racial or ethnic origin, political opinions, religious or philosophical beliefs, trade-union membership, and the processing of data concerning health or sex life."[42] These two provisions of the Directive limit the ways personal information can be used to make important decisions affecting people's lives.

Enforcement. The Fair Information Practices are broad principles, and they do not specify how they are to be carried out in practice or enforced. As I discussed earlier, individual remedies can only go so far. Of course, individual remedies are important, and people should be able to sue when injured by companies that fail to follow the Fair Information Practices. But with many of the new types of architectural harms I described—such as making people more vulnerable to fraud and identity theft—damages will be difficult to calculate. When a person actually suffers from identity theft, it is easy to comprehend the harm. When a person is made more vulnerable—such as being exposed to a greater risk of injury but not yet actually injured—it is harder to establish damages because one can't point to concrete economic loss or physical pain and suffering. Nevertheless, increased vulnerability is a palpable harm—just as weakening a person's immune system would be, or disabling her home security system. Part of the challenge for law is to begin to recognize the harms created by increased vulnerability and powerlessness. But until the law does this, enforcement must also occur through the work of government agencies tasked with policing the corporate world of information networking. Just as the Food and Drug Administration (FDA) regulates food and drugs, just as the Securities and Exchange Commission (SEC) regulates the securities markets, we need a federal agency to regulate the collection and use of personal information.[43] As I discussed in chapter 4, the Federal Trade Commission (FTC) has started to undertake this role, but it has a long way to go.

The FTC must receive expanded jurisdiction and resources to be more proactive in policing the security practices of companies. In a handful of cases thus far, the FTC has preemptively brought actions against companies for maintaining shoddy security even before information was leaked or obtained improperly. As discussed in chapter 4, the FTC brought an action against Microsoft for failing to provide adequate security for its users' personal data. In *In re Guess.com, Inc.*,[44] the FTC reached a settlement with Guess, a company that sold clothing and accessories over the Internet, for maintaining flawed security of its customers' personal information. Guess promised that all personal information "including . . . credit card information and sign-in password, are stored in an unreadable, encrypted format at all times." This statement was false, and the FTC brought an action even before there was any evidence that hackers or others improperly gained access to the data. Cases like these are promising developments, but many more need to be brought.

As discussed before, one problem with the FTC's jurisdiction is that it is triggered when a company breaches its own privacy policy. But what if a company doesn't make explicit promises about security? One hopeful development is the Gramm-Leach-Bliley (GLB) Act. The GLB Act requires a number of agencies that regulate financial institutions to promulgate "administrative, technical, and physical safeguards for personal information."[45] In other words, financial institutions must adopt a security system for their data, and the minimum specifications of this system are to be defined by government agencies. A broader but similar provision must be passed to govern all the collectors and users of personal information. It must be enforced by a federal agency that will examine each company's security practices and ensure that they are adequate. As I will discuss later, the security practices at countless companies that collect and use our personal data are notoriously insufficient, a reality that has led to the rapid growth of identity theft.

Reconceptualizing Identity Theft

Thus far, what I have said has been relatively abstract. In the remainder of this chapter, I will provide a specific demonstration of these points through the example of one of the most rapidly growing and troubling problems of the information economy—the problem of identity theft. It is a privacy problem that resembles a Kafkaesque nightmare.

The Identity Theft Problem. A person loses his wallet while on vacation in Florida. His wallet contains his driver's license and other personal information. An identity thief uses the victim's information for several years to buy and sell property, open bank accounts, establish phone service, and so on.[46] Pursuant to a Florida warrant based on the criminal conduct of the identity thief, the victim is arrested in California and imprisoned for over a week. The victim also has civil judgments issued against him.[47]

The identity of a retired 74-year-old man is stolen. Debts continue to amass on his credit reports. Although the victim lives in Maryland, a Texas bank issues a car loan to the identity thief in Texas.[48] The victim continually fights to have the debts removed from his credit reports, but he is told to take up the issues with the creditors who claim that the debts are legitimate. Even after debts are removed, they reappear on his credit reports because a different collection agency replaces them.[49]

These are examples of what has come to be called "identity theft," which is a problem involving personal information. As defined by the U.S. General Accounting Office, "identity theft or identity fraud generally involves 'stealing' another person's personal identifying information . . . and then using that information to fraudulently establish credit, run up debt, or take over existing financial accounts."[50] Identity theft is not the same as ordinary credit card fraud, where a thief steals and uses a person's credit card. In identity theft, the culprit obtains personal information and uses it in a variety of fraudulent ways to impersonate the victim. The thief gathers personal information from database companies and public records, or by stealing wallets, pilfering mail, or rooting through trash to find data on discarded documents.[51]

Identity theft is the most rapidly growing type of white-collar criminal activity.[52] According to an FTC estimate in September 2003, "almost 10 million Americans have discovered that they were the victim of some form of ID theft within the past year."[53] Identity theft can be a harrowing experience. According to estimates, a victim typically spends over two years and close to 200 hours to repair the damage that identity theft causes.[54] Victims often spend thousands of dollars to remedy the harm, and many experience great anxiety.[55] They have difficulty getting a loan, securing a mortgage, obtaining a security clearance, or even being hired for a job.[56] And victims are sometimes arrested based on warrants for the crimes of the identity thieves.[57]

Identity theft creates these problems because our digital dossiers are becoming so critical to our ability to function in modern life. Credit reporting agencies construct dossiers about us to report our financial status to creditors. Without these reports, people can't obtain loans, mortgages, or leases. Personal information is also used to establish accounts with merchants, ISPs, cable companies, phone companies, and so on.

The identity thief not only pilfers victims' personal information, but also pollutes their dossiers by adding false information, such as unpaid debts, traffic violations, parking tickets, and arrests. The harm of identity theft is not solely financial; it can seep into a person's everyday life. The victim cannot readily recover the personal information in the way that stolen property can be recovered. The victim must constantly defend against the identity thief's next move. Even after the victim cleans up her credit reports, if the identity thief remains at large, there may be further pollution. This is another way in which identity theft differs from credit card fraud or the theft of an ATM card or access card. Once the card is cancelled, the crime ends.

With identity theft, the crime can continue, for personal information works like an "access card" that cannot be readily deactivated.

Identity Theft and the Invasion Conception. Thus far, the law has viewed identity theft under the invasion conception—as a harm to individuals by criminals. Identity theft unquestionably harms individuals and certainly involves criminals. Therefore, it is no surprise that identity theft is viewed under the invasion conception and that the solutions to identity theft emerge from this model. As I will argue later, this model is deeply flawed and as a result, its solutions are ineffective.

In 1998, Congress passed the Identity Theft and Assumption Deterrence Act, which erected a comprehensive penal regime for identity theft.[58] Subsequently, the vast majority of states have passed laws to criminalize identity theft.[59] Thus, it is only recently that policymakers have turned their attention to identity theft, and the overwhelming approach is to classify identity theft as a species of crime and to focus on the actions of these criminals.

There are several problems with viewing identity theft exclusively in this manner. First, law enforcement agencies have thus far not devoted adequate resources toward investigating and prosecuting identity theft cases. In a U.S. General Accounting Office survey of 10 states, officials admitted that they have insufficient resources to respond to identity theft because violent crimes and drug offenses consume most of the resources. Additionally, the survey reported, "[i]dentity theft cases require highly trained investigators, require longer-than-usual efforts, and often end without an arrest." Identity theft often occurs across different jurisdictions, and law enforcement officials "sometimes tend to view identity theft as being 'someone else's problem.'" As a result, most identity thefts remain unsolved.[60] Research firm Gartner, Inc. estimates that less than 1 in 700 instances of identity theft result in a conviction.[61]

Second, victims experience great difficulty in obtaining redress for identity theft. Victims are often unaware that their identities have been stolen until long after the identity theft has begun. A report based on victim surveys estimates that it takes victims over a year to discover that they have been victimized.[62] According to FTC estimates, 20 percent of identity theft victims don't learn of the theft until two years later.[63] One tip-off that a person is a victim of identity theft is an unusual item on a credit report. The identity thief often takes out loans and uses lines of credit which the thief never pays back. These delinquencies show up on the victim's credit report, and destroy the victim's credit rating. Unfortunately, the Fair Credit Reporting Act (FCRA),[64] which regulates credit reporting agencies, fails to provide people with adequate resources to discover that they are being victimized or repair the damage done by identity theft. Although the FCRA permits individuals to contest the accuracy of information in their credit histories[65] and enables individuals to sue to collect damages for violations of the Act,[66] these rights often are ineffectual. One problem is that people often are unaware of the information their credit reports contain. To obtain such information, people must request a copy of their credit report from each of the three major credit reporting agencies—Experian, Equifax, and Trans Union. And if individuals want to ensure that their credit reports remain accurate, they must request reports regularly.

Credit reporting agencies have a duty to investigate consumer disputes with the accuracy of their reports, but this often is ineffective in cases of identity theft. In a compelling article, legal scholar Lynn LoPucki observes that the "victim is asked to prove a negative: namely, that he or she is not the person who borrowed from the creditor. The victim's evidence is likely to be complex and circumstantial." Creditors do not have a sufficient incentive to investigate, for if the victim is correct, creditors cannot recover on the debt. LoPucki also aptly argues that the "victim lacks a forum in which to proceed. The victim has no right to a hearing on the accuracy of the information requested." Moreover, the "FTC seldom acts on the complaint of a single customer."[67]

The FCRA does not allow people to sue for "defamation, invasion of privacy, or negligence" when the credit reporting agency discloses false information or a creditor reports false information to a credit reporting agency unless the information is "furnished with malice or willful intent to injure such consumer." Instead, the FCRA provides a cause of action for negligently failing to comply with its provisions, but a victim must bring an action within two years "from the date on which the liability arises."[68] In *TRW, Inc. v. Andrews,* the Supreme Court held that the two-year statute of limitations period begins to run when a violation occurs, even if the plaintiff remains unaware of it.[69]

In December 2003, Congress passed a law, called the Fair and Accurate Credit Transactions Act (FACTA), that revised the FCRA.[70] The FACTA makes several improvements to the FCRA. It overturns *Andrews* and expands the statute of limitations to five years from the violation or two years following the discovery of the violation. A person can ask a credit reporting agency to place a "fraud alert" in her file, and the agency must contact all the other credit reporting agencies to do the same. The Act also makes it easier for identity theft victims to obtain records from companies where the thief opened accounts or purchased goods. People can request a free credit report each year from all of the national credit reporting agencies. The Act provides consumers with the ability to opt-out of offers of prescreened credit.

However, the Act is still moored in the invasion conception. The law does not allow individuals enough involvement in the uses and dissemination of their personal information to quickly discover that they are victims of identity theft or to obtain redress after identity theft occurs. The FACTA makes it slightly easier for victims to repair the damage from identity theft, but this is akin to a better bandage. Many of the Act's protections are already being carried out voluntarily by credit reporting agencies. Prior to the FACTA, victims of identity theft could call one credit reporting agency, which would voluntarily alert the others to the fraud. Most victims could already obtain a free credit report so long as they believed in good faith that they had been defrauded. Consumers who had never been victimized had to pay only $9 for their credit report. Thus, the FACTA takes some forward steps, but it does not progress very far. FACTA's reforms are remedial; the Act does little to proactively prevent identity theft.

More disturbingly, the FACTA also gives credit reporting agencies and the companies that use our personal information a great benefit—states are barred from passing stricter laws. The states, not the federal government, had been providing stronger and more effective protection. The Act thus comes at the price of removing valuable protections to millions of individuals and preventing the states from further experimentation in combating the mounting threat of identity theft.

Viewing identity theft under the invasion conception—as a series of isolated thefts from particular individuals—results in commentators often urging individuals to take a variety of steps to avoid being victimized. Fred Cate argues that identity theft could be greatly curtailed if people exercised more care over their data:

> Despite all the bills introduced to combat the theft of identity, individual action may provide the best defense: keeping a close watch on account activity; reporting suspicious or unfamiliar transactions promptly; properly destroying commercial solicitations; storing valuable documents securely; protecting account names and passwords; and never disclosing personal information to unknown callers.[71]

A report by the FDIC suggests several tips for people to "minimize" the risk of identity theft:

> Pay attention to your billing cycles.
> Guard your mail from theft.
> Do not give out personal information.
> Keep items with personal information in a safe place.
> Give your SSN only when absolutely necessary.
> Don't carry your SSN card; leave it in a secure place.
> Order a copy of your credit report from each of the three major credit reporting agencies every year.[72]

The general advice is that if people take a number of steps, identity theft will be minimized. However, personal data is often collected unwittingly, without consent; SSNs are frequently used, and refusal to give out one's SSN results in considerable inconvenience; and many people cannot even name the three major credit reporting agencies, let alone request a copy of their credit reports. Even if people did take all these steps, the risks of identity theft are still not significantly minimized. According to an official at the FTC, "[t]here is no way you can fully immunize yourself from identity theft because the information is out there."[73]

I contend that the prevailing approach to dealing with identity theft—by relying on criminal penalties and by depending upon individuals to take great lengths to try to protect themselves—has the wrong focus. Of course, identity thieves should be prosecuted and people should avoid being careless with their data. The law has significant room to improve in prosecuting identity theft. But these solutions fail to address the foundations of the problem.

Identity Theft as Architecture. The underlying cause of identity theft is an architecture that makes us vulnerable to such crimes and unable to adequately repair the damage. This architecture is not created by identity thieves; rather, it is exploited by them. It is an architecture of vulnerability, one where personal information is not protected with adequate security, where identity thieves have easy access to data and the ability to use it in detrimental ways. We are increasingly living with digital dossiers about our lives, and these dossiers are not controlled by us but by various entities, such as private-sector companies and the government. These dossiers play a profound role in our existence in modern society. The identity thief taps into these dossiers and uses them, manipulates them, and pollutes them. The identity thief's ability to so easily access and use our personal data stems from an architecture that does not provide adequate security to our personal information and that does not afford us with a sufficient degree of participation in its collection, dissemination, and use. Consequently, it is difficult for the victim to figure out what is going on and how to remedy the situation.

The traditional legal view of identity theft fails to address this architecture, for it focuses on identity theft as a series of discrete instances of crime rather than as a larger problem about the way our personal information is handled. Even the term "identity theft" views it as an instance of crime—a "theft" rather than the product of inadequate security.

The architecture enabling identity theft emerges from the government and the private sector. With regard to the government part of the structure, the SSN and public record systems create a regime where identity is readily stolen and the consequences are severe. SSNs are a key piece of information for identity theft, for they can unlock a wealth of other information held by the government and the private sector.[74] Created in 1936 as part of the Social Security System, SSNs were not designed to be used as a general identifier. Indeed, for many years, the Social Security card stated that it was "NOT FOR IDENTIFICATION."[75] However, over time, numerous federal agencies began using the SSN for identification, as did state and local governments, schools, banks, hospitals, and other private-sector entities.[76]

In the early 1970s, the growing uses of the SSN raised serious concerns that the SSN would become a de facto universal identifier.[77] In the Privacy Act of 1974, Congress partially responded to these concerns by prohibiting government agencies from denying any right, benefit, or privilege merely because an individual refused to disclose her SSN. However, the Privacy Act did not restrict the use of SSNs by the private sector.

The use of the SSN continued to escalate after the Privacy Act. As one commentator has observed, "governmental dissemination of personal identifying numbers is still widespread, and limits on private actors are also virtually nonexistent."[78] Today, the SSN functions in the United States as a de facto identifier, and there is scant protection on its use. SSNs are often widely available. Schools frequently use student SSNs as student identifiers, which makes student SSNs available to a large number of university personnel. States often place SSNs on driver's licenses, which exposes SSNs to anyone who checks a driver's license for identification. Additionally, SSNs are requested on a wide variety of applications and forms, such as employment applications, hospital admittance forms, college applications, video store membership applications, and credit card applications.

SSNs are used as passwords to obtain access to a host of personal records from banks, investment companies, schools, hospitals, doctors, and so on.[79] The SSN is a powerful number, for with it a person can open and close accounts, change addresses, obtain loans, access personal information, make financial transactions, and more. In short, the SSN functions as a magic key that can unlock vast stores of records as well as financial accounts, making it the identity thief's best tool.

Viewed in terms of architecture, the government has created an identification number without affording adequate precautions against its misuse. In so doing, the government has exposed every citizen to significant vulnerability to identity theft and other crimes such as fraud and stalking.

Not only are the uses of SSNs inadequately controlled, but SSNs are relatively easy for the identity thief to obtain. SSNs are harvested by database firms from a number of public and non-public sources, such as court records or credit reports. It is currently legal for private firms to sell or disclose SSNs. SSNs and other personal information that assists identity thieves can be obtained from public records or the database companies that market personal data mined from public records.[80] SSNs are in fact required by law to be publicly disclosed in bankruptcy records.[81] Identity thieves thus can plunder public records, which are increasingly being made readily accessible on the Internet, for personal information to carry out their crimes. For example, recently the clerk of courts for Hamilton County, Ohio placed the county's public records on the Internet. From a speeding ticket placed on the website, an identity thief accessed a victim's SSN, address, birth date, signature, and other personal information and opened up credit card accounts in the victim's name.[82] Further, identity thieves can obtain SSNs along with a detailed dossier about their victims simply by paying a small fee to various database companies.[83]

The problem of identity theft also stems from the private sector's inadequate security measures in handling personal information. Companies lack adequate ways of controlling access to records and accounts in a person's name, and numerous companies engage in the common practice of using SSNs, mother's maiden names, and addresses for access to account information.[84] Additionally, creditors give out credit and establish new accounts if the applicant supplies a name, SSN, and address.

The credit reporting system also employs inadequate precautions to ensure against inaccuracies in credit reports and improper access to the system. Credit reporting agencies don't work for the individuals they report on; rather, they are paid by creditors. Even though the FCRA gives people certain rights with regard to credit reporting agencies, there is still a significant lack of accountability because credit reporting agencies have no incentive to compete for the business of those on whom they report. According to Lynn LoPucki, the problem emerges because "creditors and credit-reporting agencies often lack both the means and the incentives to correctly identify the persons who seek credit from them or on whom they report."[85] LoPucki aptly shifts the focus to the companies that control personal data and correctly contends that identity theft stems from the private sector's use of SSNs for identification.[86]

Viewed in terms of architecture, identity theft is part of a larger problem, which is best articulated by using the Kafka metaphor. The problem is that we have so little participation in the use of our personal data combined with the fact that it flows so insecurely and carelessly without sufficient control. The harm is not simply measured in the overt instances of identity theft and abuse, but in the fact that we are made more vulnerable to a series of errors, abuses, and dangers.

Indeed, with ever more frequency, we are hearing stories about security glitches and other instances of personal data being leaked and abused. For example, in 2002, identity thieves improperly used Ford Motor Credit Company's code to access the credit files of 13,000 of Ford's customers, which were maintained by Experian, a major credit reporting agency.[87] Citibank employed a database marketing company to collect the email addresses of its credit card customers and send them emails offering them access to their financial information.[88] This was done without verifying whether the email addresses actually belonged to the particular customers.[89]

The problems of information handling are most vividly illustrated by an incident involving Princeton University officials who improperly accessed personal information in a Yale University database. Yale established a website enabling undergraduate applicants to find out whether they had been accepted or denied admission.[90] The website invited students to enter additional information, such as their interests and hobbies.[91] To access the website, the students were asked their name, birth date, and SSN.[92] However, in April 2002, a Princeton admissions official accessed certain applicants' accounts on Yale's website by using their SSNs.[93] After discovering the unauthorized access by Princeton, Yale reported the incident to the FBI.[94] Although the shady actions of the Princeton official grabbed the most attention, the problem was created by Yale's inept security measures, ones that resemble in many ways those used by companies that hold even more sensitive personal data.

The identity thief, then, is only one of the culprits in identity theft. The government and businesses bear a significant amount of responsibility, yet this is cloaked in the conception of identity theft as a discrete crime that the victim could have prevented had she exercised more care over her personal data. Identity theft does not merely happen; rather, it is manufactured by a legally constructed architecture.

Further, the architecture contributes to the harm caused to victims of identity theft. Identity theft plunges people into a bureaucratic nightmare. The identity theft injury to victims is often caused by the frustration and sense of helplessness in attempting to stop and repair the damage caused by the identity thief. Victims experience profound difficulty in dealing with credit reporting agencies,[95] and often find recurring fraudulent entries on their credit reports even after contacting the agencies.[96] Identity theft laws do not adequately regulate the bureaucratic system that injures victims. The bureaucracies controlling personal information are often indifferent to the welfare of the individuals to whom the information pertains.

Forging a New Architecture

If we see the problem architecturally, we see an architecture of vulnerability, one with large holes, gaps, and weak spots. The harm is caused by the architecture itself. Living in a dilapidated structure—a building with flimsy walls, no locks, peepholes, inadequate fire protection, and no emergency exits—is harmful, even without a disaster occurring. Modern society is built on expectations that we will be kept secure, that our money will not be stolen, that our homes will not be invaded, that we will be protected against violence. It is difficult to imagine how we could maintain a free society if we did not have protection against rape, assault, murder, and theft. If these protections are inadequate, there is harm even without being victimized.

Effective safety is thus partly a design question. According to legal scholar Neal Katyal, physical architecture can be proactive in combating crime, for it can prevent crime. For example, "cleanliness and aesthetic appeal" can make people perceive that a place is safe and orderly, and make miscreants less likely to disrupt it.[97] In a similar manner, the architecture of information flows can be redesigned to prevent identity theft and ameliorate its effects. Identity theft is the product of an architecture that creates vulnerability and insecurity, so the most effective way to combat identity theft is to reconstruct this faulty architecture. But what should an appropriate architecture look like?

Participation and Responsibility. The problem of identity theft can be addressed with an architecture built around participation and responsibility, the key concepts of the Fair Information Practices. At the most basic level, the Fair Information Practices place the burden of addressing the identity theft problem on the entities that cause it— those using personal information. The effectiveness of the Fair Information Practices depends upon how they are applied to particular privacy problems and how they are enforced. In what follows, I will discuss how the two general aims of the Fair Information Practices— participation and responsibility—can be implemented to help grapple with the identity theft problem.

First, the architecture should allow for people to have greater participation in the collection and use of their personal information. Currently, information can be readily disseminated and transferred without a person's knowledge or consent. Few requirements exist for how secure information must be kept, and information can be used for whatever purpose the entity possessing it desires.

I recommend an architecture that requires companies gathering personal information about people to keep individuals informed about their information. Presently, even with the FCRA, credit reporting agencies are not responsive enough to the people whose information they collect and disseminate. The recently passed FACTA allows people to access their credit reports on a yearly basis, but identity theft can occur in the interim and can cause much damage even in a few months. People should be allowed to more regularly access their credit reports for free.[98] But LoPucki fears that increasing a person's ability to access information held by credit reporting agencies will also increase the identity thief's ability to gain access.[99] A more radical change in the credit reporting system may be necessary to fix this difficulty. An opt-in regime to credit reporting would significantly curtail problems of improper access to credit records. Currently, credit reporting agencies need not establish any relationship with the people on whom they report. In an opt-in regime, credit reporting agencies would have to contact individuals and would be legally accountable for improper access to credit records. Individuals could access their credit records through passwords or account numbers rather than by supplying SSNs or other personal data.

When there is an unusual change in the behavior of a record subject, such as when a person who regularly repays her loans suddenly starts defaulting, credit reporting agencies should notify that person. The architecture should empower people with an easy, quick, and convenient way to challenge inaccuracies about their personal information as well as fraudulent entries in their credit reports. Disputes can be resolved with a special arbitration system that can function quickly and inexpensively rather than resorting to expensive court proceedings.

If these measures are taken, victims will be able to discover more quickly the existence of identity theft since they will be better informed about the data collected about them and how it is being used.

The architecture should also be premised on the notion that the collection and use of personal information is an activity that carries duties and responsibilities. The law should establish specific measures of control over entities maintaining systems of personal data. For example, if a company is providing background check information about a person, it should be held responsible for any inaccuracies or deficiencies in the information.

To establish greater responsibility, the law would regulate private-sector security practices. Minimum security practices must be established for handling people's personal information or accounts. Use of a SSN, mother's maiden name, and birth date as the means of gaining access to accounts should be prohibited. Identity theft can be curtailed by employing alternative means of identification, such as passwords.

This solution does not come without difficulties, as passwords can be easily forgotten or discovered. The use of multiple questions and answers supplied by the customer at the time the account is created can be effective. Questions might include favorite songs, places a person has visited, and so on, and these questions must vary from institution to institution. If varying methods of identification are used, an identity thief will no longer be able to use a few pieces of information to access everything, which will minimize the severity of the impact of identity theft. The thief may be able to access one or two accounts, but not all of them. Unfortunately, so much personal information is already maintained by various database companies that a person's answers may exist in these databases. For example, a person might use as a password the name of her college, spouse, pet, or child. Therefore, unique and less common questions and answers will provide better security against identity theft.

The possibility that databases will eventually include the types of information that people generally use for these questions demonstrates the importance of thinking architecturally. The problem of identity theft is part of a larger structure in which companies are not effectively regulated in the collection, use, and dissemination of personal information. If database companies are regulated to prohibit the dissemination of certain types of information, then this data can be better protected from falling into the hands of an identity thief.

Of course, this method of identification is far from foolproof. But the level of sophistication and difficulty required to carry out an identity theft would be increased. Additionally, identity theft can be more readily halted. It is currently a difficult and cumbersome process to change one's SSN.[100] And a person cannot change her height, birth date, or mother's maiden name. Passwords, however, can easily be changed. Thus, once discovered, identity theft will be easier to stop and will not continue long after the victim becomes aware of it.

These suggestions pertain to already established accounts. Much identity theft, however, occurs through the identity thief opening up new accounts in the victim's name. Currently, it is far too easy to establish a new account through the mail and the Internet.[101] Pre-approved credit card applications, for example, enable the recipient to easily establish an account and change addresses. Companies that want to open a new account through the mail should verify an applicant's address, date of birth, and phone number with a credit reporting agency, and then send written confirmation both to the address listed on the application and to the address that the credit reporting agency has. Further, the company should follow-up by calling the applicant's telephone number listed with the credit reporting agency. In the event of any discrepancies in the information held by the credit reporting agency and the individual, the individual should be notified. Of course, this solution would only work well if people had greater participation in the collection and use of their information by credit reporting agencies. Many attempts at identity theft can be halted if creditors take greater care scrutinizing applications. Although the identity thief can still intercept the notification,[102] it requires additional steps to carry out the identity theft, ones that can increase the chances of the thief getting caught.

The solutions just discussed are only recommendations of the types of solutions that can be employed once we recognize that we need to focus on architecture. Viewing identity theft under the invasion conception has diverted attention from these architectural concerns. If the architecture recognizes the responsibilities of companies maintaining personal data, it will provide a strong incentive for companies to devise creative solutions and better security.

Understanding certain privacy problems as architectural demonstrates that protecting privacy involves more than protecting against isolated infractions. It is about establishing a particular social structure, one that ensures individual participation in the collection and use of personal information and responsibilities for entities that control that data. The problem of identity theft may never be completely eradicated, but in a world with the appropriate architecture, its prevalence and negative effects will be significantly curtailed.

public records

0
1 0
0 1 0
1 0 1 0
0 1 0 1 0
1 0 1 0 1 0
0 1 0 1 0 1 0
1 0 1 0 1 0
0 1 0 1 0
1 0 1 0
0 1 0
1 0
0

7 The Problem of Public Records

From the beginning of the twentieth century, we have witnessed a vast proliferation in the number of government records kept about individuals as well as a significant increase in public access to these records. These trends together have created a problematic state of affairs—a system where the government extracts personal information from the populace and places it in the public domain, where it is hoarded by private-sector corporations that assemble dossiers on almost every American citizen.

Records from Birth to Death

Today, federal, state, and local government entities maintain a smorgasbord of public records.[1] State public records cover one's life from birth to death. Birth records can contain one's name, date of birth, place of birth, full names and ages of one's parents, and mother's maiden name.[2] In particular, mother's maiden names are important because many companies use them as passwords to access more sensitive data. Shortly after birth, the federal government stamps an

individual with a SSN, which will be used throughout her life to identify her and consolidate records about her. States also maintain other
records relating to one's personal life, such as records about marriages, divorces, and death. These are often referred to collectively as
"vital records." Records of marriages, which are public in most states,[3]
contain maiden names, the date and place of birth of both spouses,
as well as their residential addresses.[4]

Beyond vital records, states keep records for almost every occasion
an individual comes into contact with the state bureaucracy. Accident
reports and traffic citation records are made publicly available by
many states. Voting records can reveal one's political party affiliation,
date of birth, place of birth, email address, home address, telephone
number,[5] and sometimes SSN.[6] In many states, this information is
publicly available.

An individual's profession and place of employment often generate
a number of records. Many professions require licenses, such as doctors, lawyers, engineers, insurance agents, nurses, police, accountants, and teachers. If an individual is injured at work, worker's
compensation records may disclose the date of birth, type of injury,
and SSN.[7] If a person is a public employee, many personal details are
released to the public by way of personnel records, including home
address, phone number, SSN, salary, sick leave, and sometimes even
email messages.[8] In Massachusetts, government officials are required
by law to maintain "street lists" containing the names, addresses,
dates of birth, veteran statuses, nationalities, and occupations of all
residents. These lists, which organize residents by the streets they live
on, are made available to the police, to all political committees and
candidates, and to businesses and other organizations.[9]

One's home and property are also a matter of public record. Property tax assessment records contain a detailed description of the
home, including number of bedrooms and bathrooms, amenities
such as swimming pools, the size of the house, and the value. Other
property ownership records unveil lifestyle information such as
whether one owns a boat, and if so, its size and type.[10]

Often, any contact with law enforcement officials will yield a
record. Arrest records can include a person's name, occupation, physical description, date of birth, and the asserted factual circumstances

surrounding the arrest.[11] Police records also contain information about victims of crime.

Court records can be very revealing. In almost all states, court records are presumed to be public.[12] Although current practice and existing physical constraints limit the extent to which personal information in court documents can be accessed, new technologies are on the verge of changing this reality.

In civil cases, court files may contain medical histories, mental health data, tax returns, and financial information.[13] For example, in an ordinary civil lawsuit over an automobile accident, the plaintiff must submit medical information, including any pre-existing conditions that might be responsible for her symptoms. This data could even include psychological information. To establish damages, the plaintiff must also reveal details about her lifestyle, activities, and employment. If this information is contained in a document filed with the court or is mentioned in a hearing or at trial, it can potentially become accessible to the public unless protected by a protective order. In addition to plaintiffs, civil defendants must also yield personal information in many instances.

Witnesses and other third parties who are involved in cases can have deeply personal details snared by discovery and later exposed in court documents. If a person serves as a juror, her name, address, spouse's name, occupation, place of employment, and answers to voir dire questions may become part of the court record.[14] Some courts have held that the public may have access to questionnaires given to jurors as part of voir dire.[15] Voir dire questions can involve sensitive matters such as whether a juror was the victim of a crime, the juror's political and religious beliefs, any medical and psychological conditions that might affect the juror's performance, and other private details.[16]

Beyond ordinary civil lawsuits, special civil proceedings, such as appeals from the denial of Social Security benefits, release much information into court records, including a person's disability, work performance, SSN, birth date, address, phone number, and medical records.[17] In federal bankruptcy courts, any "paper filed . . . and the dockets of a bankruptcy court are public records and open to examination by an entity at reasonable times without charge."[18] Information involved in bankruptcy proceedings includes one's SSN, account numbers, employment data, sources of income, expenses, debts owed, and other financial information.[19] Additionally, in certain circumstances, employees of a company that declares bankruptcy can have their personal information divulged in public bankruptcy records.[20]

In some states, family court proceedings are public. For example, a divorce proceeding can unmask the intimacies of marital relationships. As the New Hampshire Supreme Court held, "[a] private citizen seeking a divorce in this State must unavoidably do so in a public forum, and consequently many private family and marital matters become public."[21]

Parties in criminal cases have even less privacy. Beyond the personal details about a defendant released at trial or in the government's indictment or charging papers, conviction records are made public.[22] Information about victims—their lifestyles, medical data, and occupation—can also be found in court records. Pre-sentence reports prepared by probation officers about convicted defendants facing sentence are used by judges in arriving at the appropriate sentence. These reports contain a summary of the defendant's prior criminal conduct, social history, character, family environment, education, employment and income, and medical and psychological information.[23] Although in many states and in federal court, pre-sentence reports remain confidential, in some states, such as California, the pre-sentence report becomes part of the court file after sentencing.[24]

Community notification laws for sex offenders, often referred to as "Megan's Laws," require the maintenance of databases of information about prior sex offenders and disclosure of their identities and where they live. All 50 states have enacted some version of Megan's Law.[25] Sex offender records often contain SSNs, photographs, addresses, prior convictions, and places of employment.[26] A number of states have placed their sex offender records on the Internet.

Some localities are even publicizing records about individuals arrested, but not yet convicted, of certain crimes. In 1997 Kansas City initiated "John TV," broadcasting on a government-owned television station the names, photographs, addresses, and ages of people who had merely been arrested (not convicted) for soliciting prostitutes, and other cities have initiated similar programs.[27] Additionally, a growing number of states are furnishing online databases of all of their current inmates and parolees.[28]

The Impact of Technology

For a long time, public records have been accessible only in the various localities in which they were kept. A person or entity desiring to find out about the value of an individual's home would have to travel to the town or county where the property was located and search through the records at the local courthouse. Depending upon local practice, the seeker of a record might be able to obtain a copy through the mail. Court records, such as bankruptcy records, would typically be obtained by visiting a courthouse or engaging in a lengthy correspondence with the clerk's office.[29] The seeker of a record could not obtain records en masse; records could only be obtained for specific individuals.

This reality is rapidly changing. As records are increasingly computerized, entire record systems rather than individual records can be easily searched, copied, and transferred. Private-sector organizations sweep up millions of records from record systems throughout the country and consolidate them into gigantic record systems. Many websites now compile public records from across the country.[30] There are more than 165 companies offering public record information over the Internet.[31] These companies have constructed gigantic databases of public records that were once dispersed throughout different agencies, offices, and courthouses—and with the click of a mouse, millions of records can be scoured for details.[32]

The increasing digitization of documents and the use of electronic filing will soon result in much greater accessibility to court records online. Currently, most courts post only court rulings and schedules on their websites. Only a handful of courts now post complaints and other legal documents.[33] However, states are beginning to require documents to be filed electronically and to convert existing records into digital format. For example, in New Jersey, bankruptcy records (including a debtor's bankruptcy petition) are scanned into electronic format and can be accessed through the Internet.[34] Some companies are beginning to make digital images of records available over the Internet.[35] The federal court system is currently developing a system that makes full case files accessible via the Internet.[36]

Beyond greater accessibility, technology may also lead to the retention of greater amounts of personal information in public records. Under current practice, due to storage space constraints, clerks' offices often do not maintain copies of exhibits and other documents related to trials. However, as court documents such as pleadings and exhibits are filed in digital format, they will become easier to store. Further, under current practice, transcripts are typically produced only when a case is appealed. New technology enables transcripts of court proceedings to be made instantaneously without having to be transcribed. The increased use of such technology could result in the existence of more transcripts of trials, which can potentially include personal information about many parties and witnesses.

In sum, the increasing digitization of documents enables more documents to be retained by eliminating storage constraints, increases the ability to access and copy documents, and permits the transfer of documents en masse. Personal information in public records, once protected by the practical difficulties of gaining access to the records, is increasingly less obscure.

The Regulation of Public Records

As it currently stands, public records law is a complicated and diverse hodge-podge of various statutes, court practices, and common law rights that vary from state to state and leave much personal information unprotected. A broad overview of the law that governs public records reveals that it is disconnected, often outdated, and inadequate to meet the challenges of the new technologies of the Information Age.

The Common Law, Court Records, and Protective Orders. At common law, English courts rarely encountered cases involving an individual seeking to gain access to government records.[37] Only in unusual circumstances could individuals inspect government records, such as when people needed them for court proceedings.[38] Access to court records, as opposed to other public records, was broader. When documents were introduced into evidence, individuals were permitted access.[39]

Early U.S. courts followed the English practice.[40] Only if a person had a "special interest" in examining records would access be granted.[41] Later on, the common law evolved to expand the "interest" required for inspection to include redressing public wrongs and monitoring government functions.[42] The law then broadened even further to include all purposes that were not improper or harmful to others.[43] One of the most commonly mentioned improper purposes was "to satisfy idle curiosity or for the purpose of creating a public scandal."[44]

In contrast to public records, the right to inspect court records was generally broader and was shaped by the supervisory authority of the courts.[45] The courts had a long tradition of permitting open access to court records, and access was rarely limited based on the purposes for which the records were sought.[46] In 1978, in *Nixon v. Warner Communications, Inc.*, the Supreme Court noted that "[i]t is clear that the courts of this country recognize a general right to inspect and copy public records and documents, including judicial records and documents."[47] The right is justified by "the citizen's desire to keep a watchful eye on the workings of public agencies, and in a newspaper publisher's intention to publish information concerning the operation of government." The common law right of access isn't absolute, especially for court records, because "[e]very court has supervisory power over its own records and files," and can deny access when records reveal embarrassing personal information or cause harm. The decision over whether to permit access "is one best left to the sound discretion of the trial court."[48]

In the federal court system, pursuant to Federal Rule of Civil Procedure 26(c), judges have discretion "for good cause shown" to issue protective orders to shield information from disclosure where it might cause a party "annoyance, embarrassment, oppression, or undue burden or expense."[49] Protective orders allow documents to be used by parties to a case, but restrict public access. Most states have a rule similar to Rule 26(c).[50] Since court records are presumed to be publicly accessible, a party seeking a protective order must overcome the presumption.[51] Courts balance a party's interest in privacy against the public interest in disclosure.[52] If a court decides to deny access, it "must set forth substantial reasons."[53]

Courts also retain discretion to issue special orders to keep certain proceedings and information confidential. A court will sometimes, under very limited circumstances, seal court proceedings such as trials.[54] A court can allow a plaintiff to proceed anonymously with the use of a pseudonym.[55] Courts can also permit anonymous juries when jurors might otherwise be placed in danger. These decisions, however, are within the discretion of the trial court, and courts differ greatly in the exercise of their discretion. For example, one court permitted a woman who had been raped at a train station and was suing Amtrak to keep her identity secret because of the potential embarrassment she would suffer if the details of her rape became known in her community.[56] In contrast, another court held that a victim of sexual assault could not sue her assailant for civil damages under a pseudonym because "[f]airness requires that she be prepared to stand behind her charges publicly" and because she was "seeking to vindicate primarily her own interests."[57]

In sum, under modern American common law, there is a limited right to access public records so long as one's purpose is not improper. For court records, the common law right to access follows the supervisory authority of the courts, and judges have significant discretion in granting or denying access.[58]

Freedom of Information Laws. State legislatures gradually replaced or supplemented the common law right of access with open records statutes, which generally mandated broad access.[59] These statutes are called "freedom of information," "open access," "right to know," or "sunshine" laws. States were initially slow in enacting statutory public access rights; by 1940, only 12 states had open records statutes.[60] In 1966, Congress passed the Freedom of Information Act (FOIA), providing substantial public access to records of the federal government. When he signed the FOIA into law, President Lyndon Johnson declared that "democracy works best when the people have all the information that the security of the Nation permits. No one should be able to pull curtains of secrecy around decisions which can be revealed without injury to the public interest."[61] Under FOIA, "any person" (including associations, organizations, and foreign citizens) may request "records" maintained by an executive agency.[62] Requesters of records don't need to state a reason for requesting records.[63] FOIA does not apply to records kept by Congress or the Judiciary.[64]

Today, all 50 states have open records statutes, a majority of which are modeled after the FOIA.[65] Like the federal FOIA, state FOIAs are justified by a strong commitment to openness and transparency.[66] Following FOIA, many states eliminated the common law requirement that requesters establish an interest in obtaining the records. Most state FOIAs contain a presumption in favor of disclosure.[67]

Open access laws never mandate absolute disclosure. They contain exemptions, typically (although not always) including an exemption to protect individual privacy. The federal FOIA contains nine enumerated exemptions to disclosure, two of which pertain to privacy. One applies generally to records which "would constitute a clearly unwarranted invasion of personal privacy"; the other applies to law enforcement records that could "constitute an unwarranted invasion of personal privacy."[68] If possible, private information can be deleted from records, and the redacted records disclosed to the requester.

The federal FOIA doesn't require that a person be given notice that his or her personal information is encompassed within a FOIA request. Even if an individual finds out about the request, she has no right under FOIA to prevent or second-guess an agency's decision to disclose the records. FOIA does not require that the government withhold information; it is up to the government agency to assert and to litigate the individual's privacy interest.[69]

State FOIA privacy exemptions come in myriad shapes and sizes. Many state FOIAs contain privacy exemptions similar to those found in the federal FOIA, applying when disclosure would constitute a "clearly unwarranted" invasion of privacy.[70] However, not all state FOIAs have privacy exemptions. Pennsylvania's Right to Know Act does not contain a privacy exemption; it prohibits only access to records "which would operate to the prejudice or impairment of a person's reputation or personal security."[71] As one court stated, "the phrase 'personal security' does not mean 'personal privacy.'"[72] Ohio's Public Records Act does not contain any privacy exemption.[73]

In applying FOIA privacy exemptions, many states follow the federal FOIA approach and balance interests of privacy against the interests of public access.[74] However, states have adopted widely differing approaches often stemming from vastly different judicial conceptions of privacy.

Privacy Acts. The Privacy Act of 1974 regulates the record systems of federal agencies. The Act prohibits the disclosure of personal information; requires records to be kept secure; and gives people the right to review their records and to ask the agency to correct any errors.[75] People can sue if they are harmed by an agency's failure to comply with the Act. The Privacy Act has significant limitations. It is limited only to the public sector. It applies to federal, not state and local agencies. Further, the Act has been eroded by about a dozen exceptions. For example, agencies can disclose information without the consent of individuals to the Census Bureau, to law enforcement entities, to Congress, and to credit reporting agencies. When FOIA requires that information be released, the Privacy Act does not apply. Nor does the Privacy Act apply to court records.[76]

The broadest exception is that information may be disclosed for any "routine use" if disclosure is "compatible" with the purpose for which the agency collected the information.[77] The "routine use" exception has repeatedly been criticized as being a gigantic loophole.[78] As privacy law expert Robert Gellman writes, "[t]his vague formula has not created much of a substantive barrier to external disclosure of personal information."[79]

Although the Privacy Act requires an individual's permission before his or her records can be disclosed, redress for violations of the Act is virtually impossible to obtain.[80] The Privacy Act provides individuals with a monetary remedy for disclosures of personal information only if the disclosure was made "willfully and intentionally."[81] This restriction on recovery of damages fails to redress the most common form of mistakes—those due to carelessness. This leaves little incentive to bring suit against violators.[82] For example, in *Andrews v. Veterans Administration,* the Veterans Administration released inadequately redacted personnel records of nurses, resulting in what the court called a "substantial" violation of nurses' privacy. However, the agency could not be sued under the Privacy Act because it acted negligently, not willfully.[83] Moreover, less than a third of the states have enacted a general privacy law akin to the Privacy Act.[84] Paul Schwartz observes that most states lack "omnibus data protection laws" and have "scattered laws [that] provide only limited protections for personal information in the public sector."[85]

Access and Use Restrictions. Confronted with increased information trade, some states have attempted to restrict access to personal information in public records as well as certain uses of personal information obtained from public records. In the last decade, a number of states have enacted access restrictions for some of their public records, often excluding access for commercial uses, such as soliciting business or marketing services or products. For example, Georgia amended its public records law in 1991, making it unlawful to access law enforcement or motor vehicle accident records "for any commercial solicitation of such individuals or relatives of such individuals."[86] In 1992, Louisiana restricted access to accident records for commercial solicitation purposes.[87] Kentucky, in response to "a public groundswell [that] developed against the release of accident reports to attorneys and chiropractors,"[88] amended its public records law in 1994 to restrict access for these and other commercial uses.[89] In 1996, Florida barred the access of driver information in traffic citations from those seeking it for commercial solicitation purposes.[90] Colorado curtailed access to criminal justice records unless those seeking access signed a statement that such records would not be used "for the direct solicitation of business for pecuniary gain."[91] California restricted access to arrest records by providing that the records "shall not be used directly or indirectly to sell a product or service . . . and the requester shall execute a declaration to that effect under penalty of perjury."[92] Almost half of the states prohibit the commercial use of voter registration records.[93]

The federal government also has certain access and use restrictions for its public records. Pursuant to the Federal Election Campaign Act (FECA), reports of contributors to political committees are "available for public inspection . . . except that any information copied from such reports . . . may not be sold or used by any person for the purpose of soliciting contributions or for commercial purposes."[94]

In sum, although in certain contexts laws are beginning to limit access to public records for some purposes, the vast majority of public records remain virtually unrestricted in access.

Restrictions on State Information Practices. In a rare instance, the federal government has directly regulated the states' use of public records. In 1994, Congress passed the Driver's Privacy Protection Act (DPPA) to curtail states' selling their motor vehicle records to marketers.[95] In *Reno v. Condon,* the Supreme Court concluded that DPPA was a proper exercise of Congress's authority to regulate interstate commerce. Further, the Court concluded that DPPA "regulates the States as the owners of databases" and does not require them to enact regulation or to assist in enforcing federal statutes concerning private individuals.[96] Although DPPA is an important first step in bringing state public records systems under control, DPPA applies only to motor vehicle records and does not forbid the dissemination of all the other public records states maintain.

The Regulatory Regime of Public Records. As illustrated throughout this chapter, states vary significantly in what information they make publicly available. Often such decisions are made by agencies and bureaucrats or left to the discretion of the courts. Decisions as to the scope of access—whether one must obtain a record by physically going to a local agency office, by engaging in correspondence by mail, or by simply downloading it from the Internet—are often made by local bureaucrats. Frequently, it is up to the individual to take significant steps to protect privacy, such as overcoming the presumption of access to court records. In many instances, individuals are never even given notice or an opportunity to assert a privacy interest when records containing their personal information are disclosed.

Differing protection of personal information with no minimum floor of protection presents significant problems in today's age of increasing mobility and information flow. There is no federal law establishing a baseline for the regulation of public records. Thus, personal information is regulated by a bewildering assortment of state statutory protections, which vary widely from state to state.[97]

This chaotic state of affairs is troublesome in an Information Age where information so fluidly passes throughout the country and is being made more widely available through the Internet. The privacy protection that currently exists for public records is largely designed for a world of paper records and has been slow to adapt to an age where information can be downloaded from the Internet in an instant.

8 Access and Aggregation
Rethinking Privacy
and Transparency

The Tension between Transparency and Privacy

A 1998 episode of the television newsmagazine *Dateline* illustrates one way that the tension between transparency (open access to public records) and privacy can arise.[1] A man, imprisoned for murder, obtained under a state FOIA the address of a former girlfriend. When she learned that her ex-boyfriend obtained her address, the woman became quite scared because her ex-boyfriend was prone to losing his temper and held a grudge against her. She lived in fear, knowing that someday he would be released and might come after her. The prisoner, however, claimed that he was the father of her child and needed the address because he wanted to file a paternity suit. This story illustrates why it is important for people to be able to obtain certain information about others, yet also demonstrates the dangers and threat to privacy caused by the ready availability of information.

There are at least four general functions of transparency: (1) to shed light on governmental activities and proceedings; (2) to find out information about public officials and candidates for public office; (3) to facilitate certain social transactions, such as selling property or initiating lawsuits; and (4) to find out information about other individuals for a variety of purposes.

First, and perhaps most importantly, transparency provides the public with knowledge about the government and an understanding of how it functions. By promoting awareness of the workings of government, transparency serves a "watchdog" function. Open access to government proceedings ensures that they are conducted fairly. Open access exposes the government to public scrutiny and enables a check on abuse and corruption. "Sunlight is said to be the best of disinfectants," declared Justice Brandeis, "electric light the most efficient policeman."[2] Making arrest records public, for example, protects against secret arrests and government abuses.[3] Open access to public court records "allows the citizenry to monitor the functioning of our courts, thereby insuring quality, honesty, and respect for our legal system."[4] As James Madison observed: "A popular Government, without popular information, or the means of acquiring it, is but a Prologue to a Farce or a Tragedy; or, perhaps both. Knowledge will forever govern ignorance: And a people who mean to be their own Governors, must arm themselves with the power which knowledge gives."[5] According to Justice Oliver Wendell Holmes:

> It is desirable that the trial of [civil] causes should take place under the public eye not because the controversies of one citizen with another are of public concern, but because it is of the highest moment that those who administer justice should always act under the sense of public responsibility, and that every citizen should be able to satisfy himself with his own eyes as to the mode in which a public duty is performed.[6]

Access to court records permits people to examine the information considered by courts making decisions affecting the public at large. Issues raised in a product liability case could have significance for millions of others who use a product. Information about how certain types of cases are resolved—such as domestic abuse cases, medical malpractice cases, and others—is important for assessing the competency of the judicial system for resolving important social matters. Scholars and the media need to look beyond a judicial decision or a jury verdict to scrutinize the records and evidence in a case. The ability to identify jurors enables the media to question them about the reasons for their verdict. Courts and commentators have pointed out that the Watergate Scandal might never have been uncovered if the original bail hearing had been closed to the press because reporters Bob Woodward and Carl Bernstein would not have been suspicious that expensive attorneys were representing the burglars.[7]

The second function of transparency is to enable the scrutiny of public officials or candidates for public office. Information about a politician's criminal history might be informative to many voters. Information about a politician's property may provide insight into the politician's wealth, a factor that might shape the politician's values and public decisions. Some voters may find a politician's divorce records and marital history illustrative of the person's character. Other possibly informative information about a politician could include that she was sued many times or sued others many times; that she once declared bankruptcy; that she never voted in any elections; that she was formerly registered in another political party; that she owns property in other states; and so on. Open access to public records enables voters to find out such information so they may make more informed choices at the polls.

Third, transparency facilitates certain social transactions. Access to public records is an essential function for the sale and transfer of property, as it enables people to trace ownership and title in land. Public record information is useful in locating witnesses for judicial proceedings as well as locating heirs to estates. Further, access to public records can allow individuals and entities to track down individuals they want to sue and to obtain the necessary information to serve them with process.

The fourth function of transparency is to enable people to find out information about individuals for various other purposes. Public records can help verify individual identity, investigate fraud, and locate lost friends and classmates. Public records enable law enforcement officials to locate criminals and investigate crimes, and can assist in tracking down deadbeat parents. Public records can permit people to investigate babysitters or child care professionals. Employers can use public record information to screen potential employees, such as examining the past driving records of prospective truck drivers or taxicab drivers. Criminal history information might be relevant when hiring a worker in a child care facility or a kindergarten teacher.

Transparency, however, can come into tension with privacy. Can both of these important values be reconciled? Before turning to this question, I must first address how the privacy problem to which public records contribute should be understood. We must rethink certain longstanding notions about privacy before we can reach an appropriate balance between transparency and privacy.

Conceptualizing Privacy and Public Records

Access: The Public Is Private. The secrecy paradigm, as discussed in chapter 3, is deeply entrenched in information privacy law. In addition to focusing on whether information is completely secret or not, the paradigm categorizes information as either public or private. When information is private, it is hidden, and as long as it is kept secret, it remains private. When it is public, it is in the public domain available for any use. Information is seen in this black-and-white manner; either it is wholly private or wholly public.

This paradigm is outmoded in the Information Age. Unless we live as hermits, there is no way to exist in modern society without leaving information traces wherever we go. Therefore, we must abandon the secrecy paradigm. Privacy involves an expectation of a certain degree of accessibility of information. Under this alternative view, privacy entails control over and limitations on certain uses of information, even if the information is not concealed. Privacy can be violated by altering levels of accessibility, by taking obscure facts and making them widely accessible. Our expectation of limits on the degree of accessibility emerges from the fact that information in public records has remained relatively inaccessible until recently. Our personal information in public records remained private because it was a needle in a haystack, and usually nobody would take the time to try to find it. This privacy is rapidly disappearing as access to information is increasing.

In limited contexts, some courts are beginning to abandon the secrecy paradigm, although most courts still cling to it. In *United States Department of Justice v. Reporters Committee for Freedom of the Press,* the Supreme Court held that the release of FBI "rap sheets" was an invasion of privacy within the privacy exemption of FOIA. The FBI rap sheets contained the date of birth, physical description, and a history of arrests, charges, and convictions on over 24 million people. The reporters argued that the rap sheet wasn't private because it was merely a collection of data that had previously been publicly disclosed. The Court didn't agree, noting that "there is a vast difference between the public records that might be found after a diligent search of courthouse files, county archives, and local police stations throughout the country and a computerized summary located in a single clearinghouse of information."[8]

In cases involving the privacy torts, a few courts have recognized a privacy interest in information exposed to the public. In *Melvin v. Reid,* a former prostitute who was once criminally prosecuted for murder had left the prostitution business long ago and got married. When the movie *The Red Kimono,* depicted her life story and used her maiden name, she sued under the tort of public disclosure. The court held that although she could not claim that the facts about her life were private because they were in the public record, there was no need for the movie to use her real name.[9]

Likewise, in *Briscoe v. Reader's Digest Ass'n,* an article in *Reader's Digest* magazine about hijacking disclosed that the plaintiff had hijacked a truck 11 years earlier. Briscoe had rehabilitated himself, and his new friends, family, and young daughter weren't aware of his crime. The court held that although the facts of the crime could be disclosed, Briscoe could sue for the use of his name, which had no relevance to the article.[10]

Generally, however, most courts still adhere to the secrecy paradigm and do not recognize a privacy interest when information is exposed to the public. As a result, most courts have rejected the *Reid* and *Briscoe* approach.[11] In *Forsher v. Bugliosi,*[12] the court considered *Briscoe* "an exception to the more general rule that 'once a man has become a public figure, or news, he remains a matter of legitimate recall to the public mind to the end of his days.'"[13] Likewise, the Restatement for the tort of public disclosure explains: "There is no liability when the defendant merely gives further publicity to information about the plaintiff that is already public. Thus there is no liability for giving publicity to facts about the plaintiff's life which are matters of public record."[14] Similarly, for the tort of intrusion upon seclusion, the Restatement provides that "there is no liability for the examination of a public record concerning the plaintiff."[15] Further, *Briscoe* seems foreclosed by the Supreme Court's decision in *Cox Broadcasting Corp. v. Cohn,* which held that when information is disclosed in documents open to the public, the press cannot be punished for publishing it.[16]

In a number of cases, courts applying the constitutional right to information privacy have become mired in the secrecy paradigm. Courts have refused to find a constitutional right to information privacy for data exposed to the public. In *Scheetz v. Morning Call, Inc.,* a court held that a husband and wife had no constitutional right to information privacy in a police report disclosed to the press containing the wife's allegations of spousal abuse. Although her complaint to the police did not result in charges, "[t]he police could have brought charges without her concurrence, at which point all the information would have wound up on the public record, where it would have been non-confidential."[17] In *Cline v. Rogers,* the court held that police records weren't private "since arrest and conviction information are matters of public record."[18] In *Walls v. City of Petersburg,* public employees were questioned about the criminal histories of their family members, their complete marital history, including marriages, divorces, and children, and any outstanding debts or judgments against them. According to the court, the information wasn't private because it was already available in public records.[19]

Courts have also adhered to the secrecy paradigm in challenges to Megan's Laws, which mandate the public disclosure of information about prior sex offenders. In *Russell v. Gregoire,* convicted sex offenders challenged the disclosure of their picture, name, age, date of birth, crimes, and neighborhoods in which they lived. The court held that the information wasn't private because it was "already fully available to the public."[20] Likewise, in *Paul P. v. Verniero,* the court held there was no privacy interest in the names and physical descriptions of previously convicted sex offenders.[21]

In sum, although divided, most courts adhere to the secrecy paradigm. Unless the secrecy paradigm is abandoned, people will lose any ability to claim a privacy interest in the extensive personal information in public records.

Aggregation: The Digital Biography. Another longstanding notion of privacy—the invasion conception, which I discussed in chapter 6—doesn't recognize an infringement of privacy unless there is a palpable invasion. Information protected as private must be embarrassing or harmful to one's reputation. The problem with the invasion conception is that public record information often consists of fairly innocuous details—such as one's birth date, address, height, weight, and so on.

Following the invasion conception, a number of courts have rejected claims that certain information falls within state FOIA privacy exemptions because the information didn't pose immediate harms to reputation or security. One court reasoned that "[n]ames and addresses are not ordinarily personal, intimate, or embarrassing pieces of information."[22] Another court held that police payroll records containing each employee's name, gender, date of birth, salary, and other data could be disclosed because the records didn't harm their reputations.[23] Information about teacher salaries, according to one court, didn't fall within the privacy exemption because "[t]he salaries of public employees and schoolteachers are not 'intimate details . . . the disclosure of which might harm the individual.'"[24]

If the release of certain information in public records doesn't make one blush or reveal one's deepest secrets, then what is the harm? The harm stems from the aggregation effect discussed in chapter 3. Viewed in isolation, each piece of our day-to-day information is not all that telling; viewed in combination, it begins to paint a portrait about our personalities. Moreover, these digital biographies greatly increase our vulnerability to a variety of dangers. As public record information becomes more readily available, criminals can use it to gain access to a person's financial accounts. For example, one industrious criminal gained access to the financial accounts of a number of individuals on *Forbes* magazine's list of the 400 richest people in America such as Oprah Winfrey and George Lucas.[25] Identity thieves frequently obtain personal information necessary for their criminal activity through information brokers, who sell reports about individuals based on public record data combined with other information.[26] As discussed in chapter 6, the SSN is the most useful tool of the identity thief, and SSNs are often available in various public records.

Public record information also can expose people to violence. In 1989, a fan obsessed with actress Rebecca Shaeffer located her home address with the help of a private investigator who obtained it from California motor vehicles records. The fan murdered her outside her home. This killing spurred Congress to pass the Driver's Privacy Protection Act (DPPA), which restricts the states' ability to release motor vehicle records.[27] In another example, an Internet site known as the "Nuremberg Files" posted information about doctors working in abortion clinics, including names, photos, SSNs, home addresses, descriptions of their cars, and information about their families.[28] Doctors who were killed had a black line drawn through their names. Names of wounded doctors were shaded in gray. The doctors sued. At trial, they testified as to how their lives became riddled with fear, how some wore bulletproof vests and wigs in public. They won the suit and were able to block the use of their personal information on the website.[29] This case demonstrates the dangers from increased access to personal information, even relatively non-intimate information such as one's address.

At a more abstract level, the existence of digital dossiers alters the nature of the society we live in. In 1971, in his highly influential book, *The Assault on Privacy,* law professor Arthur Miller warned of the "possibility of constructing a sophisticated data center capable of generating a comprehensive womb-to-tomb dossier on every individual and transmitting it to a wide range of data users over a national network."[30] On a number of occasions, the federal government has flirted with the idea of creating a national database of personal information. The Johnson administration contemplated creating a National Data Center that would combine information collected by various federal agencies into one large computer database, but the plan was scrapped after a public outcry arose.[31] Again, in the early 1970s, an official in the General Services Administration proposed that all of the federal government's computer systems be connected in a network called FEDNET. Responding to a public outcry, Vice President Gerald Ford stopped the plan.[32]

Although these proposals have been halted due to public outcries, we have been inching toward a system of de facto national identification for some time and are precariously close to having one.[33] The

Immigration Reform and Control Act of 1986 requires new employees to supply identification and proof of U.S. citizenship before obtaining a new job.[34] In a recent effort to track down parents who fail to pay child support, the federal government has created a vast database consisting of information about all people who obtain a new job anywhere in the nation. The database contains their SSNs, addresses, and wages.[35] The ready availability of one's SSN and the ability to combine it with a host of other information about individuals will make increasingly more possible a reality where typing an individual's name into a searchable database will pull up a "womb-to-tomb" dossier.

Such a reality can pose significant dangers. "Identity systems and documents," observes political scientist Richard Sobel, "have a long history of uses and abuses for social control and discrimination."[36] Slaves were required to carry identifying papers to travel; identification cards were used by the Nazis in locating Jews; and the slaughter of Tutsis in Rwanda was aided by a system of identifiers.[37] In addition to facilitating the monitoring and control of individuals, such a dossier may make a person a "prisoner of his recorded past."[38] Records of personal information can easily be used by government leaders and officials for improper monitoring of individuals. Data can be exploited for whatever task is at hand—a tool available to anyone in power in government to use in furtherance of the current passion or whim of the day. For example, in 1942, the Census Bureau used its data from the 1940 census to assist in the effort to intern Japanese Americans during World War II.[39] Currently, we do not know the full consequences of living in a dossier society, but we are rapidly moving toward becoming such a society without sufficient foresight and preparation.

The problems and dangers just illustrated are not merely the product of the actions of the government. Rather, these troubles are caused by the way that both public- and private-sector entities are using personal information. The issue concerns more than isolated threats and harms, but is fundamentally about the structure of our society. Not only are public records altering the power that the government can exercise over people's lives, but they are also contributing to the growing power of businesses. As I discussed earlier in this book, although people may be aware that dossiers are being assembled about them, they have no idea what information the dossiers contain or how the dossiers are being used. This reality leads to unease, vulnerability, and powerlessness—a deepening sense that one is at the mercy of others, or, perhaps even more alarming, at the mercy of a bureaucratic process that is arbitrary, irresponsible, opaque, and indifferent to people's dignity and welfare.

The problem with information collection and use today is not merely that individuals are no longer able to exercise control over their information; it is that their information is subjected to a bureaucratic process that is itself out of control. Without this process being subject to regulation and control and without individuals having rights to exercise some dominion over their information, individuals will be routinely subjected to the ills of bureaucracy.

Public records contribute to this privacy problem because they are often a principal source of information for businesses in the construction of their databases. Marketers stock their databases with public record information, and the uses to which these databases are put are manifold and potentially limitless. The personal information in public records is often supplied involuntarily and typically for a purpose linked to the reason why particular records are kept. The problem is that, often without the individual's knowledge or consent, the information is then used for a host of different purposes by both the government and businesses.

Therefore, the privacy problem caused by public records concerns the structure of information flow—the way that information circulates throughout our society. The problem is not necessarily the disclosure of secrets or the injury of reputations, but is one created by increased access and aggregation of data. Privacy is an issue that concerns what type of society we want to construct for the future. Do we want to live in a Kafkaesque world where dossiers about individuals circulate in an elaborate underworld of public- and private-sector bureaucracies without the individual having notice, knowledge, or the ability to monitor or control the ways the information is used?

Transparency and Privacy: Reconciling the Tension

How can the tension between transparency and privacy be reconciled? Must access to public records be sacrificed at the altar of privacy? Or must privacy evaporate in order for government to be disinfected by sunlight?

Both transparency and privacy can be balanced through limitations on the access and use of personal information in public records. Of course, we must rethink what information belongs in public records. But we must also regulate the uses of our digital dossiers. The government is not doing enough to protect against the uses of the information that it routinely pumps into the public domain. If we abandon the notion that privacy is an exclusive status, and recognize that information in public records can still remain private even if there is limited access to it, then we can find a workable compromise for the tension between transparency and privacy. We can make information accessible for certain purposes only. When government discloses information, it can limit how it discloses that information by preventing it from being amassed by companies for commercial purposes, from being sold to others, or from being combined with other information and sold back to the government.

Much of the personal information in public records is not necessary to shed light on the way government carries out its functions. Rather, this information reveals more about the people who are the subjects of the government's regulatory machinery. Although the federal FOIA has served to shed light on government activities and has supplied critical information for hundreds of books and articles, it has also been used as a tool for commercial interests. The vast majority of FOIA requests are made by businesses for commercial purposes.[40] According to Judge Patricia Wald, FOIA turns agencies into "information brokers" rather than "a window for public assessment of how government works."[41] When weighing interests under the privacy exceptions to the federal FOIA, although courts can't consider the identity and purpose of the requester, they can take into account the relationship of the requested document to the purposes of FOIA.[42] Unlike the federal FOIA, many states routinely permit access by information brokers without looking to the purposes of their open access laws or the public interest.

State FOIAs generally do not permit any discrimination among requesters. In a number of cases, officials wanting to restrict access to people requesting records for commercial use had no statutory authority to do so. In *Dunhill v. Director, District of Columbia Department of Transportation,* a marketer of personal information about individuals sought a listing on computer tape of the names, addresses, birth dates, gender, and expiration date of drivers' permits of all people holding valid District of Columbia drivers' permits. The court held that the government had to release the information because the statute didn't authorize the government to look to the motives of the request.[43] In *In re Crawford,* a preparer of bankruptcy petitions for debtors challenged the requirement that he divulge his SSN on the petition, which would then be made public. The court recognized that although disclosure of his SSN exposed him to potential fraud and identity theft, the interest in public access "is of special importance in the bankruptcy arena, as unrestricted access to judicial records fosters confidence among creditors regarding the fairness of the bankruptcy system."[44] Thus, the court formalistically invoked the principle of transparency, relying on the vague argument that total transparency fosters "confidence."

The danger with any principle is that it can drift to different uses over time. Jack Balkin identifies this problem as "ideological drift." "Ideological drift in law means that legal ideas and symbols will change their political valence as they are used over and over again in new contexts."[45] Laws fostering transparency are justified as shedding light into the dark labyrinths of government bureaucracy to expose its inner workings to public scrutiny, and preventing the harrowing situation in Kafka's *The Trial*—a bureaucracy that worked in clandestine and mysterious ways, completely unaccountable and unchecked. These are certainly laudable goals, for they are essential to democracy and to the people's ability to keep government under control. However, freedom of information laws are increasingly becoming a tool for powerful corporations to collect information about individuals to further their own commercial interests, not to shed light on the government. A window to look in on the government is transforming into a window for the government and allied corporations to peer in on individuals. The data collected about individuals is then subject to a bureaucratic process that is often careless, uncontrolled, and clandestine. Because private-sector bureaucracies lack the transparency of government bureaucracies, there is a greater potential for personal information to be abused. Paradoxically, a right of access designed to empower individuals and protect them from the ills of bureaucracy can lead to exactly the opposite result.

There are certainly instances where information about individuals can illuminate government functioning. Examination of accident reports may reveal widespread problems with particular vehicles. Scrutiny of police records may indicate problems in police investigation and enforcement. Information about the salaries of public officials and employees allows the public to assess whether they are being over- or under-compensated. Disciplinary information about public employees allows taxpayers to scrutinize the performance of those who are earning their tax dollars. However, many of these purposes can be achieved through evaluating aggregate statistical data or by examining records with redacted personal identifying information.

The solution is not to eliminate all access to public records, but to redact personal information where possible and to regulate specific uses of information. Real property information must be made available for certain purposes, but it should not be available for all purposes. A person may need to obtain the address of a celebrity to serve process in a lawsuit; however, disclosing the address to fans or on the Internet is different.

Use restriction laws, such as those discussed in chapter 7, are a step in the right direction. These laws attempt to navigate the tension between transparency and privacy by permitting the use of public record information for certain purposes but not all purposes. One of the longstanding Fair Information Practices is purpose specification—that personal information obtained for one purpose cannot be used for another purpose without an individual's consent.[46] Often the purposes for the government collection of personal information vary widely from the purposes for which the data is used after it is disclosed in public records. Governments collecting personal information should limit such uncontrolled drift in use. Access should be granted for uses furthering traditional functions of transparency such as the watchdog function; access should be denied for commercial solicitation uses because such uses do not adequately serve the functions of transparency. Rather, these uses make public records a cheap marketing tool, resulting in the further spread of personal information, which is often resold among marketers.

Use restriction laws must go beyond basic restrictions on access for commercial solicitation. The use of public records by information brokers or other entities that aggregate personal information and sell it to others is deeply problematic for the reasons discussed earlier in this chapter. Although information brokers have brought a new level of accessibility to public records, they have also contributed greatly to the creation of digital dossiers. This type of aggregated public record information is often not used for the purposes of checking governmental abuse or monitoring governmental activities. Rather, it is used to investigate individuals. This investigation is at the behest of other individuals, private detectives, employers, and law enforcement officials. Information brokers such as ChoicePoint collect public record information and supplement it with a host of other personal information, creating a convenient investigation tool for government entities. The use of information brokers by the government to investigate citizens runs directly counter to the spirit of freedom of information laws, which were designed to empower individuals to monitor their government, not vice versa.

Certain information should be restricted from public records completely. The proposal by the Administrative Office of the U.S. Court System to separate both paper and electronic documents into a public and private file for civil cases and to restrict access to certain documents in criminal proceedings such as pre-sentence reports is a step in the right direction.[47] One example of information that should be excluded from public records is a person's SSN.[48] SSNs serve as a gateway to highly sensitive information such as financial accounts, school records, and a host of other data. As a routine practice, SSNs should be redacted from every document before being disclosed publicly.

Jurors, parties to litigation, and witnesses should all be informed of the extent to which their personal information could become a public record and must be given an opportunity to voice their privacy concerns and have information redacted.

Of course, provisions in the law can be made for people who want to consent to the disclosure of their personal information. If the requester desires personal information about a specific individual in a specific case, the agency or court can contact the individual, inform her of the purpose of the request, and ask if she consents to disclosure. People may want to consent if the data is being used by a researcher, but may not if the information is requested for marketing purposes.

The federal Privacy Act must be amended to provide more meaningful protection. Its restrictions on the use of SSNs must be strengthened to regulate and restrict the use of SSNs by the private sector. Thus, the Privacy Act should prohibit the use of SSNs as identifiers by businesses, schools, and hospitals. Further, the Privacy Act should contain meaningful remedies for violations. People should be permitted to sue for negligent infringements of the Act—not just willful ones. Rarely do government agencies willfully disclose personal information in violation of the Privacy Act; most disclosures occur because of carelessness and inadvertence. By expanding the Act in this way, agencies will have a strong incentive to treat their record systems with more care and to provide greater security for the personal information they maintain. Government agency information-handling practices should be routinely audited by a governmental oversight agency. Moreover, the "routine use" exception must be significantly tightened.

Finally, more laws like the Driver's Privacy Protection Act are necessary to ensure that states maintain adequate privacy protection in their public records law. A federal baseline should not preempt states from adopting stricter protections of privacy, but it must provide a meaningful floor of protection. Although each state should adopt its own statute akin to the federal Privacy Act, one option would be to extend the federal Privacy Act to the states.

We may never be able to achieve complete secrecy of information in many situations and, in some situations, complete secrecy would be undesirable. But we can limit accessibility and use.

Public Records and the First Amendment

Do the access and use restrictions I propose pass muster under the First Amendment? Understood broadly, the First Amendment protects openness in information flow. First, the Court has held that the First Amendment provides certain rights of access to at least some government proceedings. Restrictions on the information available in public records might infringe upon this right. Second, freedom of speech prevents the government from restricting the disclosure and dissemination of information. A close analysis of the Court's decisions, however, reveals that access and use restrictions are constitutional.

The Right of Access. The Supreme Court has held that the First Amendment mandates that certain government proceedings be open to the public. In *Richmond Newspapers, Inc. v. Virginia,* a plurality of the Court concluded that the public had a First Amendment right of access to criminal trials.[49] Two years later, in *Globe Newspaper Co. v. Superior Court,* the Court struck down a law closing criminal trials when juvenile sexual assault victims testified. According to the Court, a "major purpose" of the First Amendment is "to protect the free discussion of governmental affairs." The Court articulated a two-pronged test to determine whether the right to access applies, first looking to whether the proceeding "historically has been open to the press and general public" and then examining whether access "plays a particularly significant role in the functioning of the judicial process and the government as a whole."[50] Shortly after *Globe,* the Court extended the right to access beyond the immediate criminal trial to jury selection and to pretrial proceedings.[51] Lower courts have proclaimed that the right of access applies to hearings for pretrial suppression, due process, entrapment, and bail.[52]

Although the Court has never squarely addressed whether the right of access applies beyond the criminal arena, several lower courts have extended it to civil cases. For example, in *Publicker Industries, Inc. v. Cohen,* the court reasoned that "the civil trial, like the criminal trial, plays a particularly significant role in the functioning of the judicial process and the government as a whole."[53] Several courts have even concluded that the right to access "extends to at least some categories of court documents and records," but not all courts agree.[54] Although courts have rarely applied the right of access beyond court records, since the rationale for the right is to provide knowledge about the workings of the government, the right might logically extend to other public records. Even under such an expansive view, however, the right of access shouldn't prohibit many access and use restrictions. When public records illuminate government functioning, access to them is generally consistent with the rationale for the right of access. However, the grand purposes behind the right are not present in the context of much information gathering from public records today. Public records are becoming a tool for powerful companies to use in furtherance of commercial gain. These uses do not shed light on the government.

In fact, the Constitution does not simply require open information flow; it also establishes certain responsibilities for the way that the government uses the information it collects. The Court has held that there are circumstances where the government cannot force individuals to disclose personal information absent a compelling government interest. In *NAACP v. Alabama,* the Court struck down a statute requiring the NAACP to disclose a list of its members because this could expose them to potential economic reprisal and physical violence, thus chilling their freedom of association.[55] Similarly, in *Greidinger v. Davis,* the Fourth Circuit held that Virginia's voter registration system was unconstitutional because it forced people to publicly disclose their SSNs in order to vote, thus deterring people from voting by exposing them to potential harms such as identity theft and fraud.[56] These cases establish that government disclosure of personal information it has collected can be unconstitutional when it interferes with the exercise of fundamental rights.

Further, under the constitutional right to privacy, the Court has held that government has a duty to protect privacy when it collects personal data. In *Whalen v. Roe,* which I discussed in chapter 4, the Court held that the right to privacy encompassed the protection of personal information:

> We are not unaware of the threat to privacy implicit in the accu-
> mulation of vast amounts of personal information in computer-
> ized data banks or other massive government files. . . . The right
> to collect and use such data for public purposes is typically ac-
> companied by a concomitant statutory or regulatory duty to
> avoid unwarranted disclosures. . . . [I]n some circumstances that
> duty arguably has its roots in the Constitution.[57]

Whalen recognized that when the government collects personal information, it has a responsibility to keep it secure and confidential.

Since its creation in *Whalen,* the constitutional right to information privacy has begun to evolve in the courts, but it is still in the early
stages of growth.[58] The full extent of the government's responsibilities
in handling personal data awaits further development. Based on the
cases decided thus far, the Constitution requires public access when
information will shed light on the functioning of the government, and
it requires confidentiality when information pertains to the personal
lives of individuals.

Freedom of Speech. The First Amendment more directly fosters information flow about government activities by forbidding restrictions on
freedom of speech. Understanding how use and access restrictions
on public record information interact with the First Amendment requires a difficult navigation through a number of cases. In one series
of cases, the Court has struck down statutes prohibiting the disclosure of information gleaned from public records. In *Cox Broadcasting
Corp. v. Cohn,* the Court held that a state could not impose civil liability based upon publication of a rape victim's name obtained from a
court record: "Once true information is disclosed in public court documents open to public inspection, the press cannot be sanctioned for
publishing it." Punishing the press for publishing public record information would "invite timidity and self-censorship and very likely lead
to the suppression of many items that would otherwise be published
and that should be made available to the public."[59] In *Smith v. Daily
Mail,* the Court struck down a statute prohibiting the publication of
the names of juvenile offenders: "[I]f a newspaper lawfully obtains

truthful information about a matter of public significance then state officials may not constitutionally punish publication of the information, absent a need to further a state interest of the highest order."[60]

This line of cases culminated in *Florida Star v. B.J.F.* in which a newspaper published the name of a rape victim, which it obtained from a publicly released police report. The report was in a room with signs stating that rape victims' names weren't part of the public record and weren't to be published. The reporter even admitted that she knew she wasn't allowed to report on the information. When the story ran, many of the victim's friends learned about her rape, and a man made threatening calls to her home. As a result, she had to change her phone number and residence, seek police protection, and obtain mental health counseling. Based upon a Florida law prohibiting the disclosure of rape victims' names, a jury found the paper liable. The Supreme Court, however, held that the verdict ran afoul of the newspaper's First Amendment rights.[61] Taken together, these cases support the premise that once the government makes information public, the government cannot subsequently sanction its further disclosure.

However, in *Los Angeles Police Department v. United Reporting Publishing Co.*, the Court upheld a law restricting access for public arrestee information. Requesters of the information had to declare under penalty of perjury that the address information would not be used "directly or indirectly to sell a product or service." Rejecting a challenge that the law infringed upon commercial speech, the Court reasoned that the statute was not "prohibiting a speaker from conveying information that the speaker already possesses" but was merely "a governmental denial of access to information in its possession." As long as the government doesn't have a duty to provide access to information, it can selectively determine who can obtain it.[62]

The Court's jurisprudence thus creates a distinction between pre-access conditions on obtaining information and post-access restrictions on the use or disclosure of the information. If the government is not obligated to provide access to certain information by the First Amendment, it can amend its public access laws to establish pre-access conditions, restricting access for certain kinds of uses. Governments can make a public record available *on the condition that* certain information is not disclosed or used in a certain manner. However, once the information is made available, governments cannot establish post-access restrictions on its disclosure or use.

The Court's distinction between pre-access and post-access restrictions seems rather tenuous. States can easily redraft their statutes to get around *Florida Star*. For example, Florida could rewrite its law to make rape victims' names available on the condition that the press promise the names not be disclosed. Conditional access and use restrictions thus appear to be an end-run around *Florida Star*. Can the Court's distinction between pre- and post-access restrictions be defended?

I believe it can. First, in *Florida Star*, the Court was concerned about the government's failure "to police itself in disseminating information." The mistake was made by the police department in failing to redact the name, and thus it was unfair "to sanction persons other than the source of its release."[63] In contrast, with pre-access restrictions, the government is taking the appropriate care to protect the information itself.

Second, in both *Cox* and *Florida Star*, the Court was concerned about the chilling effects to speech from the uncertainty over whether certain public record information could be disclosed. Pre-access restrictions alleviate these concerns. Since the recipient of the information has to expressly agree to any restrictions on using the information beforehand, she will be on clear notice as to her obligations and responsibilities in handling the data.

Third, and most importantly, the distinction is a good practical compromise. Without a distinction between post- and pre-access conditions, the government would be forced into an all-or-nothing tradeoff between transparency and privacy. The government could make records public, allowing all uses of the personal information, or the government could simply not make records available at all. By making access conditional on accepting certain responsibilities when using data, the public can have access to a wide range of records while privacy remains protected at the same time.

Has the Court too quickly dispatched with the free speech implications of conditional or limited access regulation? For example, some argue that restrictions on commercial access are unconstitutional content-based restrictions on free speech because they single out specific messages and viewpoints—namely, commercial ones. Dissenting in *United Reporting Publishing Corp.*, Justice Stevens argued that the California access and use restriction improperly singled out "a narrow category of persons solely because they intend to use the information for a [commercial] purpose."[64] However, commercial access restrictions are not being applied because of disagreement with the message that commercial users wish to send. Nor do they favor a particular speaker or specific ideas. Although particular categories of use (i.e., commercial) are being singled out, avoiding viewpoint discrimination does not entail avoiding all attempts to categorize or limit uses of information. Indeed, the First Amendment constitutional regime depends upon categorizing speech. The Supreme Court protects certain categories of speech much less stringently than other forms of speech. Obscene speech, words that incite violence, and defamatory speech about private figures all receive minimal protection.[65] Commercial speech is also singled out, safeguarded with only an intermediate level of scrutiny.[66] Although there is no bright line that distinguishes when certain categories map onto particular viewpoints to such a degree as to constitute discrimination based on viewpoint, the category of commercial speech is broad enough to encompass a multitude of viewpoints and is a category that forms part of the architecture of the current constitutional regime.

Therefore, governments should be able to restrict access for certain purposes or condition access on an enforceable promise not to engage in certain uses of information. Of course, it would be improper for the government to single out particular viewpoints. Thus, for example, governments should not restrict access to public records to those who wish to use the information to advocate for certain causes rather than others. Nor could the government restrict access based on the particular beliefs or ideas of the person or entities seeking access to the information. In short, the government can't single out certain uses because it dislikes the ideas or views of a particular speaker. A limitation on commercial use is broad enough to encompass a diverse enough range of viewpoints, and the government is merely limiting uses of information rather than the expression of particular ideas.

Public Records in the Information Age. Public records are increasingly posing a serious threat to privacy in the Information Age. To understand this threat, our conceptions of privacy must be adapted to today's technological realities. We must abandon the secrecy paradigm and recognize that what is public can be private—not in the sense that it is secret, but in the limitation of the uses and disclosures of the information. Privacy is about degrees of accessibility. The threat to privacy is not in isolated pieces of information, but in increased access and aggregation, the construction of digital dossiers and the uses to which they are put. States must begin to rethink their public record regimes, and the federal government should step in to serve as the most efficient mechanism to achieve this goal. It is time for the public records laws of this country to mature to meet the problems of the Information Age.

iii government access

9 Government Information Gathering

Thus far, I have discussed how personal information is being more readily collected, stored, transferred, and combined with other information. Part I of this book discussed the problems of information flow among various businesses, and part II focused on information flows from the government to the private sector. But there is another problematic type of information flow that is rapidly escalating—data transfers from the private sector to the government. The vast digital dossiers being constructed by businesses are becoming an increasingly desirable resource for law enforcement officials. And this threatens to transform the relationship between government and citizen in some very troubling ways.

Third Party Records and the Government

Earlier in this book, I described the extensive amount of information that companies are stockpiling about us. To live in the modern world, we must enter into numerous relationships with other people and businesses: doctors, lawyers, businesses, merchants, magazines, newspapers, banks, credit card companies, employers, landlords, ISPs, insurance companies, phone companies, and cable companies. The list goes on and on. Our relationships with all of these entities generate records containing personal information necessary to establish an account and record our transactions and preferences. We are becoming a society of records, and these records are not held by us, but by third parties.

These record systems are becoming increasingly useful to law enforcement officials. Personal information can help the government detect fraud, espionage, fugitives, drug distribution rings, and terrorist cells. Information about a person's financial transactions, purchases, and religious and political beliefs can assist the investigation of suspected criminals and can be used to profile people for more thorough searches at airports.

The government, therefore, has a strong desire to obtain personal information found in records maintained by third parties. For instance, from pen registers and trap and trace devices, the government can obtain a list of all the phone numbers dialed to or from a particular location, potentially revealing the people with whom a person associates. From bank records, which contain one's account activity and check writing, the government can discover the various companies and professionals that a person does business with (ISP, telephone company, credit card company, magazine companies, doctors, attorneys, and so on). Credit card company records can reveal where one eats and shops. The government can obtain one's travel destinations and activities from travel agent records. From hotel records, it can discover the numbers a person dialed and the pay-per-view movies a person watched.[1] The government can obtain one's thumbprint from car rental companies that collect them to investigate fraud.[2] From video stores, the government can access an inventory of the videos that a person has rented.

The government can also glean a wealth of information from the extensive records employers maintain about their employees.[3] Employers frequently monitor their employees.[4] Some use software to track how employees surf the Internet.[5] Employers often record information about an employee's email use, including back-up copies of the contents of email. A number of employers also conduct drug test-

ing, and many require prospective employees to answer questionnaires asking about drug use, finances, psychological treatment, marital history, and sexuality.[6] Some even require prospective hires to
take a psychological screening test.[7]

Landlords are another fertile source of personal information.
Landlord records often contain financial, employment, and pet information, in addition to any tenant complaints. Many landlords also
maintain log books at the front desk where visitors sign in. Some
apartment buildings use biometric identification devices, such as
hand scanners, to control access to common areas such as gyms.

Increasingly, companies and entities that we have never established any contact with nevertheless have dossiers about us. Credit
reporting agencies maintain information relating to financial transactions, debts, creditors, and checking accounts. The government can
also find out details about people's race, income, opinions, political
beliefs, health, lifestyle, and purchasing habits from the database
companies that keep extensive personal information on millions of
Americans.

Beyond the records described here, the Internet has the potential
to become one of the government's greatest information gathering
tools. There are two significant aspects of the Internet that make it
such a revolutionary data collection device. First, it gives many individuals a false sense of privacy. The secrecy and anonymity of the Internet is often a mirage. Rarely are people truly anonymous because
ISPs keep records of a subscriber's screen name and pseudonyms. ISP
account information includes the subscriber's name, address, phone
numbers, passwords, information about web surfing sessions and
durations, and financial information.[8] By learning a person's screen
name, the government can identify who posted messages in news-
groups or conversed in chatrooms.

At the government's request, an ISP can keep logs of the email addresses with which a person corresponds. Further, if a person stores
email that is sent and received with the ISP, the government can obtain the contents of those emails.

Second, the Internet is unprecedented in the degree of information
that can be gathered and stored. It is one of the most powerful gener-
ators of records in human history. As discussed in chapter 2, websites

often accumulate a great deal of information about their users, from transactional data to information collected through cookies. The government can glean a substantial amount of information about visitors to a particular website. From Internet retailers, the government can learn about the books, videos, music, and electronics that one purchases. Some Internet retailers, such as Amazon.com, record all the purchases a person has made throughout many years. Based on this information, the government can discover a consumer's interests, political views, religious beliefs, and lifestyle.

The government may also obtain information from websites that operate personalized home pages. Home pages enable users to keep track of the stocks they own, favorite television channels, airfares for favorite destinations, and news of interest. Other websites, such as Microsoft Network's calendar service, allow users to maintain their daily schedule and appointments. Further, as discussed in chapter 2, there are database companies that amass extensive profiles of people's websurfing habits.

While life in the Information Age has brought us a dizzying amount of information, it has also placed a profound amount of information about our lives in the hands of numerous entities. As discussed earlier, these digital dossiers are increasingly becoming digital biographies, a horde of aggregated bits of information combined to reveal a portrait of who we are based upon what we buy, the organizations we belong to, how we navigate the Internet, and which shows and videos we watch. This information is not held by trusted friends or family members, but by large bureaucracies that we do not know very well or sometimes do not even know at all.

Government–Private-Sector Information Flows

In late 2002, the news media reported that the Department of Defense was planning a project known as Total Information Awareness (TIA). The project was to be run by John Poindexter, who had been convicted in 1990 for his activities during the Iran-contra scandal. TIA envisioned the creation of a gigantic government database of personal information, including data culled from private-sector entities concerning finances, education, travel, health, and so on. This information would then be analyzed under various models to detect patterns and profiles for terrorist activities.[9] The website for the project contained the symbol of a pyramid with beams of light emanating from an eye at the top. Next to the pyramid was a globe, illuminated by the light. Underneath the image were the words *scientia est potentia*—"knowledge is power."[10]

When TIA broke as a major news story, civil liberties groups and many commentators and politicians voiced stinging criticism. In a *New York Times* editorial, William Safire wrote that Poindexter "is determined to break down the wall between commercial snooping and secret government intrusion. . . . And he has been given a $200 million budget to create computer dossiers on 300 million Americans."[11] After these outcries, the pyramid and eye logo was quickly removed from the Department of Defense website. The Senate amended its spending bill in January 2003 to temporarily suspend funding for TIA until the details of the program were explained to Congress.[12] In May 2003, the Department of Defense issued its report to Congress, renaming the program "Terrorism Information Awareness" and declaring (without specifying how) that it would protect privacy. Later on, in July, the Senate voted unanimously to stop funding for TIA. The program had been killed.

But TIA is only one part of the story of government access to personal information and its creation of dossiers on American citizens. In fact, for quite some time, the government has been increasingly contracting with businesses to acquire databases of personal information. Database firms are willing to supply the information and the government is willing to pay for it. Currently, government agencies such as the FBI and IRS are purchasing databases of personal information from private-sector companies.[13] A private company called ChoicePoint, Inc. has amassed a database of 10 billion records and has contracts with at least 35 federal agencies to share the data with them. In 2000, the Justice Department signed an $8 million contract with ChoicePoint, and the IRS reached a deal with the company for between $8 and $12 million. ChoicePoint collects information from public records from around the country and then combines it with information from private detectives, the media, and credit reporting firms. This data is indexed by people's SSNs. The Center for Medicare and Medicaid Services uses ChoicePoint's data to help it identify fraudulent Medicare claims by checking health care provider addresses against ChoicePoint's list of "high-risk and fraudulent business addresses." ChoicePoint's information is not only used by government agencies but also by private-sector employers to screen new hires or investigate existing employees.[14]

ChoicePoint's information is a mixture of fact and fiction. There are a number of errors in the records, such as when a ChoicePoint report falsely indicated that a woman was a convicted drug dealer and shoplifter, resulting in her being fired from her job.[15] Database Technologies (DBT), a company later acquired by ChoicePoint, had a hand in the 2000 presidential election problems in Florida. DBT supplied Florida officials with a list of 8,000 "ex-felons" to eliminate from their voter lists.[16] However, many of the 8,000 were not guilty of felonies, only misdemeanors, and were legally eligible to vote. Although the error was discovered prior to the election and officials tried to place the individuals back on the voter rolls, the error may have led to some eligible voters being turned away at the polls.

Additionally, many states have joined together to create a database system called Multi-State Anti-Terrorism Information Exchange, or MATRIX for short. Run by SeisInt, Inc., a private-sector company in Florida, MATRIX contains personal information gathered from public records and from businesses. In its vast fields of data, MATRIX includes people's criminal histories, photographs, property ownership, SSNs, addresses, bankruptcies, family members, and credit information. The federal government has provided $12 million to help support the program.[17]

A second form of information flow from the private sector to the government emerges when the government requests private-sector records for particular investigations or compels their disclosure by subpoena or court order. Voluntary disclosure of customer information is within the third party company's discretion. Further, whether a person is notified of the request and given the opportunity to challenge it in court is also within the company's discretion.

The September 11, 2001 terrorist attacks changed the climate for private sector-to-government information flows. Law enforcement officials have a greater desire to obtain information that could be helpful in identifying terrorists or their supporters, including information about what people read, the people with whom they associate, their religion, and their lifestyle. Following the September 11 attack, the FBI simply requested records from businesses without a subpoena, warrant, or court order.[18] Recently, Attorney General John Ashcroft has revised longstanding guidelines for FBI surveillance practices. Under the previous version, the FBI could monitor public events and mine the Internet for information only when "facts or circumstances reasonably indicate that a federal crime has been, is being, or will be committed."[19] Under the revised version, the FBI can engage in these types of information gathering without any requirement that it be part of a legitimate investigation or related in any manner to criminal wrongdoing. The FBI can now collect "publicly available information, whether obtained directly or through services or resources (whether nonprofit or commercial) that compile or analyze such information; and information voluntarily provided by private entities."[20] Further, the FBI can "carry out general topical research, including conducting online searches and accessing online sites and forums."[21]

In conjunction with the government's greater desire for personal information, the private sector has become more willing to supply it. Background check companies, for instance, experienced a large boost in business after September 11.[22] Several large financial companies developed agreements to provide information to federal law enforcement agencies.[23] Indeed, in times of crisis or when serious crimes are at issue, the incentives to disclose information to the government are quite significant. Shortly after September 11, around 200 universities admitted to giving the FBI access to their records on foreign students—often without a subpoena or court order.[24] In violation of its privacy policy, JetBlue Airlines shared the personal data of 1 million customers with Torch Concepts, an Alabama company contracting with the Defense Department to profile passengers for security risks. Torch combined the JetBlue data with SSNs, employment information, and other details obtained from Acxiom, Inc., a database marketing company.[25] In a similar incident, Northwest Airlines secretly turned over to NASA its customer data—including addresses, phone numbers, and credit card information—for use in a government data mining project.[26] In a December 2002 survey of nearly 800 chief security officers, almost 25 percent said that they would supply information to the government without a court order, with 41 percent doing so in cases involving national security.[27]

When businesses refuse to cooperate, the government can compel production of the information by issuing a subpoena or obtaining a court order. These devices are very different from warrants because they offer little protection to the individual being investigated. Notification of the target of the investigation is often within the discretion of the third party. Further, it is up to the third party to challenge the subpoena. So, rather than spend the money and resources to challenge the subpoena, companies can simply turn it over or permit the government to search their records. Since September 11, AOL and Earthlink, two of the largest ISPs, have readily cooperated with the investigation of the terrorist attacks.[28] Often, ISPs have their own technology to turn over communications and information about targets of investigations. If they lack the technology, law enforcement officials can install devices such as "Carnivore" to locate the information.[29] Carnivore, now renamed to the more innocuous "DCS1000," is a computer program installed by the FBI at an ISP.[30] It can monitor all ISP email traffic and search for certain keywords in the content or headers of the email messages.

These developments are troubling because private-sector companies often have weak policies governing when information may be disclosed to the government. The privacy policy for the MSN network, an affiliation of several Microsoft, Inc. websites such as Hotmail (an email service), Health, Money, Newsletters, eShop, and Calendar, states:

> MSN Web sites will disclose your personal information, without notice, only if required to do so by law or in the good faith belief that such action is necessary to: (a) conform to the edicts of the law or comply with legal process served on Microsoft or the site.[31]

Though somewhat unclear, this privacy policy appears to require a subpoena or court order for the government to obtain personal data.

Amazon.com's privacy policy reads: "We release account and other personal information when we believe release is appropriate to comply with law . . . or protect the rights, property, or safety of

Amazon.com, our users, or others."[32] It is unclear from this policy the extent to which Amazon.com, in its discretion, can provide information to law enforcement officials.

EBay, a popular online auction website, has a policy stating that

> [it] cooperates with law enforcement inquiries, as well as other third parties to enforce laws, such as: intellectual property rights, fraud and other rights. We can (and you authorize us to) disclose any information about you to law enforcement or other government officials as we, in our sole discretion, believe necessary or appropriate, in connection with an investigation of fraud, intellectual property infringements, or other activity that is illegal or may expose us or you to legal liability.[33]

This policy gives eBay almost complete discretion to provide the government with whatever information it deems appropriate.

Truste.com, a nonprofit organization providing a "trustmark" for participating websites that agree to abide by certain privacy principles, has drafted a model privacy statement that reads: "We will not sell, share, or rent [personal] information to others in ways different from what is disclosed in this statement."[34] The statement then says that information may be shared with "an outside shipping company to ship orders, and a credit card processing company to bill users for goods and services." Personal data is also shared with third parties when the user signs up for services that are provided by those third parties. This policy, however, does not contain any provision about supplying information to the government. Further, the policy does not inform people that under existing law, information must be disclosed to the government pursuant to a subpoena or court order.

The government is also increasing information flow from the private sector by encouraging it to develop new information gathering technologies. Private-sector firms stand to profit from developing such technologies. Since September 11, companies have expressed an eagerness to develop national identification systems and face-recognition technology.[35] In addition, the federal government has announced a "wish list" for new surveillance and investigation technologies.[36] Companies that invent such technologies can obtain lucrative government contracts.

The government has also funded private-sector information gathering initiatives. For instance, a company that began assembling a national database of photographs and personal information as a tool to guard against consumer fraud has received $1.5 million from the Secret Service to aid in the development of the database.[37]

In certain circumstances, where institutions do not willingly cooperate with the government, the law requires their participation. For example, the Bank Secrecy Act of 1970 forces banks to maintain records of financial transactions to facilitate law enforcement needs—in particular, investigations and prosecutions of criminal, tax, or regulatory matters.[38] All federally insured banks must keep records of each customer's financial transactions and must report to the government every financial transaction in excess of $10,000.[39] The Personal Responsibility and Work Opportunity Reconciliation Act of 1996 requires employers to report personal information from all new employees including SSNs, addresses, and wages.[40] The Communications Assistance for Law Enforcement Act of 1994 requires telecommunications service providers to develop technology to assist government surveillance of individuals.[41] Passed in 2001, the USA-PATRIOT Act authorizes the FBI to obtain a court order to inspect or seize "books, records, papers, documents, or other items" for use in an investigation for terrorism or intelligence activities.[42] This provision contains a gag order, prohibiting anybody from disclosing that the FBI has sought or obtained anything.[43]

All of this suggests that businesses and government have become allies. When their interests diverge, the law forces cooperation. The government can increasingly amass gigantic dossiers on millions of individuals, conduct sweeping investigations, and search for vast quantities of information from a wide range of sources, without any probable cause or particularized suspicion. Information is easier to obtain, and it is becoming more centralized. The government is increasingly gaining access to the information in our digital dossiers. As Justice Douglas noted in his dissent when the Court upheld the constitutionality of the Bank Secrecy Act:

> These [bank records] are all tied to one's SSN; and now that we have the data banks, these other items will enrich that store-

house and make it possible for a bureaucrat—by pushing one button—to get in an instant the names of the 190 million Americans who are subversives or potential and likely candidates.[44]

Thus, we are increasingly seeing collusion, partly voluntary, partly coerced, between the private sector and the government. While public attention has focused on the Total Information Awareness project, the very same goals and techniques of the program continue to be carried out less systematically by various government agencies and law enforcement officials. We are already closer to Total Information Awareness than we might think.

The Orwellian Dangers

Although there are certainly many legitimate needs for law enforcement officials to obtain personal data, there are also many dangers to unfettered government access to information. There are at least two general types of harms, some best captured by the Orwell metaphor and others that are more fittingly described with the Kafka metaphor. I turn first to the Orwellian dangers.

Creeping toward Totalitarianism. Historically, totalitarian governments have developed elaborate systems for collecting data about people's private lives.[45] Although the possibility of the rise of a totalitarian state is remote, if our society takes on certain totalitarian features, it could significantly increase the extent to which the government can exercise social control. Justice Brandeis was prescient when he observed that people "are naturally alert to repel invasion of their liberty by evil-minded rulers. The greatest dangers to liberty lurk in the insidious encroachment by men of zeal, well-meaning but without understanding."[46]

Democracy and Self-Determination. Even if government entities are not attempting to engage in social control, their activities can have collateral effects that harm democracy and self-determination. Paul Schwartz illustrates this with his theory of "constitutive privacy." According to Schwartz, privacy is essential to both individuals and communities: "[C]onstitutive privacy seeks to create boundaries about personal information to help the individual and define terms of life within the community." As a form of regulation of information flow, privacy shapes "the extent to which certain actions or expressions of identity are encouraged or discouraged." Schwartz contends that extensive government oversight over an individual's activities can "corrupt individual decision making about the elements of one's identity."[47] Likewise, Julie Cohen argues that a "realm of autonomous, unmonitored choice . . . promotes a vital diversity of speech and behavior." The lack of privacy "threatens not only to chill the expression of eccentric individuality, but also, gradually, to dampen the force of our aspirations to it."[48]

Freedom of Association. Government information collection interferes with an individual's freedom of association. The Court has held that there is a "vital relationship between freedom to associate and privacy in one's associations."[49] In a series of cases, the Court has restricted the government's ability to compel disclosure of membership in an organization.[50] In *Baird v. State Bar*,[51] for example, the Court has declared: "[W]hen a State attempts to make inquiries about a person's beliefs or associations, its power is limited by the First Amendment. Broad and sweeping state inquiries into these protected areas . . . discourage citizens from exercising rights protected by the Constitution."[52] The government's extensive ability to glean information about one's associations from third party records without any Fourth Amendment limitations threatens the interests articulated in these cases.[53]

Anonymity. Extensive government information gathering from third party records also implicates the right to speak anonymously. In *Talley v. California,* the Court struck down a law prohibiting the distribution of anonymous handbills as a violation of the First Amendment. The Court held that "[p]ersecuted groups and sects from time to time throughout history have been able to criticize oppressive practices and laws either anonymously or not at all." Further, the Court reasoned, "identification and fear of reprisal might deter perfectly peaceful discussions of public matters of importance."[54] The Court has reiterated its view of the importance of protecting anonymous speech in subsequent cases.[55] From third parties, especially ISPs, the government can readily obtain an anonymous or pseudonymous speaker's identity. Only computer-savvy users can speak with more secure anonymity. Although private parties attempting to identify an anonymous speaker through subpoenas have been required to satisfy heightened standards,[56] no such heightened standards have yet been applied when the government seeks to obtain the information.

Further, beyond typical anonymity is the ability to receive information anonymously. As Julie Cohen persuasively contends: "The freedom to read anonymously is just as much a part of our tradition, and the choice of reading materials just as expressive of identity, as the decision to use or withhold one's name."[57] The lack of sufficient controls on the government's obtaining the extensive records about how individuals surf the web, the books and magazines they read, and the videos or television channels they listen to can implicate this interest.

Additionally, the increasing information flow between the private sector and the government not only impacts the privacy of the target of an investigation, but can also affect the privacy of other individuals. The names, addresses, phone numbers, and a variety of data about a number of individuals can be ensnared in records pertaining to the target.

These types of harms can inhibit individuals from associating with particular people and groups and from expressing their views, especially unpopular ones. This kind of inhibition is a central goal of Orwell's Big Brother. Although it certainly does not approach the same degree of oppressiveness as Big Brother, it reduces the robustness of dissent and weakens the vitality of our communication.

The Kafkaesque Dangers

The second general type of danger promoted by government information gathering consists of the harms routinely arising in bureaucratic settings: decisions without adequate accountability, dangerous pockets of unfettered discretion, and choices based on short-term goals without consideration of the long-term consequences or the larger social effects. These bureaucratic harms have similarities to those I discussed earlier when discussing the Kafka metaphor, although these harms take on some new dimensions with government law enforcement bureaucracy. As in Kafka's *The Trial*, dossiers circulate throughout a large government bureaucracy, and individuals are not informed how their information is used and how decisions are made based on their data. The existence of dossiers of personal information in government bureaucracies can lead to dangers such as hasty judgment in times of crisis, the disparate impact of law enforcement on particular minorities, cover-ups, petty retaliation for criticism, blackmail, framing, sweeping and disruptive investigations, racial or religious profiling, and so on.

The most frequent problem is not that law enforcement agencies will be led by corrupt and abusive leaders, although this arguably happened for nearly 50 years when J. Edgar Hoover directed the FBI. The problem is the risk that judgment will not be exercised in a careful and thoughtful manner. In other words, it stems from certain forms of government information collection shifting power toward a bureaucratic machinery that is poorly regulated and susceptible to abuse. This shift has profound social effects because it alters the balance of power between the government and the people, exposing individuals to a series of harms, increasing their vulnerability and decreasing the degree of power they exercise over their lives.

When the Fourth Amendment was ratified, organized police forces did not exist.[58] Colonial policing was the "business of amateurs."[59] Sheriffs did not have a professional staff; they relied heavily on ordinary citizens to serve as constables or watchmen, whose primary duties consisted of patrolling rather than investigating.[60] The government typically became involved in criminal investigations only after an arrest was made or a suspect was identified, and in ordinary criminal cases, police rarely conducted searches prior to arrest.[61]

Organized police forces developed during the nineteenth century, and by the middle of the twentieth century, policing reached an unprecedented level of organization and coordination.[62] At the center of the rise of modern law enforcement was the development of the FBI. When the FBI was being formed in 1908, there was significant opposition in Congress to a permanent federal police force.[63] Members of Congress expressed trepidation over the possibility that such an investigatory agency could ascertain "matters of scandal and gossip" that could wind up being used for political purposes.[64] These concerns related to the potential dangers of the agency's information gathering capabilities, and as will be discussed later, the fears eventually became realities.

Today, we live in an endless matrix of law and regulation, administered by a multitude of vast government bureaucracies. Like most everything else in modern society, law enforcement has become bureaucratized. There are large police departments armed with sophisticated technology that coordinate with each other. There are massive agencies devoted entirely to investigation and intelligence gathering. One of the distinctive facets of law enforcement bureaucracy in the United States is that low-ranking officials exercise a profound degree of discretion, and most of their discretionary decisions are undocumented.[65]

Many factors make it difficult for law enforcement officials to strike a delicate balance between order and liberty. Among them, there are tremendous pressures on law enforcement agencies to capture criminals, solve notorious crimes, keep crime under control, and prevent acts of violence and terrorism. This highly stressful environment can lead to short cuts, bad exercises of discretion, or obliviousness and insensitivity to people's freedom. One of the most crucial aspects of keeping government power under control is a healthy scrutiny. Most law enforcement officials, however, are unlikely to view themselves with distrust and skepticism. Police and prosecutors are too enveloped in the tremendous responsibilities and pressures of their jobs to remain completely unbiased.

In short, one need not fear the rise of a totalitarian state or the inhibition of democratic activities to desire strong controls on the power of the government in collecting personal information. The Kafka metaphor more aptly captures what is harmful about these types of bureaucratic realities. The harm is that our personal data is stored within a bureaucratic system, where we are vulnerable to abuses, careless errors, and thoughtless decisions.

Leaks, Lapses, and Vulnerability. As more private-sector data becomes available to the government, there could be a de facto national database, or a large database of "suspicious" individuals.[66] Federal governmental entities have engaged in extensive data gathering campaigns on various political groups throughout the twentieth century. From 1940 through 1973, for example, the FBI and CIA conducted a secret domestic intelligence operation, reading the mail of thousands of citizens. The FBI's investigations extended to members of the women's liberation movement and prominent critics of the Vietnam War, and the FBI obtained information about personal and sexual relationships that could be used to discredit them. During the McCarthy era and again in the 1980s, the FBI sought information from libraries about the reading habits of certain individuals. Between 1967 and 1970, the U.S. Army conducted wide-ranging surveillance, amassing extensive personal information about a broad group of individuals. The impetus for the Army's surveillance was a series of riots that followed Dr. Martin Luther King, Jr.'s assassination. The information collected involved data about finances, sexual activity, and health. In 1970, Congress significantly curtailed the Army's program, and the records of personal information were eventually destroyed.[67]

The danger of these information warehousing efforts is not only that it chills speech or threatens lawful protest, but also that it makes people more vulnerable by exposing them to potential future dangers such as leaks, security lapses, and improper arrests. For example, during the late 1960s and early 1970s, the Philadelphia Police Department (PPD) compiled about 18,000 files on various dissident individuals and groups. During a national television broadcast, PPD officials disclosed the names of some of the people on whom files were kept.[68]

Automated Investigations and Profiling. Government agencies are using personal information in databases to conduct automated investigations. In 1977, in order to detect fraud, the federal government began matching its computer employee records with those of people receiving federal benefits.[69] With the use of computers to match records of different government entities, the government investigated millions of people. Some matching programs used data obtained from merchants and marketers to discover tax, welfare, and food stamp fraud as well as to identify drug couriers.[70] This sharing of records between different government agencies, ordinarily a violation of the Privacy

Act, was justified under the "routine use" exception.[71] Computer matching raised significant concerns, and in 1988, Congress finally passed a law regulating this practice.[72] The law has been strongly criticized as providing scant substantive guidance and having little practical effect.[73]

This type of automated investigation is troubling because it alters the way that government investigations typically take place. Usually, the government has some form of particularized suspicion, a factual basis to believe that a particular person may be engaged in illegal conduct. Particularized suspicion keeps the government's profound investigative powers in check, preventing widespread surveillance and snooping into the lives and affairs of all citizens. Computer matches, Priscilla Regan contends, investigate everyone, and most people who are investigated are innocent.[74]

With the new information supplied by the private sector, there is an increased potential for more automated investigations, such as searches for all people who purchase books about particular topics or those who visit certain websites, or perhaps even people whose personal interests fit a profile for those likely to engage in certain forms of criminal activity. Profiles work similarly to the way that Amazon.com predicts which products customers will want to buy. They use particular characteristics and patterns of activity to predict how people will behave in the future. Of course, profiles can be mistaken, but they are often accurate enough to tempt people to rely on them. But there are even deeper problems with profiles beyond inaccuracies. Profiles can be based on stereotypes, race, or religion. A profile is only as good as its designer. Profiles are often kept secret, enabling prejudices and faulty assumptions to exist unchecked by the public. As Oscar Gandy observes, the use of profiling to form predictive models of human behavior incorrectly assumes that "the identity of the individual can be reduced, captured, or represented by measurable characteristics." Profiling is an "inherently conservative" technology because it "tends to reproduce and reinforce assessments and decisions made in the past."[75] Spiros Simitis explains that a profiled individual is "necessarily labeled and henceforth seen as a member of a group, the peculiar features of which are assumed to constitute her personal characteristics. Whoever appears in the lists as a 'tax-evader,' 'assistance-chiseler,' or 'porno-film viewer' must be constantly aware of being addressed as such."[76]

Profiling or automated investigations based on information gathered through digital dossiers can result in targets being inappropriately singled out for more airport searches, police investigations, or even arrest or detention. Indeed, the federal government recently announced the creation of CAPPS II, the Computer Assisted Passenger Prescreening System, which employs computer databases to profile individuals to determine their threat level when flying. Based on their profiles, airline passengers are classified as green, yellow, or red. Passengers labeled green are subject to a normal security check; those in the yellow category receive additional searching; and those branded as red are not permitted to fly.[77] The government has not released details about what information is gathered, how people are profiled, whether race or nationality is a factor, or what ability, if any, people will have to challenge their classification.

People ensnared in the system face considerable hassle and delay. For example, in 2003, a 29-year-old member of the U.S. national rowing team was stopped at the gate when flying from Newark to Seattle. Although born in the United States, the young rower had a Muslim last name, which was probably a factor that led him to be placed on the no-fly list. When officials investigated, they cleared him, but it was too late—his flight had already left. This wasn't an isolated incident; it happened to him a few months earlier as well.[78] With no way to clear his name, he remains at risk of being detained, hassled, and delayed every time he goes to an airport.

Overreacting in Times of Crisis. The government can use dossiers of personal information in mass roundups of distrusted or suspicious individuals whenever the political climate is ripe. As legal scholar Pamela Samuelson observed: "One factor that enabled the Nazis to efficiently round up, transport, and seize assets of Jews (and others they viewed as 'undesirables') was the extensive repositories of personal data available not only from the public sector but also from private sector sources."[79] In the United States, information archives greatly assisted the roundups of disfavored groups, including Japanese Americans during World War II. Following the bombing of Pearl

Harbor on December 7, 1941, the FBI detained thousands of Japanese American community leaders in internment camps. These initial roundups were facilitated by an index of potentially subversive people of Japanese descent compiled by the Justice Department beginning in the late 1930s. In 1942, in the name of national security, about 120,000 people of Japanese descent living on the West Coast were imprisoned in internment camps. The Census Bureau prepared special tabulations of Japanese Americans, which assisted in the relocation.[80]

The acquisition of personal data also facilitated the Palmer Raids (or "Red Scare") of 1919–1920. A bomb blew up at the doorstep of Attorney General A. Mitchell Palmer's home.[81] Shortly thereafter, bombs went off in eight other cities. Letter bombs were mailed to many elites, but most were halted at the post office due to inadequate postage.[82] In a climate rife with fear of "Reds," anarchists, and labor unrest, Congress tasked the Bureau of Investigation (the organization that became the FBI in 1935) with addressing these terrorist threats.[83] Under the direction of a young J. Edgar Hoover, the Bureau of Investigation developed an extensive index of hundreds of thousands of radicals.[84] This data was used to conduct a massive series of raids, in which over 10,000 individuals suspected of being Communists were rounded up, many without warrants.[85] The raids resulted in a number of deportations, many based solely on membership in certain organizations.[86] When prominent figures in the legal community such as Roscoe Pound, Felix Frankfurter, and Zechariah Chafee, Jr., criticized the raids, Hoover began assembling a dossier on each of them.[87]

Additionally, personal information gathered by the FBI enabled the extensive hunt for Communists during the late 1940s and 1950s—a period of history that has since been criticized as a severe over-reaction, resulting in the mistreatment of numerous individuals, and impeding the reform agenda begun in the New Deal.[88] According to historian Ellen Schrecker, federal agencies' "bureaucratic interests, including the desire to present themselves as protecting the community against the threat of internal subversion, inspired them to exaggerate the danger of radicalism."[89] Senator Joseph R. McCarthy, the figure who epitomized the anti-Communism of the 1950s, received substantial assistance from Hoover, who secretly released information about suspected Communists to McCarthy.[90] Further, the FBI supplied a steady stream of names of individuals to be called before the House Un-American Activities Committee (HUAC).[91] As historian Richard Powers observes, "information derived from the [FBI's] files was clearly the lifeblood of the Washington anti-communist establishment."[92] The FBI also leaked information about suspected individuals to employers and the press.[93] Public accusations of being a Communist carried an immense stigma and often resulted in a severe public backlash.[94] Individuals exposed as Communists faced retaliation in the private sector. Numerous journalists, professors, and entertainers were fired from their jobs and blacklisted from future employment.[95]

In short, government entities have demonstrated substantial abilities to gather and store personal information. Combined with the extensive data available about individuals in third party records, this creates a recipe for similar or greater government abuses in the future.

Changing Purposes and Uses. Information obtained by the government for one purpose can readily be used for another. For example, suppose the government is investigating whether a prominent critic of the war against terrorism has in any way assisted terrorists or is engaged in terrorism. In tracking an individual's activities, the government does not discover any criminal activity with regard to terrorism, but discovers that a popular website for downloading music files has been visited and that copyright laws have been violated. Such information may ultimately be used to prosecute copyright violations as a pretext for the government's distaste for the individual's political views and beliefs. Further, dossiers maintained by law enforcement organizations can be selectively leaked to attack critics.

Indeed, it is not far-fetched for government officials to amass data for use in silencing or attacking enemies, critics, undesirables, or radicals. For example, J. Edgar Hoover accumulated an extensive collection of files with detailed information about the private lives of numerous prominent individuals, including presidents, members of Congress, Supreme Court justices, celebrities, civil rights leaders, and attorney generals.[96] Hoover's data often included sexual activities.[97] Hoover used this information to blackmail people or to destroy their reputations by leaking it. Often, however, he did not even have to make any explicit threats. Politicians—and even presidents—feared that Hoover had damaging information about them and would avoid criticizing Hoover or attempting to remove him as FBI director. Indeed, on one of the tapes President Nixon recorded in the Oval Office, he declared that he could not fire Hoover because Hoover knew too much information about him.[98]

We live in a world of mixed and changing motives. Data that is obtained for one purpose can be used for an entirely different purpose as motives change. For example, for several years, the FBI extensively wiretapped Martin Luther King, Jr.[99] They wiretapped his home, his office, and the hotel rooms that he stayed at when traveling.[100] Based on the wiretaps, the FBI learned of his extensive partying, extramarital affairs, and other sexual activities. A high-level FBI official even anonymously sent him a tape with highlights of the FBI's recordings, along with a letter that stated:

> King, there is only one thing left for you to do. You know what it is. You have just 34 days in which to do (this exact number has been selected for a specific reason, it has definite practical significant [sic]). You are done. There is but one way out for you. You better take it before your filthy, abnormal fraudulent self is bared to the nation.[101]

Hoover's motive is disputed. One theory is that King was wiretapped because he was friendly with a person who had previously been a member of the Communist Party.[102] Another theory is that Hoover despised King personally. Hoover's longstanding hatred of King is evidenced by his nasty public statements about King, such as calling King "the most notorious liar" in the nation.[103] This was probably due, in part, to King's criticism of the FBI for inadequately addressing the violence against blacks in the South, Hoover's overreaction to any criticism of the FBI, and the FBI's practice of consistently targeting its critics.[104] As David Garrow hypothesizes, the original reason that the FBI began collecting information about King was due to fears of Communist ties; however, this motivation changed once these fears proved unfounded and several powerful individuals at the FBI expressed distaste for King's sexual activities and moral behavior.[105]

Protecting Privacy with Architecture

The dangers discussed previously illustrate why privacy is integral to freedom in the modern state. As I discussed in chapter 6, we should move away from the invasion conception and seek to protect privacy through architectural solutions that regulate power in our various relationships. Protecting privacy through architecture differs from protecting it as an individual right. Viewing privacy as an individual right against government information gathering conceives of the harm to privacy as emanating from the invasion into the lives of particular people. But many of the people asserting a right to privacy against government information gathering are criminals or terrorists, people we do not have a strong desire to protect. In modern Fourth Amendment law, privacy protection is often initiated at the behest of specific individuals, typically those accused of crimes. Often these individuals' rights conflict with the need for effective law enforcement and the protection of society. Why should one individual's preference for privacy trump the social goals of security and safety? This question is difficult to answer if privacy is understood as a right possessed by particular people.

In contrast, architecture protects privacy differently and is based on a different conception of privacy. Privacy is not merely a right possessed by individuals, but is a form of freedom built into the social structure. It is thus an issue about the common good as much as it is about individual rights. It is an issue about social architecture, about the relationships that form the structure of our society.

One might dismiss the abuses of government information gathering as caused by a few rogue officials. But according to David Garrow, the FBI that targeted Martin Luther King, Jr. was not a "deviant institution in American society, but actually a most representative and faithful one."[106] In other words, the FBI reflected the mindset of many Americans, embodying all the flaws of that mindset. We like to blame individuals, and certainly the particular abusers are worthy of admonition, but we cannot overlook the fact that the causes of abuse often run deeper than the corrupt official. Abuse is made possible by a bureaucratic machinery that is readily susceptible to manipulation. Thus, the problem lies in institutional structures and architectures of power. In the latter half of the twentieth century, and continuing to the present, one of the aspects of this architecture has been the lack of control over government information gathering.

What is the most effective architecture to structure the way that the government can access personal information held by third parties? In the next chapter, I discuss two architectures, that of the Fourth Amendment, which the Court has concluded doesn't apply to data held by third parties, and that of the statutory regime which has arisen in its place.

10 The Fourth Amendment, Records, and Privacy

The Architecture of the Fourth Amendment

The Purposes and Structure of the Fourth Amendment. For better or for worse, we currently regulate law enforcement in the United States with a constitutional regime, comprised primarily by the Fourth, Fifth, and Sixth Amendments. A significant part of this regime applies to government information gathering. The Fifth Amendment affords individuals a privilege against being compelled to testify about incriminating information. The Fourth Amendment regulates the government's power to obtain information through searches and seizures. Specifically, the Amendment provides:

> The right of the people to be secure in their persons, houses, papers, and effects, against unreasonable searches and seizures, shall not be violated, and no warrants shall issue, but upon probable cause, supported by oath or affirmation, and particularly describing the place to be searched, and the persons or things to be seized.[1]

Although the Fourth Amendment applies to government activity in both the civil and criminal contexts,[2] it is limited to activities that constitute "searches" and "seizures." Certain activities, such as seeing things exposed openly to public view, are not searches.[3] The Fourth

Amendment only governs searches where an individual has "a reasonable expectation of privacy."[4]

If the Fourth Amendment applies, a search or seizure must be "reasonable." Although technically the two clauses of the Fourth Amendment are separate, the Court has interpreted the requirement that a search or seizure be reasonable as related to the warrant requirement. To obtain a warrant, the police must demonstrate to a neutral judge or magistrate that they have "probable cause," which means they must provide "reasonably trustworthy information" that the search will reveal evidence of a crime.[5] Generally, searches and seizures without a warrant are per se unreasonable—which means that they are deemed invalid.[6] This has become known as the "per se warrant rule."[7]

The Court has made numerous exceptions to the per se warrant rule.[8] For example, the Court held in *Terry v. Ohio* that the police could stop and frisk an individual without a warrant or probable cause.[9] Further, the Court has held that "special needs" in schools and workplaces make the warrant and probable cause requirements impracticable.[10] In the words of legal scholars Silas Wasserstrom and Louis Michael Seidman, the per se warrant rule "is so riddled with exceptions, complexities, and contradictions that it has become a trap for the unwary."[11]

The Fourth Amendment is enforced primarily through the exclusionary rule. Evidence obtained in violation of the Amendment must be excluded from trial.[12] Without the exclusionary rule, Justice Holmes observed, the Fourth Amendment would be a mere "form of words."[13] According to law professor Arnold Loewy: "The exclusionary rule protects innocent people by eliminating the incentive to search and seize unreasonably."[14] The exclusionary rule, however, has long been a sore spot in Fourth Amendment jurisprudence, engendering extensive debate over its desirability and efficacy.[15]

Fourth Amendment Scope: Privacy. As applied by the Court, the Fourth Amendment has focused on protecting against invasions of privacy,[16] although some commentators contend this focus is misguided. According to legal scholar William Stuntz, criminal procedure is "firmly anchored in a privacy value that had already proved inconsistent with the modern state."[17] For Stuntz, privacy vis-à-vis the government is impracticable given the rise of the administrative state, with its extensive health and welfare regulation. Stuntz asserts that robust Fourth Amendment protection of privacy will prevent the government from regulating industry, uncovering white-collar crime, and inspecting industrial facilities. The government must collect information to enforce certain regulations, such as securities laws and worker safety protections.[18] "By focusing on privacy," Stuntz argues, "Fourth Amendment law has largely abandoned the due process cases' concern with coercion and violence."[19] "The problem," argues Stuntz, "is not information gathering but [police] violence."[20]

Legal scholar Scott Sundby offers a different critique of the Fourth Amendment's focus on privacy. Although designed to expand Fourth Amendment protection, privacy has "turned out to contain the seeds for the later contraction of Fourth Amendment rights."[21] "The Fourth Amendment as a privacy-focused doctrine has not fared well with the changing times of an increasingly nonprivate world and a judicial reluctance to expand individual rights."[22]

However, Sundby assumes that "privacy" means what the Court says it means. Many current problems in Fourth Amendment jurisprudence stem from the Court's failure to conceptualize privacy adequately, both in method and substance. Methodologically, the Court has attempted to adhere to a unified conception of privacy. Conceptualizing privacy by attempting to isolate its essence or common denominator has inhibited the Court from conceptualizing privacy in a way that can adapt to changing technology and social practices.[23] Substantively, the Court originally conceptualized privacy in physical terms as protecting tangible property or preventing trespasses. The Court then shifted to viewing privacy with the secrecy paradigm. In each of these conceptual paradigms, the Court has rigidly adhered to a single narrow conception and has lost sight of the Fourth Amendment's larger purposes.

In contrast, I contend that the Fourth Amendment provides for an architecture, a structure of protection that safeguards a range of different social practices of which privacy forms an integral dimension. Those like Stuntz and Sundby who contend that the Fourth Amendment should not concern itself with privacy fail to see the importance of privacy in the relationship between the government and the People. The private life is a critical point for the exercise of power. Privacy shields aspects of our lives and social practices where people feel vulnerable, uneasy, and fragile, where social norms and judgment are particularly oppressive and abrasive. It is also implicated when information relates to our basic needs and desires: finances, employment, entertainment, political activity, sexuality, and family. Indeed, the great distopian novels of the twentieth century—George Orwell's *1984*, Aldous Huxley's *Brave New World*, and Franz Kafka's *The Trial*— all illustrate how government exercises of power over the private life stifle freedom and well-being.

Although Stuntz contends that the Fourth Amendment must forsake privacy because of the rise of the administrative state, this is the very reason why protecting privacy is imperative. The administrative state threatens to equip the government with excessive power that could destroy the Framers' careful design to ensure that the power of the People remains the strongest.[24] In particular, the extensive power of modern bureaucracies over individuals depends in significant part on the collection and use of personal information. While Stuntz is correct that the Fourth Amendment should not be cabined exclusively to protecting privacy and should address other values such as coercion and violence, he errs in treating privacy and police coercion as mutually exclusive.[25]

Robust Fourth Amendment protection need not be inconsistent with the administrative state, as a significant amount of modern administrative regulation concerns business and commercial activities which lack Fourth Amendment rights equivalent to those guaranteed to individuals.[26] Stuntz retorts that for individuals to have a meaningful protection of privacy, they must be provided with privacy within institutions, which "is almost the same as giving the institution itself a protectible privacy interest."[27] Beyond this, Stuntz contends, "a great deal of government information gathering targets individuals," such as the information that is gathered in tax forms.[28] However, one need not adopt an all-or-nothing approach to Fourth Amendment privacy. The Fourth Amendment does not categorically prohibit the government from compelling certain disclosures by individuals or institutions. If it did, then the tax system and much corporate regulation would be nearly impossible to administer. But the fact that the government can compel certain disclosures does not mean that it can compel people to disclose the details of their sexual lives or require them to send in their diaries along with their tax forms. The government's power to inspect factories for safety violations does not mean that the government should be able to search every employee's office, locker, or bag. Therefore, although misconceptualizing privacy, the Court has correctly made it a focal point of the Fourth Amendment.

Fourth Amendment Structure: Warrants. Before eroding it with dozens of exceptions, the Court made the Fourth Amendment's warrant requirement one of the central mechanisms to ensure that the government was responsibly exercising its powers of information collection. Some critics, however, view warrants as relatively unimportant in the Fourth Amendment scheme. According to constitutional law expert Akhil Amar, the Fourth Amendment "does not require, presuppose, or even prefer warrants—it *limits* them. Unless warrants meet certain strict standards, they are per se unreasonable."[29] Amar contends that the colonial revolutionaries viewed warrants with disdain because judges were highly influenced by the Crown and warrants immunized government officials from civil liability after conducting a search.[30] Therefore, according to Amar, "[t]he core of the Fourth Amendment, as we have seen, is neither a warrant nor probable cause, but reasonableness."[31]

Amar is too dismissive of warrants. Merely looking to colonial precedents is insufficient, because the Fourth Amendment did not follow colonial precedents (since general searches were rampant) but rejected them.[32] My aim, however, is not to quarrel about original intent. Even if Amar is right about the Framers' intent, warrants are an important device in our times since, as Scott Sundby observes, "the Founders could not have foreseen the technological and regulatory reach of government intrusions that exists today."[33]

The warrant requirement embodies two important insights of the Framers that particularly hold true today. First, the warrant requirement aims to prevent searches from turning into "fishing expeditions."[34] Accordingly, the warrant clause circumscribes searches and seizures. As the Fourth Amendment states, a warrant must describe with "particular[ity] . . . the place to be searched and the persons or things to be seized."[35]

The Framers included the warrant clause because of their experience with writs of assistance and general warrants.[36] A writ of assistance was a document that allowed British customs officials to force local officials and even private citizens to search and seize prohibited goods.[37] Writs of assistance didn't need to specify a particular person or place to be targeted; anyone could be searched under their authority; and they resulted in "sweeping searches and seizures without any evidentiary basis."[38] Like writs of assistance, general warrants had a very broad scope, and they did not need to mention specific individuals to target or specific locations to be searched. They "resulted in 'ransacking' and seizure of the personal papers of political dissenters, authors, and printers of seditious libel."[39] As Patrick Henry declared: "They may, unless the general government be restrained by a bill of rights, or some similar restrictions, go into your cellars and rooms, and search, ransack, and measure, everything you eat, drink, and wear. They ought to be restrained within proper bounds."[40]

Second, warrants reflect James Madison's vision of the appropriate architecture for a society in which the power of the People remains paramount. Writing about separation of powers in *Federalist No. 51*, Madison observed:

> But what is government itself but the greatest of all reflections on human nature? If men were angels, no government would be necessary. If angels were to govern men, neither external nor internal controuls on government would be necessary. In framing a government which is to be administered by men over men, the great difficulty lies in this: You must first enable the government to controul the governed; and in the next place, oblige it to controul itself. A dependence on the people is no doubt the primary controul on the government; but experience has taught mankind the necessity of auxiliary precautions.[41]

The profound insight of Madison and the Framers was that by separating government powers between different entities and pitting them against each other, government could be controlled. As legal scholar Raymond Ku aptly observes, the Framers adopted the Fourth Amendment based on concerns about limiting executive power.[42] Madison was acutely aware that the "parchment barriers" of the Constitution would fail to check government encroachments of power, and he explained how both the legislative and executive branches could overstep their bounds.[43] He arrived at an architectural solution: Power should be diffused among different departments of government, each afforded "the necessary constitutional means, and personal motives, to resist encroachments of the others." Government will be kept in check only if its parts consist of "opposite and rival interests."[44] As historian Gordon Wood describes the Madisonian vision:

> It was an imposing conception—a kinetic theory of politics— such a crumbling of political and social interests, such an atomization of authority, such a parceling of power, not only in the governmental institutions but in the extended sphere of the society itself, creating such a multiplicity and a scattering of designs and passions, so many checks, that no combination of parts could hold, no group of evil interests could long cohere. Yet out of the clashing and checking of this diversity, Madison believed the public good, the true perfection of the whole, would somehow arise.[45]

The warrant requirement reflects Madison's philosophy of government power by inserting the judicial branch in the middle of the executive branch's investigation process.[46] Although warrants have been criticized as ineffective because judges and magistrates often defer to the police and prosecutor's determination, criminal procedure expert Christopher Slobogin aptly contends that warrants raise the "standard of care" of law enforcement officials by forcing them to "document their requests for authorization."[47] According to Stuntz, warrants make searching more expensive, because they require law enforcement officials to "draft affidavits and wait around courthouses."[48] Because officers must devote time to obtaining a warrant, they are unlikely to use them unless they think it is likely that they will find what they are looking for.[49] As Justice Douglas has explained for the Court:

> [T]he Fourth Amendment has interposed a magistrate between the citizen and the police. This was done neither to shield criminals nor to make the home a safe haven for illegal activities. It was done so that an objective mind might weigh the need to invade that privacy in order to enforce the law. The right of privacy was deemed too precious to entrust to the discretion of those whose job is the detection of crime and the arrest of criminals. Power is a heady thing; and history shows that the police acting on their own cannot be trusted. And so the Constitution requires a magistrate to pass on the desires of the police before they violate the privacy of the home.[50]

Further, the requirement of prior approval prevents government officials from "dreaming up post hoc rationalizations"[51] and judges from experiencing hindsight bias when evaluating the propriety of a search after it has taken place.[52]

My purpose is not to defend the existing structure of the Fourth Amendment as perfect. For the purposes of this discussion, it is sufficient to agree (1) that the Fourth Amendment regime serves an important function by establishing an architecture that aims to protect privacy in addition to other values, and (2) that one of the central features of this architecture requires neutral and external oversight of the executive branch's power to gather and use personal information.

Even if its efficacy is limited, the structure of the Fourth Amendment is better than a void. Few commentators have suggested that the Fourth Amendment be repealed or that its larger purposes in controlling government power are inimical to a well-functioning society. Outside the realm of the Fourth Amendment is a great wilderness, a jungle of government discretion and uncontrolled power. Thus, the issue of the applicability of the Fourth Amendment is an important one, and to that issue I now turn.

The Shifting Paradigms of Fourth Amendment Privacy

Some notion of privacy has always been the trigger for Fourth Amendment protection, at least since the late nineteenth century. In 1886, in *Boyd v. United States*,[53] an early case delineating the meaning of the Fourth and Fifth Amendments, the government attempted to subpoena a person's private papers for use in a civil forfeiture proceeding. The Court held that the subpoena violated the Fourth and Fifth Amendments, since it invaded the individual's "indefeasible right of personal security, personal liberty and private property."[54]

Commentators have characterized *Boyd* as protecting property and as consistent with the exaltation of property and contract during the *Lochner* era.[55] The *Lochner* era was a period of Supreme Court jurisprudence lasting from about 1899 through 1937. The case that epitomized this era was *Lochner v. New York,* where the Court struck down a law restricting the number of hours that bakery employees could work to 60 a week. The Court concluded that the law infringed upon the constitutional guarantee of liberty of contract.[56] When the Court also nullified many other progressive laws and New Deal statutes for similar reasons, it was denounced for adhering too strictly to an ideology of laissez faire and unbridled commercial activity.[57]

Although *Boyd* certainly furthers the ideology of the *Lochner* Court, it should not merely be dismissed as the product of *Lochner*-like activism. *Boyd* follows a conception of privacy that the Court consistently adhered to in the late nineteenth century and the first half of the twentieth century. Under this conception, the Court viewed invasions of privacy as a type of physical incursion. For example, nine years prior to *Boyd,* in 1877, the Court held in *Ex Parte Jackson* that the Fourth Amendment applied to the opening of letters sent through the postal system: "The constitutional guaranty of the right of the people to be secure in their papers against unreasonable searches and seizures extends to their papers, thus closed against inspection, wherever they may be."[58] Additionally, privacy also concerned physical bodily intrusions. In *Union Pacific Railway Company v. Botsford,* an 1891 case concerning privacy but not directly involving the Fourth Amendment, the Court held that a court could not compel a female plaintiff in a civil action to submit to a surgical examination:

> The inviolability of the person is as much invaded by a compulsory stripping and exposure as by a blow. To compel any one, and especially a woman, to lay bare the body, or to submit it to

the touch of a stranger, without lawful authority, is an indignity, an assault, and a trespass.[59]

Consistent with *Boyd* and *Ex Parte Jackson*, the Court readily recognized the injury caused by physical intrusions such as trespassing into homes, rummaging through one's things, seizing one's papers, opening and examining one's letters, or physically touching one's body. Indeed, in 1890, when Warren and Brandeis authored their famous article *The Right to Privacy*, they observed that the law, which had long recognized physical and tangible injuries, was just beginning to recognize incorporeal ones.[60] Warren and Brandeis argued that privacy was more than simply a physical intrusion, a view increasingly recognized in the common law of torts in the early twentieth century. However, in its Fourth Amendment jurisprudence, the Court held fast to its physical intrusion conception of privacy.

The Court's view that Fourth Amendment privacy constituted protection from physical intrusions came to a head in 1928 in *Olmstead v. United States*.[61] There, the Court held that the tapping of a person's home telephone outside a person's house did not run afoul of the Fourth Amendment because it did not involve a trespass inside a person's home: "The Amendment does not forbid what was done here. There was no searching. There was no seizure. The evidence was secured by the use of the sense of hearing and that only. There was no entry of the houses or offices of the defendants."[62] *Olmstead* relied upon the Court's physical intrusion conception of privacy. Since there was no trespassing, opening, or rummaging, there was no invasion of Fourth Amendment privacy.

Justice Louis Brandeis vigorously dissented, chastising the Court for failing to adapt the Constitution to new problems. He observed: "When the Fourth and Fifth Amendments were adopted, the form that evil had theretofore taken had been necessarily simple."[63] The government "could secure possession of [a person's] papers and other articles incident to his private life—a seizure effected, if need be, by breaking and entry."[64] But technological developments, Brandeis argued, have created new threats to privacy:

> [T]ime works changes, brings into existence new conditions and purposes. Subtler and more far-reaching means of invading privacy have become available to the government. Discovery and invention have made it possible for the government, by means far more effective than stretching upon the rack, to obtain disclosure in court of what is whispered in the closet.[65]

The Court, however, continued to follow the *Olmstead* conception of privacy in subsequent cases. In *Goldman v. United States,* for example, the police placed a device called a "detectaphone" on the wall next to a person's office, enabling them to eavesdrop on the conversations inside the office. The Court concluded that since there had been no physical trespass into the office, the Fourth Amendment had not been violated.[66]

In 1967, nearly 40 years after *Olmstead,* the Court in *Katz v. United States* finally abandoned the physical intrusion conception of privacy and adopted the Fourth Amendment approach employed today. *Katz* involved the electronic eavesdropping of a telephone conversation made by a person in a phone booth. Explicitly overruling *Olmstead* and *Goldman,* the Court declared: "What a person knowingly exposes to the public, even in his own home or office, is not a subject of Fourth Amendment protection. But what he seeks to preserve as private, even in an area accessible to the public, may be constitutionally protected."[67]

The Court's approach to determining the applicability of the Fourth Amendment emerged from Justice Harlan's concurrence in *Katz.* The "reasonable expectation of privacy test" looks to whether (1) a person exhibits an "actual or subjective expectation of privacy" and (2) "the expectation [is] one that society is prepared to recognize as 'reasonable.'"[68]

Brandeis's dissent in *Olmstead* only partially won the day in *Katz.* Instead of adopting a conception of privacy that was adaptable to new technology, as the reasonable expectation of privacy test initially promised to be, the Court rigidified its approach with a particular conception of privacy—the secrecy paradigm. The Court based this new conception on the language in *Katz* that privacy turned on what a person exposed to the public. In this way, privacy was conceptualized as a form of secrecy, and people couldn't have a reasonable expectation of privacy in information that was not kept secret.

The full implications of this new conception of privacy are discussed in the next section. Before turning to this issue, it is important to observe the effects of the Court's failure to reconceptualize privacy in *Olmstead*. As a result of the nearly 40 years between *Olmstead* and *Katz*, there was little control over the burgeoning use of electronic surveillance, one of the most powerful technological law enforcement tools developed during the twentieth century. The Fourth Amendment stood by silently as this new technology proliferated.

At the time of *Olmstead*, many viewed wiretapping with great unease. Justice Holmes called it a "dirty business."[69] Even J. Edgar Hoover, who later became one of the greatest abusers of wiretapping, testified in 1929 that wiretapping was "unethical" and that he would fire any FBI employee who engaged in it.[70]

In 1934, just six years after *Olmstead*, Congress enacted §605 of the Federal Communications Act, making wiretapping a federal crime. However, §605 was practically impotent. It did not apply to wiretapping by state police or private parties. Nor did it apply to bugging. Further, it only precluded the disclosure of tapped communications in court proceedings.[71] Thus, the FBI could wiretap so long as it didn't try to use any of the results in court.[72]

Gradually, presidents gave the FBI increasing authority to wiretap.[73] In World War II, the FBI gained authorization to engage in wiretapping to investigate national security threats. Later, the authorization expanded to encompass domestic security. The fear of communism during the 1950s allowed the FBI to intensify its use of electronic surveillance.[74]

Widespread abuses began to occur. Hoover's misconduct was egregious. He wiretapped critics of the FBI, enemies of his political allies, and practically anybody whose political views he disliked. As discussed earlier, he engaged in massive electronic surveillance of Martin Luther King, Jr. Presidents also misused the FBI's wiretapping power for their own political purposes. President Nixon ordered extensive wiretapping, including surveillance of his own speechwriter, William Safire.[75] Presidents Kennedy and Johnson also ordered electronic surveillances inappropriately.[76] With regard to pre-*Katz* wiretapping by the states, an influential study led by Samuel Dash concluded that 90 percent of state wiretapping lacked court authorization and that state regulation of wiretapping had been largely ineffective against abuses.[77]

Thus, for 40 years, the government's power to engage in electronic surveillance fell outside of the reach of the Fourth Amendment, and the legislation that filled the void was ineffective. Today, history is in the process of repeating itself. The Court has made a mistake similar to *Olmstead*, and it is one with severe and far-reaching implications.

The New *Olmstead*

Although we have moved from the *Olmstead* physical intrusion conception of privacy to a new regime based upon expectations of privacy, there is a new *Olmstead*, one that is just as shortsighted and rigid in approach. The Court's new conception of privacy is the secrecy paradigm. If any information is exposed to the public or if law enforcement officials can view something from any public vantage point, then the Court has refused to recognize a reasonable expectation of privacy.

For example, in *Florida v. Riley,* the Court held that a person did not have a reasonable expectation of privacy in his enclosed greenhouse because a few roof panels were missing and the police were able to fly over it with a helicopter.[78] In *California v. Greenwood,* the police searched plastic garbage bags that the defendant had left on the curb to be collected by the trash collector. The Court held that there was no reasonable expectation of privacy in the trash because "[i]t is common knowledge that plastic bags left on or at the side of a public street are readily accessible to animals, children, scavengers, snoops, and other members of the public."[79] Trash is left at the curb "for the express purpose of conveying it to a third party, the trash collector, who might himself have sorted through [the] trash or permitted others, such as the police, to do so."[80]

Consistent with this conception of privacy, the Court held that there is no reasonable expectation in privacy for information known or exposed to third parties. In *United States v. Miller,* federal agents presented subpoenas to two banks to produce the defendant's financial records. The defendant argued that the Fourth Amendment required a warrant, not a subpoena, but the Court concluded that the Amendment didn't apply. There is no reasonable expectation of privacy in the records, the Court reasoned, because the information is "revealed to a third party."[81] Thus, "checks are not confidential communications but negotiable instruments to be used in commercial transactions. All of the documents obtained, including financial statements and deposit slips, contain only information voluntarily conveyed to the banks and exposed to their employees in the ordinary course of business."[82]

The Court used similar reasoning in *Smith v. Maryland.* Without a warrant, the police asked a telephone company to use a pen register, which is a device installed at the phone company to record the numbers dialed from the defendant's home. The Court concluded that since people "know that they must convey numerical information to the phone company," they cannot "harbor any general expectation that the numbers they dial will remain secret."[83]

Miller and *Smith* establish a general rule that if information is in the hands of third parties, then an individual lacks a reasonable expectation of privacy in that information, which means that the Fourth Amendment does not apply.[84] Individuals thus probably do not have a reasonable expectation of privacy in communications and records maintained by ISPs or computer network administrators.[85] The third party record doctrine stems from the secrecy paradigm. If information is not completely secret, if it is exposed to others, then it loses its status as private. *Smith* and *Miller* have been extensively criticized throughout the past several decades. However, it is only recently that we are beginning to see the profound implications of the third party doctrine. *Smith* and *Miller* are the new *Olmstead* and *Goldman.* Gathering information from third party records is an emerging law enforcement practice with as many potential dangers as the wiretapping in *Olmstead.* "The progress of science in furnishing the government with means of espionage is not likely to stop with wiretapping," Justice Brandeis observed in his *Olmstead* dissent. "Ways may some day be developed by which the government, without removing papers from secret drawers, can reproduce them in court, and by which it will be enabled to expose to a jury the most intimate occurrences of the home."[86]

That day is here. The government's harvesting of information from the extensive dossiers being assembled with modern computer technology poses one of the most significant threats to privacy of our times.[87]

The Emerging Statutory Regime and Its Limits

Throughout the twentieth century, when the Supreme Court held that the Fourth Amendment was inapplicable to new practices or technology, Congress often responded by passing statutes that afforded some level of protection. Through a series of statutes, Congress has established a regime regulating government access to third party records. This regime erects a particular architecture significantly different from that of the Fourth Amendment. Unfortunately, this regime is woefully inadequate.

Procedural Requirements to Obtain Information. The most significant deficiency is that a majority of the statutes permit government access to third party records with only a court order or subpoena—a significant departure from the Fourth Amendment, which generally requires warrants supported by probable cause to be issued by a neutral and detached judge. Unlike warrants, subpoenas do not require probable cause and can be issued without judicial approval. Prosecutors, not neutral judicial officers, can issue subpoenas.[88] According to Stuntz: "[W]hile searches typically require probable cause or reasonable suspicion and sometimes require a warrant, subpoenas require nothing, save that the subpoena not be unreasonably burdensome to its target. Few burdens are deemed unreasonable."[89] According to legal scholar Ronald Degnan, subpoenas are not issued "with great circumspection" and are often "handed out blank in batches and filled in by lawyers."[90] As Stuntz contends, federal subpoena power is "akin to a blank check."[91]

Prosecutors can also use grand jury subpoenas to obtain third party records.[92] Grand jury subpoenas are "presumed to be reasonable" and may only be quashed if "there is no reasonable possibility that the category of materials the Government seeks will produce information relevant to the general subject of the grand jury investigation."[93] As Stuntz observes, grand jury subpoenas "are much less heavily regulated" than search warrants:

> As long as the material asked for is relevant to the grand jury's investigation and as long as compliance with the subpoena is not too burdensome, the subpoena is enforced. No showing of probable cause or reasonable suspicion is necessary, and courts measure relevance and burden with a heavy thumb on the government's side of the scales.[94]

Therefore, courts "quash or modify" subpoenas only "if compliance would be unreasonable or oppressive."[95] Further, "judges decide these motions by applying vague legal standards case by case."[96]

Court orders under most of the statutes are not much more constrained than subpoenas. They typically require mere "relevance" to an ongoing criminal investigation, a standard significantly lower and looser than probable cause.

The problem with subpoenas and court orders is that they supply the judiciary with greatly attenuated oversight powers. The role of the judge in issuing or reviewing subpoenas is merely to determine whether producing records is overly burdensome. With this focus, financial hardship in producing information would give courts more pause when reviewing subpoenas than would threats to privacy. The role of the judiciary in court orders is also quite restricted. Instead of requiring probable cause, court orders require the government to demonstrate that records are "relevant" to a criminal investigation, a much weaker standard. In short, judicial involvement with subpoenas and court orders amounts to little more than a rubber stamp of judicial legitimacy.

Wiretapping and Bugging. When the Court held in *Olmstead* that the Fourth Amendment did not apply to wiretapping, Congress responded six years later by enacting §605 of the Federal Communications Act of 1934. As discussed earlier, §605 was far too narrow and limited. In 1968, a year after the Court in *Katz* declared that the Fourth Amendment applied to wiretapping, Congress enacted Title III of the

Omnibus Crime Control and Safe Streets Act,[97] which greatly strengthened the law of wiretapping, extending its reach to state officials and private parties. In 1986, Congress amended Title III with the Electronic Communications Privacy Act (ECPA). The ECPA restructured Title III into three parts, known as the "Wiretap Act," which governs the interception of communications; the "Stored Communications Act," which covers access to stored communications and records; and the "Pen Register Act," which regulates pen registers and trap and trace devices.[98]

The Wiretap Act covers wiretapping and bugging. It applies when a communication is intercepted during transmission. The Act has strict requirements for obtaining a court order to engage in electronic surveillance.[99] In certain respects, the Wiretap Act's requirements are stricter than those for a Fourth Amendment search warrant.[100] It also requires that the surveillance "minimize the interception of communications" not related to the investigation. The Act is enforced with an exclusionary rule.[101]

However, the interception of electronic communications not involving the human voice (such as email) is not protected with an exclusionary rule. Although the Wiretap Act has substantial protections, it covers ground already protected by the Fourth Amendment. In areas not protected by the Fourth Amendment, the architecture of the statutory regime is much weaker and more porous.

Stored Communications. Communications service providers frequently store their customers' communications. ISPs temporarily store email until it is downloaded by the recipient. Many ISPs enable users to keep copies of previously read email on the ISP's server, as well as copies of their sent emails. Since a third party maintains the information, the Fourth Amendment may not apply.[102]

The Stored Communications Act provides some protection, but unfortunately it is quite confusing and its protection is limited. Electronic storage is defined as "any *temporary, intermediate* storage of a wire or electronic communication incidental to the electronic transmission thereof," and "any storage of such communication by an electronic communication service for purposes of backup protection."[103] This definition clearly covers email that is waiting on the ISP's server to be downloaded. But what about previously read email that remains on the ISP's server? According to the Department of Justice's (DOJ) interpretation of the Act, the email is no longer in *temporary* storage, and is therefore "simply a remotely stored file."[104] The Act permits law enforcement officials to access it merely by issuing a subpoena to the ISP.[105] And in contrast to the Wiretap Act, the Stored Communications Act does not have an exclusionary rule.

Communications Service Records. The Stored Communications Act also regulates government access to a customer's communications service records, which consist of the customer's name, address, phone numbers, payment information, and services used.[106] One of the most important pieces of information in ISP records is the customer's identity. An ISP may have information linking a customer's screen name to her real name. Thus, an ISP often holds the key to one's ability to communicate anonymously on the Internet. The government often wants to obtain this information to identify a particular speaker. To access customer records, the government must obtain a court order, which requires "specific and articulable facts showing that there are reasonable grounds to believe that . . . the records or other information sought, are relevant and material to an ongoing criminal investigation."[107] Further, since the Act lacks an exclusionary rule, information obtained in violation of the law can still be introduced in court.[108]

Pen Registers, Email Headers, and Websurfing. The Pen Register Act attempts to fill the void left by *Smith v. Maryland* by requiring a court order to use a pen register or trap and trace device.[109] Whereas a pen register records the phone numbers a person dials from her home, a trap and trace device creates a list of the telephone numbers of incoming calls. The USA-PATRIOT Act, passed in 2001 shortly after the September 11th attacks, expanded the scope of the Pen Register Act. The definition of a pen register now extends beyond phone numbers to also encompass addressing information on emails and IP addresses. An IP address is the unique address assigned to a particular computer connected to the Internet. All computers connected to the Internet have one. Consequently, a list of IP addresses accessed reveals the various websites that a person has visited. Because websites are often distinctively tailored to particular topics and interests, a comprehensive list of them can reveal a lot about a person's life. The court order to obtain this information, however, only requires the government to demonstrate that "the information likely to be obtained . . . is relevant to an ongoing criminal investigation."[110] Courts cannot look beyond the certification nor inquire into the truthfulness of the facts in the application. Once the government official makes the proper certification, the court must issue the order.[111] As one court has observed, the "judicial role in approving use of trap and trace devices is ministerial in nature."[112] Finally, there is no exclusionary rule for Pen Register Act violations.

Financial Records. Two years after *United States v. Miller,* Congress filled the void with the Right to Financial Privacy Act (RFPA) of 1978, which requires the government to obtain a warrant or subpoena to access records from banks or other financial institutions.[113] However, the subpoena merely requires a "reason to believe that the records sought are relevant to a legitimate law enforcement inquiry."[114] When subpoena authority is not available to the government, the government need only submit a formal written request for the information.[115]

In addition to banks, credit reporting agencies have detailed records for nearly every adult American consumer. Under the Fair Credit Reporting Act (FCRA) of 1970, a consumer reporting agency "may furnish identifying information respecting any consumer, limited to his name, address, former addresses, places of employment, or former places of employment, to a governmental agency."[116] Thus, the government can simply request this information without any court involvement. And the government can obtain more information with a court order or grand jury subpoena.[117] Since the FCRA focuses on credit reporting agencies, it doesn't prohibit the recipients of credit reports from disclosing them to the government.

Although the RFPA and FCRA protect financial information maintained by banks and credit reporting agencies, the government can obtain financial information from employers, landlords, merchants, creditors, and database companies, among others. Therefore, financial records are protected based only on which entities possess them. Thus, the statutory regime merely provides partial protection of financial data.

Electronic Media Entertainment Records. The statutory regime protects records pertaining to certain forms of electronic media entertainment. Under the Cable Communications Policy Act (Cable Act) of 1984,[118] a government official must obtain a court order in order to obtain cable records. The government must offer "clear and convincing evidence that the subject of the information is reasonably suspected of engaging in criminal activity and that the information sought would be material evidence in the case."[119] People can "appear and contest" the court order.[120] This standard is more stringent than the Fourth Amendment's probable cause and warrant requirements. However, there is no exclusionary rule under the Cable Act.

In addition to cable records, the statutory regime also protects videotape rental records. The Video Privacy Protection Act (VPPA) of 1988 states that a videotape service provider may disclose customer records to law enforcement officials "pursuant to a warrant . . . , an equivalent State warrant, a grand jury subpoena, or a court order."[121] Unlike the Cable Act, the level of protection under the VPPA is much less stringent.

Although the statutory regime protects the records of certain forms of electronic media entertainment, it fails to protect the records of many others. For example, records from music stores, electronics merchants, and Internet media entities are afforded no protection.

Medical Records. Our medical records are maintained by third parties. Could the third party doctrine extend to medical records? On the one hand, given the considerable privacy protection endowed upon the patient-physician relationship, the third party doctrine may stop at the hospital door.[122] On the other hand, the doctrine applies to records of financial institutions, which also have a tradition of maintaining the confidentiality of their customers' information.[123] Unless the patient-physician relationship is distinguished from banks, the third party doctrine logically could apply to medical records. However, the Supreme Court has yet to push the doctrine this far.

The federal health privacy rules under the Health Insurance Portability and Accountability Act (HIPAA) of 1996 apparently view medical records as falling under the third party doctrine. The rules permit law enforcement officials to access medical records with a mere subpoena.[124] Health information may also be disclosed "in response to a law enforcement official's request for such information for the purpose of identifying or locating a suspect, fugitive, material witness, or missing person."[125]

Moreover, not all health records are covered by HIPAA. Only records maintained by health plans, health care clearinghouses, and health care providers are covered.[126] Although doctors, hospitals, pharmacists, health insurers, and HMOs are covered, not all third parties possessing our medical information fall under HIPAA. For example, the sale of nonprescription drugs and the rendering of medical advice by many Internet health websites are not covered by HIPAA.[127] Therefore, while certain health records are protected, others are not.

Holes in the Regime. Federal statutes provide some coverage of the void left by the inapplicability of the Fourth Amendment to records held by third parties. Although the statutes apply to communication records, financial records, entertainment records, and health records, these are only protected when in the hands of particular third parties. Thus, the statutory regime does not protect records based on the type of information contained in the records, but protects them based on the particular types of third parties that possess them.

Additionally, there are gaping holes in the statutory regime of protection, with classes of records not protected at all. Such records include those of merchants, both online and offline. Records held by bookstores, department stores, restaurants, clubs, gyms, employers, and other companies are not protected. Additionally, all the personal information amassed in profiles by database companies is not covered. Records maintained by Internet retailers and websites are often not considered "communications" under the ECPA; the government can access these records and the ECPA doesn't apply. Thus, the statutory regime is limited in its scope and has glaring omissions and gaps. Further, the statutes are often complicated and confusing, and their protection turns on technical distinctions that can leave wide fields of information virtually unprotected.

Therefore, the current statutory regime is inadequate. As warrants supported by probable cause are replaced by subpoenas and court orders supported by "articulable facts" that are "relevant" to an investigation, the role of the judge in the process is diminished to nothing more than a decorative seal of approval. And since there are numerous holes in the regime, there are many circumstances when neither court orders nor subpoenas are required. The government can simply ask for the information. An individual's privacy is protected only by the vague and toothless privacy policies of the companies holding their information.

11 Reconstructing the Architecture

Today, much of our personal information is finding its way into the hands of third parties. Moreover, given the Court's current conception of privacy under the Fourth Amendment, the architecture that regulates many of the government's information gathering practices is increasingly that of a confusing and gap-riddled statutory regime.

One solution to fill the void is for the Court to reverse *Smith v. Maryland* and *United States v. Miller.* Although Fourth Amendment architecture is significantly more protective than that of the statutory regime, the problem of how to regulate government access to third party records is not adequately addressed by Fourth Amendment architecture alone. As discussed earlier, the principal remedy for Fourth Amendment violations is the exclusionary rule, which prevents the government from introducing improperly obtained data during a criminal prosecution. However, many information acquisition abuses often occur in the absence of prosecutions. Therefore, the exclusionary rule alone is not sufficiently protective.

A better architecture to regulate government information gathering from third parties should be constructed. In particular, such an architecture should prevent the types of problems associated with government information gathering discussed earlier in chapter 9. An architecture should strive for three goals: minimization, particularization, and control.

First, government information gathering should be minimized. Sweeping investigations and vast stores of personal data in the hands of government entities present significant opportunities for the problematic uses discussed earlier.

Second, efforts at amassing data should be particularized to specific individuals suspected of criminal involvement. Particularization requires law enforcement officials to exercise care in selecting the individuals who should be investigated, and it prevents dragnet investigations that primarily involve innocent people. One of the most important aspects of keeping the government under control is to prevent its investigatory powers from being turned loose on the population at large.

Third, government information gathering and use must be controlled. There must be some meaningful form of supervision over the government's information gathering activity to ensure that it remains minimized and particularized. The government's use of information must be controlled to prevent abuses and security lapses.

The aims of the architecture, however, are not the most difficult issue. Substantively, the architecture needs a scope. Which information gathering activities should be regulated? Procedurally, the architecture needs a mechanism for carrying out its aims. What type of structural controls should an architecture adopt?

Scope: System of Records

An architecture begins with substance. It must provide guidance about which information gathering activities it governs. What is the appropriate scope of an architecture that regulates government information gathering? In particular, should the architecture cover all instances where the government gathers personal data from third parties? Restricting all information collection from third parties would prevent law enforcement officials from eliciting initial information essential to develop sufficient evidence to establish probable cause. In the early stages of an investigation, the police frequently talk to victims, witnesses, friends, and neighbors. The police often find out about a crime when people voluntarily report suspicious activity. These examples all involve third parties who possess information about the person being investigated. If the architecture encompasses all third parties, then it might unduly constrain police investigations.

Consequently, a line must be drawn to distinguish the instances where third parties can voluntarily supply information to the government and where the government will be prohibited from accessing information. Although we may want to prevent Amazon.com from divulging to the government the log of books a person bought, we may not want to prohibit a person's neighbor or a stranger from telling the police which books she happened to observe the person reading.

Where should we draw the line? One way is to focus on the type of data involved, distinguishing between "private" and "nonprivate" information. The architecture would protect all personal information that is private. But how is privacy to be defined?[1] Following the secrecy paradigm, the Court has defined privacy as total secrecy. But this definition obviously doesn't work since it would exclude information held by third parties.

Another way to define private information is to focus on "intimate" information. A number of commentators, such as philosophers Julie Inness and Tom Gerety, have contended that intimacy is the essential characteristic of privacy.[2] But what constitutes "intimate" information? Without an adequate definition, "intimate" becomes nothing more than a synonym for "private." Some commentators, such as Inness, define "intimacy" as involving loving and caring relationships.[3] However, much private information, such as financial and health data, doesn't pertain to these types of relationships.

The more fundamental problem with focusing on whether information is private is that privacy is contextual and historically contingent. Easy distinctions such as intimate versus nonintimate and secret versus nonsecret fail to account for the complex nature of what is considered private. Privacy is a dimension of social practices, activities, customs, and norms that are shaped by history and culture. The matters that are considered private and public have changed throughout history. Privacy is not an inherent property of particular forms of information, since even the most sensitive and revealing information is not private under all circumstances. Even if ordinarily a person's sex life or medical history is private, it wouldn't be private if that person were a public figure who routinely discussed these matters openly in public. Certainly, public disclosure does not eliminate the privacy of information; indeed, even information that is exposed to others may retain its private character. Nevertheless, privacy depends upon degrees of accessibility of information, and under certain circumstances, even highly sensitive information may not be private.

Additionally, focusing on the type of information does not solve the problem of distinguishing between the neighbor's telling the police what books he sees a person reading and Amazon.com's providing the police with a complete inventory of the books the person has purchased. By attempting to draw a line based upon the type of information, these two instances would be treated similarly. Another example more radically illustrates the problem. Many would deem information about a person's genitals to be private information. Should the police be required to obtain a warrant before talking to a victim of a sexual assault about an assailant's genitals? This would be absurd. On the other hand, many would express serious objections if the police, without probable cause, could simply compel information from the person's doctor.

Another way a line could be drawn is based upon people's expectations. Such an approach would draw from the Court's notion of "reasonable expectations of privacy." The problem with this approach, however, is that an empirical evaluation of expectations alone could gradually lead to the diminishment of privacy as more and more people come to expect that the records held by third parties can be readily obtained by the government.[4]

If a line cannot be drawn based upon the type of information involved or people's expectations of privacy, then how should the line be drawn? The answer must focus on relationships. Privacy is not independent of the relationships in which it is a part. Individuals readily share information in certain private relationships, such as the family. In particular relationships people undertake certain risks, including the risk of betrayal by one with whom confidences are shared.

The fact that there are expectations and risks, however, does not mean that they must be the exclusive focus of our inquiry.

The issue is not the *conceivable* risk of betrayal, but rather which risks people *ought to assume* and which risks people *should be insured against*. This determination has a normative dimension. When a patient discloses an ailment to a doctor, arguably the patient assumes the risk that the doctor will disclose the information to the public. However, there are several protections against this risk. Patient-physician confidentiality is protected by ethical rules, which if violated could result in the loss of the doctor's license to practice medicine.[5] Confidentiality is also protected with an evidentiary privilege.[6] Courts have created tort law causes of action against physicians who disclose personal information.[7] Finally, states have passed laws that protect against the disclosure of medical information.[8] Thus, in numerous ways, the law structures the patient-physician relationship to protect against the risk of disclosure. Similarly, the law of evidence has recognized the importance of protecting the privacy of communications between attorney and client, priest and penitent, husband and wife, and psychotherapist and patient.[9] Our expectations in these relationships are the product of both existing norms and the norm-shaping power of the law. As Christopher Slobogin notes, "in a real sense, we only assume those risks of unregulated government intrusion that the courts tell us we have to assume."[10]

Therefore, the scope of the architecture should be shaped by considerations regarding social relationships. The architecture's scope should encompass all instances when third parties share personal information contained within a "system of records." This term is taken from the Privacy Act, which defines a "system of records" as "a group of any records . . . from which information is retrieved by the name of the individual or by some identifying number, symbol, or other identifying particular assigned to the individual."[11] A "system of records" is used to distinguish between collecting information by speaking with specific individuals versus obtaining it through the vast stores of records held by companies.

Focusing on systems of records targets at least two sets of relationships that must be regulated: our relationships with the government and our relationships with the companies, employers, and other entities that possess personal information.

In relationships with the government, the focus should be on what society wants the *government* to be able to know rather than whether certain matters are public or private based on the extent of their exposure to others. The Court's conception of privacy assumes that the government stands in the same shoes as everybody else, which is clearly not the case. If we allow a loved one to read our diary, do we also want the government to be able to read it? As Anthony Amsterdam has observed: "For the tenement dweller, the difference between observation by neighbors and visitors who ordinarily use the common hallways and observation by policemen who come into hallways to 'check up' or 'look around' is the difference between all the privacy that his condition allows and none."[12]

Indeed, the existence of Fourth Amendment protection indicates that the government stands in a different position than ordinary citizens or private-sector organizations. The possibility of aggregation and the rise of digital dossiers argue in favor of regulating the government's access to information.

The focus should be on the goals of the architecture rather than on technical distinctions over whether information is intimate enough or secret enough. These questions should not derail attention from the important issue of whether government information gathering activities present sufficient actual and potential dangers to warrant protection. The problems discussed earlier regarding information flows from the private sector to the government stem from the extensiveness of the personal information that businesses are reaping today. Focusing on "systems of records" targets the type of information flow that raises concern. Because the problem of modern government information gathering is caused by the increasing dossiers maintained in private-sector record systems, the architecture targets those third parties that store data in record systems.

Our relationships with the entities that maintain record systems about us differ from other social relationships. Though it is possible for the government to obtain personal data by interviewing friends and others, the information in records is more permanent in nature and is readily aggregated. Record systems are particularly dangerous because of how easily data can be gathered, combined, stored, and analyzed.

Further, entities that maintain systems of records collect data in a power dynamic where information disclosure is often not consensual. A person can take considerable steps to prevent a stranger from collecting data without consent. For example, a person who is overzealous in gathering information can be subject to laws prohibiting stalking or harassment.

Relationships to employers and landlords, however, are different than those with our friends, neighbors, and even strangers. Currently, employers and landlords have a substantial amount of power to extort personal information. They often stand in an unequal position to that of the individual employees or tenants. The nature of the relationship with employers and landlords provides them with a significantly greater amount of power and control. If people aren't willing to supply the information, then they may not be hired or approved as a tenant.

Relationships with merchants and communications providers might not be as directly coercive as those with the entities that govern our livelihoods and dwellings. Because these relationships are more impersonal, should it be left up to the market to decide this issue? Some might argue that if consumers demanded that companies protect their information from the government, then the market would reflect these demands.

Thus far, however, the market has not been responsive to this issue. As discussed earlier, privacy policies are often vague about information flows to the government. Individuals are usually unaware of the extent to which information about them is collected. People have difficulty bargaining over privacy, and the market fails to afford sufficient incentives to rectify this problem.[13] Further, many companies have never established a relationship with the people whose data they have collected—and thus, there isn't even the opportunity to bargain.

Even if people are informed, they have little choice but to hand over information to third parties. Life in the Information Age depends upon sharing information with a host of third party companies. The

Supreme Court in *Smith* and *Miller* has suggested that if people want to protect privacy, they should not share their information with third parties. However, refraining from doing so may result in people living as Information Age hermits, without credit cards, banks, Internet service, phones, and television. The market does not seem to offer a wide array of choices for people about the amount of privacy they would like to protect. As discussed in chapter 5, there is little hope that the market alone will achieve the appropriate level of protection.

Therefore, the scope of the architecture must be defined broadly to encompass any third party that maintains a "system of records." This definition of scope is not perfect, and there may be hard cases that call for exceptions. However, this rule would provide clear guidance to law enforcement officials when gathering information from third parties. Clarity is a virtue. Unlike the existing statutory architecture, which is complicated and often full of notable gaps, this architecture has clear and simple boundaries.

Structure: Mechanisms of Oversight

Many different procedural mechanisms are available to control government information gathering, and they fall on a spectrum from no control to complete restriction. In the middle of the spectrum are mechanisms of oversight—where the government can access information only if it can make certain showings before a neutral and external party. This middle course will work the best.

No Control. On the "no control" end of the spectrum, businesses may voluntarily disclose personal information to the government. If it so desired, Amazon.com could connect its computers to the FBI's. If a private-sector entity does not volunteer information, then the government can compel its production with a mere subpoena. The entity need not contest the subpoena or provide notice to the person to whom the information pertains. Whether the entity does so would be left up to market forces—to contracts between the entity and the consumer or privacy policies. The problem with "no control" is that it does nothing to solve the problems caused by government information gathering.

Mechanisms of Restriction. On the other end of the spectrum are architectural mechanisms of restriction—prohibitions on government collection and use of information. These mechanisms are embodied in the architecture of the Fifth Amendment.[14] The Fifth Amendment provides that "[n]o person . . . shall be compelled in any criminal case to be a witness against himself."[15] The Fifth Amendment's privilege against self-incrimination prevents the government from compelling individuals to testify against themselves, and completely bars use of the information obtained in violation of the right at trial. In contrast, under current Fourth Amendment architecture, evidence is admissible at trial so long as the government obtains it with a valid search warrant.

At one point in its history, the Fourth Amendment used to rely heavily on mechanisms of restriction. Early cases, such as *Boyd v. United States,*[16] and *Gouled v. United States,*[17] held that the government could seize a person's private papers only if they were instrumentalities of a crime—in other words, only if they were actually used to commit the crime. If they were merely evidence of a crime, however, the government couldn't obtain them—even with a warrant. This rule became known as the "mere evidence" rule. The Court later overturned it.[18]

Perhaps the mere evidence rule should be resurrected and applied to third party records. This would effectively bar the government from obtaining the records. The problem with this solution is that it would cripple modern criminal investigation. As William Stuntz observes: "Government regulation require[s] lots of information, and *Boyd* came dangerously close to giving regulated actors a blanket entitlement to nondisclosure. It is hard to see how modern health, safety, environmental, or economic regulation would be possible in such a regime."[19] Because *Boyd* rested in part on the Fifth Amendment, it completely prevented the government from obtaining and using the papers against the defendant no matter what procedure the government had used to obtain them. This approach is far too restrictive when it comes to most personal information maintained in third party records.

Mechanisms of Oversight. In the middle of the spectrum are mechanisms of oversight. An architecture containing this type of mechanism is preferable to regulate government access of records held by third parties maintaining "systems of records." Mechanisms of oversight allow the government to gather information, but the government must first justify its need to do so by presenting facts and evidence before a neutral detached judge or magistrate. Oversight is embodied in the Fourth Amendment's per se warrant rule. The warrant requirement achieves the aims of minimization, particularization, and control. Collection is minimized by the requirement that the government justify that its information gathering is legitimate and necessary. The warrant ensures particularization with its requirement that there be probable cause that a particular person be engaged in criminal activity or that particular place contains evidence of a crime. Finally, the warrant achieves control (at least over the collection efforts) by having a neutral and detached party authorize the collection.

In many cases, warrants are the best regulatory device for government information gathering. Often, at the point during an investigation when certain information from third parties becomes important to obtain, there is already enough evidence to support a warrant. In both *Smith* and *Miller* there was probably sufficient evidence for the police to secure warrants. Therefore, the requirement of a warrant prevents cases of illegitimate abuses—such as large-scale information sweeps and investigations without particularized suspicion—without unduly interfering with legitimate law enforcement activities. Further, third party records have few of the dangers that make warrants inefficient. For example, because third parties maintain the records, there are fewer opportunities for a suspect to hide or destroy documents during the time law enforcement officials obtain a warrant.

However, as discussed previously, merely applying the Fourth Amendment to government access to third party records proves inadequate. The exclusionary rule only provides a remedy at trial, and many of the abuses associated with government information gathering extend far beyond criminal trials. Therefore, I recommend a fusion between warrants and subpoenas.

Despite being far more permissive for government information collection purposes, subpoenas have certain protections not available with search warrants. Unlike warrants, they can be challenged prior to the seizure of the documents. The subpoenaed party can refuse to comply and make a motion to quash before a judge. Further, subpoenas permit the target to produce the documents rather than have government agents rummage through a person's home or belongings.[20] The advantages of subpoenas over search warrants are best illustrated in *Zurcher v. The Stanford Daily*,[21] where the police searched a newspaper's offices for evidence relating to a criminal suspect. The newspaper was not involved in the alleged crime; it merely possessed evidence. The Court upheld the search because the police obtained a valid warrant. Dissenting justices contended that there were First Amendment concerns with searches of newspaper offices because they would disrupt journalistic activities and result in "the possibility of disclosure of information received from confidential sources, or of the identity of the sources themselves."[22] Congress responded to *Zurcher* by passing the Privacy Protection Act of 1980, which restricts the use of search warrants for offices of newspapers and other media entities for evidence of crimes of other parties.[23] In effect, the Act requires the use of subpoenas in addition to warrants to obtain such evidence.

The benefits of subpoenas, however, often do not apply when they are issued on the third parties to produce an individual's records. The third party does not need to notify the individual or may not have any incentive to challenge the subpoena in court. Further, as discussed earlier, subpoenas have many weaknesses compared to warrants, such as a lack of requiring particularized suspicion and little protection by way of oversight by the judiciary.

Therefore, the Fourth Amendment architecture should be resurrected statutorily, by creating a requirement that the government obtain a special court order—a fusion between a warrant and a subpoena. From warrants, the standard of probable cause should be used. This threshold would require government officials to go before a judge with specific facts and evidence that a particular person is involved in criminal activity. For example, a probable cause standard would prevent government officials from scouring through databases to locate all people who bought books about bomb making or drug manufacturing. Such a search is akin to the types of general searches that the Framers wanted to forbid. From subpoenas, advance notice should be provided to the person whose records are involved, and that person should be able to challenge the order in court. This statutory regime would incorporate the exclusionary rule, a minimum statutory damages provision, and a framework for disciplining offending law enforcement officials.

Moreover, third parties maintaining personal information in a "system of records" should be restricted from voluntarily disclosing an individual's personal information to the government except under special circumstances. Exceptions might include allowing disclosure to prevent an imminent threat of harm to another. Another exception would allow the individual to whom the records pertain to authorize the government to obtain them from the third party. For example, if a victim of computer hacking wanted to permit the government to access the victim's own ISP records, the victim could authorize the government to do so.

Regulating Post-Collection Use of Data

Another problem that must be addressed is the way personal information is used once it has been collected. As Stuntz astutely observes: "Fourth Amendment law regulates the government's efforts to uncover information, but it says *nothing* about what the government may do with the information it uncovers. Yet as the Clinton investigation shows, often the greater privacy intrusion is not the initial disclosure but the leaks that follow."[24] Legal scholar Carol Steiker notes: "Unlike other countries in North America and Western Europe, the United States [has] never developed a national plan to organize a 'system' of policing or to provide for centralized control over police authority."[25] Once information is collected, the Fourth Amendment's architecture of oversight no longer applies. This is problematic, as many of the abuses of information by the government occur after the information has been collected.

The Privacy Act of 1974 provides some limited regulation of records maintained by law enforcement entities. But as discussed earlier in chapter 8, the Act contains many exceptions and loopholes that have limited its effectiveness. Government entities often can share information widely with each other.[26] Additionally, the Act applies only to the federal government.

The Privacy Act is an important first step in reining in the vast stores of data that government entities collect. There remains, however, much room for the Privacy Act to be improved and strengthened. One possible safeguard is to mandate the destruction of data after a certain period of time or, mandate the transfer of data to the judicial branch after a certain period of time for access only under special circumstances. Another way is to adopt a meaningful purpose specification restriction. This means that, with certain reasonable exceptions, information collected from third party records may only be used for the particular purpose for which it is collected.

Developing an Architecture

The government's increasing access to our digital dossiers is one of the most significant threats to privacy of our times, and it is inadequately regulated. The Court's Fourth Amendment jurisprudence has been mired in the difficulties of conceptualizing privacy, thus preventing the application of the Fourth Amendment. A statutory regime has arisen to fill the void, but it is severely flawed. A new architecture must be constructed, one that effectively regulates the government's collection and use of third party records. The process toward developing an appropriate architecture should begin by regulating both the government's acquisition of personal data and its downstream uses of it. As for acquiring personal information stored in a system of records, the government should be required to obtain a special court order that combines the benefits of subpoenas and warrants. As for downstream uses, specific limits must be established for how long the government can keep personal information and for what the government can do with it. The task of developing an architecture is not easy in a rapidly changing society that is adjusting to the new dimensions of the Information Age. This proposed solution is thus a beginning of the process.

12 Conclusion

The problems arising from the emergence of digital dossiers are profoundly important. They affect the power of individuals, institutions, and the government; and they pervade numerous relationships that form the framework of modern society. The way we respond to these problems will significantly shape the type of society we are constructing. Digital dossiers will affect our freedom and power; they will define the very texture and tenor of our lives.

Ideally, technology empowers us, gives us greater control over our lives, and makes us more secure. But digital technologies of data gathering and use are having the opposite effect. Increasingly, companies and the government are using computers to make important decisions about us based on our dossiers, and we are frequently not able to participate in the process.

As discussed throughout this book, the law of information privacy has not yet effectively grappled with these problems. Certainly, information privacy law has had positive effects. It would be far too simple to conclude that the law has failed. But the law has not been sufficiently successful, and the problems have grown much more troubling during the law's watch.

One response to these developments is a cynical one. Some commentators argue that things have already progressed too far for law to grapple with the problems of digital dossiers. Scott McNealy, CEO of Sun Microsystems, famously quips: "You already have zero privacy. Get over it."[1] Amitai Etzioni observes that "as long as Americans wish to enjoy the convenience of using credit cards and checks (as opposed to paying cash) and of ordering merchandise over the phone and the Internet (rather than shopping in person), they will leave data trails that are difficult to erase or conceal."[2] "To be realistic," Etzioni states, "the probability of returning the genie to the bottle is nil."[3]

Too often, discussions of privacy parade a horde of horribles, raising fears of new technologies developing too fast for the law to handle. We are left with a sense of hopelessness—technology will continue to erode privacy and there is little we can do to stop it. To the contrary, I believe that there is much cause for optimism. We are still in the early days of the Information Age, and we still have the ability to shape the networks of information flow.

In fact, technology isn't the primary culprit—many of the privacy problems I discussed are caused in large part because of the law. The law plays a profound role not just in solving the problems of digital dossiers, but in manufacturing them as well. The law is not merely reactive to new technologies that threaten privacy, but is also a shaping force behind these technologies as well as the amount of privacy we experience today. We often see privacy as naturally occurring and threatened by rapidly developing technology. Law must intervene to protect privacy. However, law creates and constructs the world we live in. This is particularly true with privacy. To a significant degree, privacy is legally constructed. Law already shapes our ability to hide information and it shapes information accessibility. Law makes certain information publicly available; it keeps places (such as the home) private by enforcing trespass and property laws. Law also shapes our expectations of privacy in many contexts.[4]

The law also influences much of the loss of privacy. Many privacy problems are the product of legal decisions that have been made over the past century as we have shaped our modern information economy. Once we understand the full extent of the legal construction of privacy, we will realize that privacy is not passively slipping away but is being actively eliminated by the way we are constructing the information economy through the law.

In the nineteenth century, Americans faced many significant privacy problems. For example, since colonial times, the privacy of the mail was a vexing problem. Sealing letters was difficult.[5] Benjamin Franklin, who was in charge of the colonial mails, required his employees to swear an oath not to open mail.[6] Nevertheless, significant concerns persisted about postal clerks reading people's letters. Thomas Jefferson, Alexander Hamilton, and George Washington frequently complained about the lack of privacy in their letters, and they would sometimes write in code.[7] As Thomas Jefferson wrote: "[T]he infidelities of the post office and the circumstances of the times are against my writing fully and freely."[8]

These problems persisted in the nineteenth century. As Ralph Waldo Emerson declared, it was unlikely that "a bit of paper, containing our most secret thoughts, and protected only by a seal, should travel safely from one end of the world to the other, without anyone whose hands it had passed through having meddled with it."[9] The law responded to these problems. Congress passed several strict laws protecting the privacy of the mail.[10] And in 1877, in *Ex Parte Jackson,* the Supreme Court held that the Fourth Amendment prohibited government officials from opening letters without a warrant.[11]

In the nineteenth century, one might have simply concluded that people shouldn't expect privacy in their letters, and that they should "get over it." But privacy isn't just found but constructed. It is the product of a vision for a future society. By erecting a legal structure to protect the privacy of letters, our society shaped the practices of letter-writing and using the postal system. It occurred because of the desire to make privacy an integral part of these practices rather than to preserve the status quo.

Similar examples abound in the nineteenth and early twentieth centuries. When the increasing amount of information collected by the U.S. census sparked a public outcry, Congress took action by passing powerful laws to safeguard the confidentiality of census information.[12] After Warren and Brandeis's 1890 article, *The Right to Privacy,*[13] raised concern over new technologies in photography and an increasingly sensationalistic press, courts and legislatures responded by creating many new privacy laws.

Today, we face new technological challenges. Many of the problems we currently encounter are created by the profound growth in the creation and use of digital dossiers. Part of the difficulty we are experiencing in dealing with these problems is that they are not as easy to capture in a soundbite, and they often do not quickly materialize as concrete injuries. When a scandalous secret is disclosed or a hidden video camera is installed in one's bedroom, we can easily recognize and describe the privacy harms. The troubles caused by digital dossiers are of a different sort. These harms are complex and abstract, which is why I invoked the metaphor of Kafka's *The Trial,* since Kafka was so adept at depicting these types of harms. Today, like the all-encompassing Court system that assembled a dossier about Joseph K., large organizations we know little about are producing digital dossiers about us. The dossiers capture a kind of digital person—a personality translated into digitized form, composed of records, data fragments, and bits of information. Our digital dossiers remain woefully insecure, at risk of being polluted by identity thieves or riddled with careless errors. And all the while, we are like Joseph K.—powerless, uncertain, and uneasy—constantly kept on the outside while important decisions about us are being made based on our dossiers.

I have argued that we need to rethink traditional notions of privacy in order to solve these problems. Protecting privacy in the Information Age is a question of social design. It is about designing an architecture for the information networks that are increasingly constitutive of modern society. The law must restructure our relationships with the entities collecting and using our personal information. These relationships are not naturally occurring—it is the law that has defined our relationships to various businesses and institutions, and it is thus the law that is at least partly responsible for our powerlessness and vulnerability. Changing our relationships with bureaucracies can't be achieved through isolated lawsuits. We need a regulatory system, akin to the ones we have in place regulating our food, environment, and financial institutions.

The law actively contributes to the creation of our dossiers by compelling people to give up personal data, placing it in public records, and then allowing it to be amassed by database companies. The solution is for the law to place greater controls on its public records by limiting the degree to which personal information in these records can be accessed and used.

The increasing government access and use of our digital dossiers is also the product of legal decisions made during the past century. The Supreme Court has interpreted the Fourth Amendment in a short-sighted way, and the use of dossiers threatens a profound end-run around Fourth Amendment protections. The law that fills the void fails to adequately control the government's tapping into our digital dossiers. The solution is to create a legal structure for keeping government access to our digital dossiers in check. The government should be required to obtain a special court order when it wants to access personal data that is maintained in a business's record systems.

All of these solutions are not absolutist ones. I am not advocating that businesses be forbidden from collecting personal data or that public records be made inaccessible or that the government be prohibited from obtaining personal information. These absolutist solutions are not practical in an information society. In this respect, those that say the genie can't be stuffed back into the bottle are correct. We will not suddenly turn into Luddites and throw away our credit cards, stop surfing the Internet, and return to using paper records. We are in an Information Age, and there is no turning back. But this does not mean that privacy is destined for extinction. We can have the benefits of an information-driven world without sacrificing privacy. The solutions I propose do not stop the flow of data. Companies can still gather information; public records can be made widely available; and the government can obtain personal information. But when companies collect our data, the law should impose weighty responsibilities and should allow people to have greater participation in how the data is used. When public records are made available, the law should do so along with demanding restrictions on access and use. When the government wants to obtain personal data, the law should mandate that it demonstrate before a neutral judicial official that it has a factual basis that the search will reveal evidence of a particular person's criminal activity.

The law *can* protect privacy. This does not require that the law become involved in areas in which it currently has been absent—the law is *already* involved. The choices we make in shaping the law are of critical importance. The law is currently making choices, and it is attempting to balance privacy against countervailing interests such as efficiency, transparency, free speech, and safety. As I have demonstrated throughout this book, however, our understandings of privacy must be significantly rethought. Once privacy is reconceptualized, we can find ways to accommodate both privacy and its opposing interests. With an understanding of privacy appropriate for the problems we now face, the law will be better able to build privacy into our burgeoning information society.

Notes

Notes to Chapter 1

1. See generally Joel R. Reidenberg, "Resolving Conflicting International Data Privacy Rules in Cyberspace," 52 Stan. L. Rev. 1315 (2000).
2. Marcia Stepanek, "How the Data-Miners Want to Influence Your Vote," Business Week Online, Oct. 26, 2000, at http://www.businessweek.com/bwdaily/dnflash/oct2000/nf20001026_969.htm.
3. http://www.acxiom.com.
4. John Dewey, *Logic: The Theory of Inquiry* (1938), in 12 *Later Works* 1, 108 (Jo Ann Boydston ed., 1991)

Notes to Chapter 2

1. For example, in the eleventh century, William the Conqueror collected information about his subjects for taxation in the Doomsday Book. *See* Priscilla M. Regan, *Legislating Privacy: Technology, Social Values, and Public Policy* 69 (1995).
2. Robert Ellis Smith, *Ben Franklin's Web Site: Privacy and Curiosity from Plymouth Rock to the Internet* 12 (2000). Record-keeping by state and local governments became increasingly prevalent during the nineteenth century. Note, "The Right to Privacy in Nineteenth Century America," 94 Harv. L. Rev. 1892, 1906–07 (1981).
3. See Regan, *Legislating Privacy,* 46.
4. Id., 46.
5. See id., 47.
6. Martin Campbell-Kelly & William Aspray, *Computer: A History of the Information Machine* 21 (1996).
7. Simson Garfinkel, *Database Nation: The Death of Privacy in the 21st Century* 17–18 (2000).
8. Campbell-Kelly & Aspray, *Computer,* 26.

9. Id., 44–52; Garfinkel, *Database Nation,* 18.
10. See Campbell-Kelly & Aspray, *Computer,* 52.
11. Garfinkel, *Database Nation,* 19.
12. Arthur R. Miller, *The Assault on Privacy* 55 (1971).
13. Philippa Strum, *Privacy: The Debate in the United States since 1945,* at 46 (1998).
14. Id., 47; Charles J. Sykes, *The End of Privacy* 52 (1999). For a listing of the increasing authorized uses of SSNs, see Garfinkel, *Database Nation,* 33–34.
15. See, e.g., Vance Packard, *The Naked Society* (1964); Alan Westin, *Privacy and Freedom* (1967); Arthur Miller, *The Attack on Privacy* (1971); Kenneth L. Karst, "'The Files': Legal Controls over the Accuracy and Accessibility of Stored Personal Data," 31 L. & Contemp. Probs. 342 (1966); Symposium, "Computers, Data Banks, and Individual Privacy," 53 Minn. L. Rev. 211–45 (1968).
16. See Regan, *Legislating Privacy,* 82.
17. U.S. Department of Health, Education, and Welfare, Records, Computers, and the Rights of Citizens: Report of the Secretary's Advisory Comm. on Automated Personal Data Systems 29 (1973).
18. See Beth Givens, *The Privacy Rights Handbook* 116 (1997).
19. See Personal Responsibility and Work Opportunity Reconciliation Act of 1996, Pub. L. No. 104-193, 110 Stat. 2105 (1996).
20. Roland Marchand, "Customer Research as Public Relations: General Motors in the 1930s," in *Getting and Spending: European and American Consumer Societies in the Twentieth Century* 85, 86 (Susan Strasser, Charles McGovern, & Matthias Judt eds., 1998).
21. Id., 92–109.
22. Arthur M. Hughes, *The Complete Database Marketer* 51 (2d ed. 1996).
23. Id., 57.
24. See id., 267–68, 278–88.
25. See id., 156.
26. Cliff Allen, Deborah Kania, & Beth Yaeckel, *Internet World Guide to One-to-One Web Marketing* 3 (1998).
27. Erik Larson, *The Naked Consumer: How Our Private Lives Become Public Commodities* 41 (1992). The connection between the Census Bureau and marketers remains a very close one. Presidents have frequently appointed former marketers to serve as the head of the Census Bureau. Since the 1970s, the Census Bureau has been run by a former director of marketing at General Motors, an executive at a political polling firm, a research manager for Sears, and a past president of the American Marketing Association. Id., 44. Companies have made special deals with the Census Bureau to ask certain questions and to perform tabulations of census data in ways that will be useful to marketers. Indeed, the Census Bureau has been accused of being too influenced by the needs and wants of corporate America. Id., 44–46.
28. See Allen, Kania, & Yaeckel, *One-to-One,* 3; Hughes, *Database Marketer,* 295.
29. Hughes, *Database Marketer,* 298–99.
30. See id., 300.
31. Id., 5.
32. Michael McCarthy, "Direct Marketing Gets Cannes Do Spirit; 'It's About Time' Advertising Sector Recognized, Says a Founding Father," USA Today, June 17, 2002, at B4. See generally William J. Fenrich, Note, "Common Law Protection of Individ-

uals' Rights in Personal Information," 65 Fordham L. Rev. 951, 956 (1996); Ian Ayres & Matthew Funk, "Marketing Privacy," 20 Yale J. on Reg. 77 (2003).

33. Susan Headden, "The Junk Mail Deluge," U.S. News & World Rep., Dec. 8, 1997, at 40. Junk mail sent to each home averages about 34 pounds per year. Id. See also Givens, *Privacy Rights*, 16.

34. Headden, "Junk Mail."

35. Wendy Melillo, "Can You Hear Me Now? With the Help of the FTC, Consumers Prepare to Hit Back at Telemarketers," Adweek, Apr. 21, 2003, at 24.

36. Board of Governors of the Federal Reserve System, Report to the Congress Concerning the Availability of Consumer Identifying Information and Financial Fraud 7 (Mar. 1997).

37. See Hughes, *Database Marketer*, 365 (20 cents to 1 dollar per name); Headden, *Junk Mail* (3–20 cents per name).

38. Susan E. Gindin, "Lost and Found in Cyberspace: Informational Privacy in the Age of the Internet," 34 San Diego L. Rev. 1153, 1162 (1997). For more background about the companies that mine for personal data and the processes they use to do it, see Tal Z. Zarsky, "'Mine Your Own Business!': Making the Case for the Implications of the Data Mining of Personal Information in the Forum of Public Opinion," 5 Yale J. L. & Tech. 4 (2003).

39. Fenrich, "Common Law," 956.

40. Anne Wells Branscomb, *Who Owns Information? From Privacy to Public Access* 11 (1994).

41. Robert O'Harrow, Jr., "Behind the Instant Coupons, a Data-Crunching Powerhouse," Wash. Post, Dec. 31, 1998, at A20.

42. Leslie Wayne, "Voter Profiles Selling Briskly as Privacy Issues Are Raised," N.Y. Times, Sept. 9, 2000, at A1.

43. Marcia Stepanek, "How the Data-Miners Want to Influence Your Vote," Business Week Online, Oct. 26, 2000, at http://www.businessweek.com/bwdaily/dnflash/oct2000/nf20001026_969.htm.

44. Hughes, *Database Marketer*, 354.

45. See, e.g., Garfinkel, *Database Nation*, 137; Givens, *Privacy Rights*, 83.

46. *See* Peter P. Swire, "Financial Privacy and the Theory of High-Tech Government Surveillance," 77 Wash. U. L.Q. 461, 464–69 (1999).

47. Smith, *Franklin's Web Site*, 314.

48. Steven L. Nock, *The Costs of Privacy: Surveillance and Reputation in America* 3 (1993).

49. For example, Experian has information on 205 million Americans. See http://www.experian.com/corporate/factsheet.html.

50. See Givens, *Privacy Rights*, 83.

51. http://www.regulatorydatacorp.com/ourservices.html.

52. Tyler Hamilton, "Getting to Know You: Opening a Bank Account Gives Regulatory DataCorp a Window on Your Life," Toronto Star, June 18, 2003.

53. http://www.focus-usa-1.com/lists_az.html.

54. Id.

55. Id.

56. http://www.datacardcentral.com/dataindex-r.cfm

57. http://www.hippodirect.com/ListSubjectsN_1.asp?lSubject=37. For a terrific discussion of various databases such as the ones discussed in this section, see

Electronic Privacy Information Center, "Privacy and Consumer Profiling," http://www/epic.org/privacy/profiling/.

58. See Standards for Privacy of Individually Identifiable Health Information: Preamble, 65 Fed. Reg. 82461 (Dec. 28, 2000).

59. Jim Sterne, *What Makes People Click: Advertising on the Web* 179 (1997).

60. For more background on cookies, see A. Michael Froomkin, "The Death of Privacy?" 52 Stan. L. Rev. 1461, 1486–87 (2000). For a discussion of data collection about women on the Internet, see Ann Bartow, "Our Data, Ourselves: Privacy, Propertization, and Gender," 34 U.S.F. L. Rev. 633 (2000).

61. Heather Green, "Privacy Online: The FTC Must Act Now," Bus. Wk., Nov. 29, 1999, at 48.

62. See Robert O'Harrow, Jr., "Fearing a Plague of 'Web Bugs'; Invisible Fact-Gathering Code Raises Privacy Concerns," Wash. Post, Nov. 13, 1999, at E1.

63. See Leslie Walker, "Bugs That Go through Computer Screens," Wash. Post, Mar. 15, 2001, at E1; see also Richard M. Smith, "FAQ: Web Bugs," http://www.privacyfoundation.org/resources/webbug.asp.

64. James R. Hagerty & Dennis K. Berman, "Caught in the Net: New Battleground over Web Privacy: Ads That Snoop," Wall St. J., Aug. 27, 3003.

65. Julie E. Cohen, "DRM and Privacy," 18 Berkeley Tech. L.J. 575, 585 (2003); see also Julie E. Cohen, "The Right to Read Anonymously: A Closer Look at 'Copyright Management' in Cyberspace," 28 Conn. L. Rev. 981 (1996).

66. Chris Gulker, "The View from Silicon Valley," The Independent, May 21, 2003.

67. Mike Crissey, "In War with Bad Bots, A Secret Weapon: Humans," Miami Herald, Dec. 24, 2002.

68. Sterne, *People Click,* 255.

69. J.D. Lasica, "The Net NEVER Forgets," Salon, Nov. 25, 1998, at http://www.salon.com/21st/feature/1998/11/25feature.html.

Notes to Chapter 3

1. See, e.g., Florida v. Riley, 488 U.S. 445, 466 (1989) (Brennan, J., dissenting) (quoting passage from *1984* to criticize the majority's holding that viewing the defendant's greenhouse from a low-flying helicopter wasn't a search); United States v. Kyllo, 190 F.3d 1041, 1050 (9th Cir. 1999) *rev'd* 121 S. Ct. 2038 (Noonan, J., dissenting) ("The first reaction when one hears of the Agema 210 [thermal imaging device used to detect heat emissions from the home] is to think of George Orwell's *1984.*"); Lorenzana v. Superior Court, 511 P.2d 33, 41 (Cal. 1973) (en banc) ("Surely our state and federal Constitutions and the cases interpreting them foreclose a regression into an Orwellian society").

2. See, e.g., United States v. Falls, 34 F.3d 674, 680 (8th Cir. 1994) (video surveillance "results in a very serious, some say Orwellian, invasion of privacy."); United States v. Cuevas-Sanchez, 821 F.2d 248, 251 (5th Cir. 1987) (stating that "indiscriminate video surveillance raises the spectre of the Orwellian state."); United States v. Marion, 535 F.2d 697, 698 (2d Cir. 1976) (Congress enacted Title III of the Omnibus Crime Control and Safe Streets Act of 1968 to "guard against the realization of Orwellian fears."); People v. Teicher, 422 N.E.2d 506, 513 (N.Y. 1981) ("Certainly the Orwellian overtones involved in this activity demand that close scrutiny be given to any application for a warrant permitting video electronic surveillance").

3. See, e.g., Capua v. City of Plainfield, 643 F. Supp. 1507, 1511 (D.N.J. 1986) (stating that drug testing is "George Orwell's 'Big Brother' Society come to life"); Edward M. Chen, Pauline T. Kim, & John M. True, "Common Law Privacy: A Limit on an Employer's Power to Test for Drugs," 12 Geo. Mason L. Rev. 651, 674 (1990) (characterizing drug testing as "George Orwell's 'Big Brother' Society come to life").

4. Steven L. Winter, *A Clearing in the Forest: Law, Life, and Mind* 65 (2001).

5. George Lakoff & Mark Johnson, *Metaphors We Live By* 145–46 (1980).

6. Id., 5.

7. J.M. Balkin, *Cultural Software: A Theory of Ideology* 247, 248 (1998).

8. Winter, *Clearing,* 65 (metaphor is a cognitive "process by which the mind projects a conceptual mapping from one knowledge domain to another").

9. Balkin, *Software,* 9, 141.

10. See, e.g., A. Michael Froomkin, "The Metaphor Is the Key: Cryptography, the Clipper Chip, and the Constitution," 143 U. Pa. L. Rev. 709, 718 (1995) (Internet law "depends critically on the legal metaphors used to understand the Internet"); Orin S. Kerr, "The Problem of Perspective in Internet Law," 91 Geo. L.J. 386–89 (2003).

11. Richard A. Posner, "Orwell versus Huxley: Economics, Technology, Privacy, and Satire," 24 Philosophy and Literature 1, 31 (2000).

12. See, e.g., William Branigin, "Employment Database Proposal Raises Cries of 'Big Brother,'" Wash. Post, Oct. 3, 1995, at A17; James Gleick, "Big Brother Is Us: Our Privacy Is Disappearing, But Not by Force. We're Selling It, Even Giving It Away," N.Y. Times Magazine, Sept. 29, 1996, at 130; Priscilla M. Regan, *Legislating Privacy* 93 (1995) (a House committee held hearings called "1984 and the National Security State" to examine the growing computerization of records); 140 Cong. Rec. H9797, H9810 (statement of Rep. Kennedy) ("the promise of the information highway has given way to an Orwellian nightmare of erroneous and unknowingly disseminated credit reports"); J. Roderick MacArthur Found. v. FBI, 102 F.3d 600, 608 (D.C. Cir. 1996) (Tatel, J., dissenting) ("Congress passed the Privacy Act to give individuals some defenses against governmental tendencies towards secrecy and 'Big Brother' surveillance."); McVeigh v. Cohen, 983 F. Supp. 215, 220 (D.D.C. 1998) ("In these days of 'big brother,' where through technology and otherwise the privacy interests of individuals from all walks of life are being ignored or marginalized, it is imperative that statutes explicitly protecting these rights be strictly observed").

13. George Orwell, *1984,* at 3 (1949).

14. Id., 4.

15. Id., 20.

16. Dennis H. Wrong, *Power: Its Forms, Bases and Uses* 115 (1979).

17. David Lyon, *The Electronic Eye: The Rise of the Surveillance Society* 62 (1994).

18. Michel Foucault, *Discipline and Punish: The Birth of the Prison* 200 (Alan Sheridan trans., Pantheon Books ed. 1977).

19. Id., 201.

20. Sampson v. Murray, 415 U.S. 61, 96 n.2 (1974) (Douglas, J., dissenting) (quoting Arthur Miller, "Computers, Data Banks and Individual Privacy: An Overview," 4 Colum. Hum. Rts. L. Rev. 1, 2 [1972]).

21. White v. California, 95 Cal. Rptr. 175, 181 (Cal. Ct. App. 1971) (1971) (Friedman, J., concurring in part and dissenting in part).

22. See, e.g., Charles N. Faerber, "Book versus Byte: The Prospects and Desirability of a Paperless Society," 17 J. Marshall J. Computer & Info. L. 797, 798 (1999) ("Many are terrified of an Orwellian linkage of databases."); Bryan S. Schultz,

"Electronic Money, Internet Commerce, and the Right to Financial Privacy: A Call for New Federal Guidelines," 67 U. Cin. L. Rev. 779, 797 (1999) ("As technology propels America toward a cashless marketplace . . . society inches closer to fulfilling George Orwell's startling vision."); Alan F. Westin, "Privacy in the Workplace: How Well Does American Law Reflect American Values," 72 Chi.-Kent L. Rev. 271, 273 (1996) (stating that Americans would view the idea of government data protection boards to regulate private sector databases as "calling on 'Big Brother' to protect citizens from 'Big Brother.'"); Wendy Wuchek, "Conspiracy Theory: Big Brother Enters the Brave New World of Health Care Reform," 3 DePaul J. Health Care L. 293, 303 (2000).

23. William G. Staples, *The Culture of Surveillance: Discipline and Social Control in the United States* 129–34 (1997).

24. Abbe Mowshowitz, "Social Control and the Network Marketplace," in *Computers, Surveillance, and Privacy* 79, 95–96 (David Lyon & Elia Zureik eds., 1996).

25. See, e.g., Dorothy Glancy, "At the Intersection of Visible and Invisible Worlds: United States Privacy Law and the Internet," 16 Santa Clara Computer & High Tech. L.J. 357, 377 (2000) (describing privacy problem created by the private sector as the "little brother" problem); Marsha Morrow McLauglin & Suzanne Vaupel, "Constitutional Right of Privacy and Investigative Consumer Reports: Little Brother Is Watching You," 2 Hastings Const. L.Q. 773 (1975); Hon. Ben F. Overton & Katherine E. Giddings, "The Right of Privacy in Florida in the Age of Technology and the Twenty-First Century: A Need for Protection from Private and Commercial Intrusion," 25 Fla. St. U. L. Rev. 25, 27 (1997) ("In his book, 1984, we were warned by George Orwell to watch out for 'Big Brother.' Today, we are cautioned to look out for 'little brother' and 'little sister.'"); Thomas L. Friedman, "Foreign Affairs: Little Brother," N.Y. Times, Sept. 26, 1999; Wendy R. Leibowitz, "Personal Privacy and High Tech: Little Brothers Are Watching You," Nat'l L.J., Apr. 7, 1997, at B16.

26. David Lyon, *The Electronic Eye: The Rise of the Surveillance Society* 78 (1994).

27. Katrin Schatz Byford, "Privacy in Cyberspace: Constructing a Model of Privacy for the Electronic Communications Environment," 24 Rutgers Computer & Tech. L.J. 1, 50 (1998).

28. Reg Whitaker, *The End of Privacy: How Total Surveillance Is Becoming a Reality* 160–75 (1999).

29. Paul M. Schwartz, "Privacy and Democracy in Cyberspace," 52 Vand. L. Rev. 1609, 1657 n.294 (1999).

30. David H. Flaherty, *Protecting Privacy in Surveillance Societies* 9 (1989).

31. Oscar H. Gandy, Jr., *The Panoptic Sort: A Political Economy of Personal Information* 10 (1993).

32. Jerry Kang, "Information Privacy in Cyberspace Transactions," 50 Stan. L. Rev. 1193, 1261 (1998).

33. Roger Clarke, "Information Technology and Dataveillance," 3 (1987), at http://www.anu.edu.au/people/Roger.Clarke/DV/CACM88.html.

34. Colin J. Bennet, "The Public Surveillance of Personal Data: A Cross-National Analysis," in *Computers, Surveillance, and Privacy* 237 (David Lyon & Elia Zureik eds., 1996).

35. Kang, "Information Privacy," 1260.

36. Paul M. Schwartz, "Privacy and Participation: Personal Information and Public Sector Regulation in the United States," 80 Iowa L. Rev. 553, 560 (1995).

37. Foucault, *Discipline and Punish*, 217.

38. In an early paper describing the problem of computer databases, Paul Schwartz aptly quoted from Kafka's *The Trial*. See Paul Schwartz, "Data Processing and Government Administration: The Failure of the American Legal Response to the Computer," 43 Hastings L.J. 1321 (1992).

39. Kafka, *The Trial*, 16–17.

40. Id., 146.

41. Id., 199.

42. Id., 42–43.

43. Id., 147–48, 157.

44. See, e.g., Max Weber, *From Max Weber: Essays in Sociology* 196 (H. H. Gerth & C. Wright Mills, trans. & eds., 1946); see also Max Weber, *The Theory of Social and Economic Organization* 329–41 (A.M. Henderson & Talcott Parsons trans., 1947).

45. Max Weber, *Economy and Society* 957–58 (Guenther Roth & Claus Wittich eds., 1978).

46. Id. at 223.

47. Schwartz, "Data Processing," 1325.

48. Weber, *From Max Weber*, 216.

49. Id., 1348, 1365.

50. Weber, "Economy and Society," 992.

51. See Aldous Huxley, *Brave New World* 20–32 (1932). For Huxley's own commentary on his novel, see Aldous Huxley, *Brave New World Revisited* (1958). For an insightful comparison between Huxley and Orwell, see Neil Postman, *Amusing Ourselves to Death* vii (1986).

52. John Gilliom, *Overseers of the Poor: Surveillance, Resistance, and the Limits of Privacy* (2001).

53. Friedrich Dürrenmatt, *The Assignment* 109 (Joel Agee trans., 1989).

54. John Schwartz, "DoubleClick Takes It on the Chin; New Privacy Lawsuit Looms; Stock Price Drops," Wash. Post, Feb. 18, 2000, at E1 (quoting Dana Sherman).

55. Helen Nissenbaum, "Protecting Privacy in the Information Age: The Problem of Privacy in Public," 17 Law & Phil. 559 (1998); see also Anita L. Allen, *Uneasy Access: Privacy for Women in a Free Society* 123–25 (1998).

56. Julie E. Cohen, "Examined Lives: Informational Privacy and the Subject as Object," 52 Stan. L. Rev. 1373, 1398 (2000).

57. Stan Karas, "Privacy, Identity, Databases," 52 Am. U. L. Rev. 393, 426–27 (2002).

58. See id., 435.

59. See id., 438–39.

60. Henry James, *Portrait of a Lady* 253 (1882) (Penguin ed. 1984).

61. As legal scholar Arthur Miller observes, an "individual who is asked to provide a simple item of information for what he believes to be a single purpose may omit explanatory details that become crucial when his file is surveyed for unrelated purposes." Miller, *Assault on Privacy*, 34.

62. W.H. Auden's poem, "The Unknown Citizen" aptly describes this phenomenon. A person's life is chronicled through the various records kept about him; we learn a lot about the person, but at the end of the poem, Auden demonstrates that the records reveal little about his happiness or quality of life. W.H. Auden, "The Unknown Citizen," in *Collected Poems* 201 (Edward Mendelson ed., 1976).

63. Cohen, "Information Privacy," 1405.

64. *Brazil* (Universal Pictures 1985).

65. Eugene L. Meyer, "Md. Woman Caught in Wrong Net; Data Errors Link Her to Probes, Cost 3 Jobs," Wash. Post, Dec. 15, 1997, at C1.

66. Hire Check, "Welcome to Hirecheck," at http://www.hirecheck.com/ flashintro/index.html (last viewed July 1, 2002).

67. Hire Check, "Background Screening," at http://www.hirecheck.com/ProductsAndServices/backgroundScreening.html (last viewed July 1, 2002).

68. Kenneth L. Karst, "'The Files': Legal Controls over the Accuracy and Accessibility of Stored Personal Data," 31 L. & Contemp. Probs. 342, 361 (1966).

69. Jeffrey Rosen, *The Unwanted Gaze: The Destruction of Privacy in America* 8 (2000).

70. See, e.g., Richard A. Posner, *Cardozo: A Study in Reputation* 74–91 (1990) (measuring Benjamin Cardozo's reputation by a Lexis search counting mentions of his name).

71. See, e.g., Fred R. Shapiro, "The Most-Cited Law Review Articles Revised," 71 Chi-Kent L. Rev. 751, 751 (1996) (listing the "one hundred most-cited legal articles of all time"). For a humorous critique of this enterprise, see J.M. Balkin & Sanford Levinson, "How to Win Cites and Influence People," 71 Chi-Kent L. Rev. 843 (1996).

72. See, e.g., Robert M. Jarvis & Phyllis G. Coleman, "Ranking Law Reviews: An Empirical Analysis Based on Author Prominence," 39 Ariz. L. Rev. 15 (1997).

73. See, e.g., Jane B. Baron, "Law, Literature, and the Problems of Interdisciplinarity," 108 Yale L.J. 1059, 1061 n.9 (1999) (comparing Westlaw search of law reviews for terms "law and economics" and "law and literature" to measure comparative influence of each of these academic movements).

74. See Oscar H. Gandy, Jr., "Exploring Identity and Identification in Cyberspace," 14 Notre Dame J.L. Ethics & Pub. Pol'y 1085, 1100 (2000) (arguing that profiles are "inherently conservative" because such profiles "reinforce assessments and decisions made in the past").

75. H. Jeff Smith, *Managing Privacy: Information Technology and Corporate America* 121 (1994).

76. *See* Larry Selden & Geoffrey Colvin, *Angel Customers and Demon Customers* (2003).

77. *See* Bruce Mohl, "Facing Their Demons," Boston Globe, July 27, 2003, at F1.

78. Smith, *Managing Privacy,* 123.

79. Chris Jay Hoofnagle, Letter to Senator Richard Shelby Regarding Senate Banking Committee Hearing on the Accuracy of Credit Report Information and the Fair Credit Reporting Act (July 7, 2003).

80. Robert O'Harrow, Jr., "Survey Says: You're Not Anonymous," Wash. Post, June 9, 1999, at E1.

81. See, e.g., Givens, *Privacy Rights,* 23; Hughes, *Database Marketer,* 318.

82. See Erik Larson, *The Naked Consumer: How Our Private Lives Become Public Commodities* 134–35 (1992).

83. Robert O'Harrow, Jr., "Bargains at a Price: Shoppers' Privacy; Cards Let Supermarkets Collect Data," Wash. Post, Dec. 31, 1998, at A1.

84. Robert O'Harrow, Jr., "Survey Asks Readers to Get Personal, and 400,000 Do," Wash. Post, Dec. 16, 1998, at C18.

85. Smith, *Managing Privacy,* 55, 67, 93.

86. See In re Geocities, 1999 FTC LEXIS 17 (Feb. 5, 1999).

87. In re Liberty Financial Companies, No. 9823522, 1999 FTC LEXIS 99 (May 6, 1999).

88. Whitaker, *End of Privacy*, 132–33; Nina Bernstein, "Lives on File: The Erosion of Privacy—A Special Report," N.Y. Times, June 12, 1997, at A1.

89. Givens, *Privacy Rights*, 176.

90. 983 F. Supp. 215 (D.D.C. 1998).

91. 10 U.S.C. § 654.

92. 816 A.2d 1001 (N.H. 2003).

93. Barb Albert, "Patients' Medical Records Inadvertently Posted on Net," Indianapolis Star, Mar. 30, 1999, at A1.

94. Charles J. Sykes, *The End of Privacy: Personal Rights in the Surveillance Society* 100 (1999).

95. Robert O'Harrow, Jr., "Hacker Accesses Patient Records," Wash. Post, Dec. 9, 2000, at E1.

96. *See* FTC v. Eli Lilly, No. 012-3214, available at http://www.ftc.gov/opa/2002/01/elililly.com.

97. *See* Charles Pillar, "Web Mishap: Kids' Psychological Files Posted," L.A. Times, Nov. 7, 2001.

98. Chris Jay Hoofnagle, Testimony before the Subcomm. on Social Security of the Comm. on Ways and Means, U.S. House of Representatives, Hearing on Use and Misuse of the Social Security Number (July 10, 2003).

99. Id.

Notes to Chapter 4

1. Ken Gormley, "One Hundred Years of Privacy," 1992 Wis. L. Rev. 1335, 1357 (1992).

2. For more background about Warren and Brandeis, see Philippa Strum, *Brandeis: Beyond Progressivism* (1993); Lewis J. Paper, *Brandeis* (1983); Daniel J. Solove & Marc Rotenberg, *Information Privacy Law* 3–5 (2003); Dorothy Glancy, "The Invention of the Right to Privacy," 21 Ariz. L. Rev. 1, 25–27 (1979).

3. Samuel D. Warren & Louis D. Brandeis, "The Right to Privacy," 4 Harv. L. Rev. 193 (1890).

4. According to legal philosopher Roscoe Pound, the article did "nothing less than add a chapter to our law." Alpheus Mason, *Brandeis: A Free Man's Life* 70 (1946). First Amendment scholar Harry Kalven, Jr. called it the "most influential law review article of all." Harry Kalven, Jr., "Privacy in Tort Law—Were Warren and Brandeis Wrong?" 31 L. & Contemp. Probs. 326, 327 (1966).

5. William L. Prosser, "Privacy," in *Philosophical Dimensions of Privacy: An Anthology* 104, 104 (Ferdinand David Schoeman ed., 1984).

6. Warren & Brandeis, "Right to Privacy," 195–96.

7. Id., 195.

8. Id., 198, 205.

9. See, e.g., Irwin R. Kramer, "The Birth of Privacy Law: A Century since Warren and Brandeis," 39 Cath. U. L. Rev. 703, 704 (1990).

10. Prosser, "Privacy," 107.

11. See Restatement (Second) of Torts §§ 652B, 652C, 652D, 652E (1976) (discussing intrusion, appropriation, publicity of private facts, and false light).

12. See Lake v. Wal-Mart Stores, Inc., 582 N.W.2d 231, 235 (Minn. 1998) (recognizing a common law tort action for invasion of privacy and noting that Minnesota had remained one of the few hold-outs).

13. Restatement (Second) of Torts § 652B (1976).

14. Seaphus v. Lilly, 691 F. Supp. 127, 132 (N.D. Ill. 1988) (unlisted number); Shibley v. Time, Inc., 341 N.E.2d 337, 339 (Ohio Ct. App. 1975) (subscription list); Tureen v. Equifax, Inc., 571 F.2d 411, 416 (8th Cir. 1978) (insurance history).

15. Restatement (Second) of Torts § 652D (1976).

16. Daily Times Democrat v. Graham, 162 So.2d 474 (Ala. 1964) (dress); Barber v. Time, Inc., 159 S.W.2d 291 (Mo. 1942) (unusual disease); Brents v. Morgan, 299 S.W. 967 (Ky. 1927) (debt).

17. Restatement (Second) of Torts § 652E (1976).

18. Restatement (Second) of Torts § 652C (1976).

19. Restatement (Second) of Torts § 652C cmt. a (1976). According to legal scholar Jonathan Kahn, the "early association of appropriation claims with such intangible, non-commensurable attributes of the self as dignity and the integrity of one's persona seems to have been lost, or at least misplaced, as property-based conceptions of the legal status of identity have come to the fore." Jonathan Kahn, "Bringing Dignity Back to Light: Publicity Rights and the Eclipse of the Tort of Appropriation of Identity," 17 Cardozo Arts & Ent. L.J. 213, 223 (1999).

20. Because their identities are lucrative for marketing purposes, celebrities often sue under this tort. For an interesting illustration, see *Carson v. Here's Johnny Portable Toilets, Inc.*, 698 F.2d 831 (6th Cir. 1983), where Johnny Carson successfully sued a portable toilet company that used the name "Here's Johnny Portable Toilets."

21. 652 N.E.2d 1351, 1356 (Ill. App. Ct. 1995).

22. 341 N.E.2d 337 (Ohio Ct. App. 1975).

23. As legal scholar Bruce Sanford contends: "A stake-out by a group of unrelated reporters should be viewed as no more than the sum of its separate parts." Bruce W. Sanford, *Libel and Privacy* § 11.2, at 541 (2d ed. 1991).

24. See, e.g., Alaska Const. art. I, § 22; Cal. Const. art. I, § 1; Fla. Const. art. I, § 23; Ariz. Const. art. II, § 8; Mont. Const. art. II, § 10; Haw. Const. art. I, § 6; Ill. Const. art. I, §§ 6, 12; La. Const. art. I, § 5; S.C. Const. art. I, § 10; Wash. Const. art. I, § 7.

25. See NAACP v. Alabama, 357 U.S. 449 (1958); Shelton v. Tucker, 364 U.S. 479 (1960).

26. NAACP v. Alabama, 357 U.S. 449, 463 (1958); Bates v. City of Little Rock, 361 U.S. 516, 524 (1960).

27. See McIntyre v. Ohio Election Comm'n, 514 U.S. 334 (1995); Watchtower Bible & Tract Society v. Village of Stratton, 122 S. Ct. 2080 (2002).

28. See Julie E. Cohen, "The Right to Read Anonymously: A Closer Look at 'Copyright Management' in Cyberspace," 28 Conn. L. Rev. 981, 1020 (1996) (arguing that when federal law punishes people for modifying copyright management technology to preserve their anonymity, this may constitute state action).

29. U.S. Const. Amend. IV.

30. Schmerber v. California, 384 U.S. 757, 767 (1966).

31. U.S. Const. Amend. V.

32. 116 U.S. 616 (1886).

33. Id., 630.

34. William J. Stuntz, "Privacy's Problem and the Law of Criminal Procedure," 93 Mich. L. Rev. 1016, 1050 (1995).

35. See Warden v. Hayden, 387 U.S. 294 (1967) (overturning the mere evidence rule in Boyd); Shapiro v. United States, 355 U.S. 1 (1948) (holding that the Fifth Amendment does not prohibit the government from requiring that a person produce her records).

36. 442 U.S. 735 (1979).

37. Id., 743.

38. 425 U.S. 435, 442–43 (1976).

39. 318 U.S. 479 (1965).

40. 410 U.S. 113 (1973).

41. 429 U.S. 589, 599–600 (1977).

42. Id., 601–02.

43. Id., 603.

44. 72 F.3d 1133 (3d Cir. 1995).

45. Id., 1139–40.

46. Directive of the European Parliament and the Council of Europe on the Protection of Individuals with Regard to the Processing of Personal Data and on the Free Movement of Such Data (1996). For an analysis of the Directive, see Peter P. Swire & Robert E. Litan, *None of Your Business: World Data Flows, Electronic Commerce, and the European Privacy Directive* (1998).

47. 15 U.S.C. § 1681.

48. Robert Ellis Smith, *Ben Franklin's Web Site: Privacy and Curiosity from Plymouth Rock to the Internet* 23 (2000); Priscilla M. Regan, *Legislating Privacy: Technology, Social Values, and Public Policy* 101 (1995).

49. See Susan E. Gindin, "Lost and Found in Cyberspace: Informational Privacy in the Age of the Internet," 34 San Diego L. Rev. 1153, 1157 (1997).

50. Pub. L. No. 93-579, 88 Stat. 1896 (codified at 5 U.S.C. § 552a).

51. Pub. L. No. 93-380, 88 Stat. 484 (codified at 20 U.S.C. § 1232g).

52. 47 U.S.C. § 551.

53. 18 U.S.C. §§ 2510–2522; 2701–10.

54. 154 F. Supp.2d 497 (S.D.N.Y. 2001).

55. Pub. L. No. 100-618, 102 Stat. 3195 (codified at 18 U.S.C. §§ 2710-11).

56. §§ 2710(b)(1), (c)(1).

57. Pub. L. No. 102-243, 105 Stat. 2394 (codified at 47 U.S.C. § 227).

58. See 18 U.S.C. § 2721(b)(12).

59. Pub. L. No. 104-191, 110 Stat. 1936 (1996).

60. 45 C.F.R. § 164.508(a).

61. 15 U.S.C. §§ 6501–06.

62. § 6502(b)(1)(A).

63. Anita L. Allen, "Minor Distractions: Children, Privacy and E-Commerce," 38 Houston L. Rev. 751, 769, 775 (2001).

64. Pub. L. No. 106-102, 113 Stat. 1338 (codified at 15 U.S.C. §§ 6801–6809).

65. 15 U.S.C. § 6802(a), (b).

66. See Smith, *Franklin's Web Site*, at 327.

67. Edward J. Janger & Paul M. Schwartz, "The Gramm-Leach-Bliley Act, Information Privacy, and the Limits of Default Rules," 86 Minn. L. Rev. 1219, 1232 (2002).

68. Id., 1241. But see Peter P. Swire, "The Surprising Virtues of the New Financial Privacy Law," 86 Minn. L. Rev. 1263, 1315–16 (2002) (arguing that the GLB Act works quite well and forces financial institutions to take stock of their privacy practices).

69. As Paul Schwartz observes, "personal information in the private sector is often unaccompanied by the presence of basic legal protections. Yet, private enterprises now control more powerful resources of information technology than ever before." Paul M. Schwartz, "Privacy and Democracy in Cyberspace," 52 Vand. L. Rev. 1609, 1633 (1999).

70. See Joel Reidenberg, "Setting Standards for Fair Information Practice in the U.S. Private Sector," 80 Iowa L. Rev. 497 (1995).

71. Joel R. Reidenberg, "Privacy in the Information Economy: A Fortress or Frontier for Individual Rights?" 44 Fed. Comm. L.J. 195 (1992).

72. Colin J. Bennett, "Convergence Revisited: Toward a Global Policy for the Protection of Personal Data?" in *Technology and Privacy: The New Landscape* 99, 113 (Philip E. Agre & Marc Rotenberg eds., 1997).

73. 15 U.S.C. § 45.

74. See Daniel J. Solove & Marc Rotenberg, *Information Privacy Law* 541–53 (2003). Legal scholar Steven Hetcher notes that the FTC has influenced many websites to create privacy policies. Steven Hetcher, "The FTC as Internet Privacy Norm Entrepreneur," 53 Vand. L. Rev. 2041 (2000); see also Steven Hetcher, "Changing the Social Meaning of Privacy in Cyberspace," 15 Harv. J. L. & Tech. 149 (2001); Steven A. Hetcher, "Norm Proselytizers Create a Privacy Entitlement in Cyberspace," 16 Berkeley Tech. L.J. 877 (2001).

75. For a discussion of FTC jurisprudence over privacy policies, see Jeff Sovern, "Protecting Privacy with Deceptive Trade Practices Legislation," 69 Fordham L. Rev. 1305 (2001).

76. See, e.g., In re Liberty Financial Companies, No. 9823522, 1999 FTC LEXIS 99 (May 6, 1999) (operator of website falsely promised that personal data collected from children and teens would be kept anonymous); FTC v. ReverseAuction.com, Inc., No. 99-CV-32 (D.D.C. Jan. 6, 2000) (company improperly obtained personal information from eBay and used it to spam eBay customers); In re GeoCities, 1999 FTC LEXIS 17 (Feb. 5, 1999) (website falsely promised that it never provided information to others without customer permission).

77. *See In the Matter of Microsoft Corp.*, No. 012-3240.

78. Schwartz, "Privacy and Democracy," 1638. The relatively recent GLB Act provides a rare exception, for it requires financial institutions to develop "safeguards for personal information." *See* 15 U.S.C. §§ 6801(b); 6805(b)(2). This is a rather general mandate, and the agency regulations do not provide much greater specificity. Ultimately, the strength of the GLB Act's security protections will depend upon how they are enforced.

79. Schwartz, "Privacy and Democracy," 1639.

80. David Brin, *The Transparent Society* 8–9 (1998).

81. Id., 23.

82. Id., 23–24.

Notes to Chapter 5

1. Alan Westin, *Privacy and Freedom* 7 (1967).

2. See, e.g., Arthur Miller, *The Assault on Privacy* 25 (1971) ("[T]he basic attribute of an effective right to privacy is the individual's ability to control the circulation of information relating to him"). Randall P. Bezanson, "The Right to Privacy Revisited: Privacy, News, and Social Change, 1810–1990," 80 Calif. L. Rev. 1133, 1135 (1992)

("I will advance a concept of privacy based on the individual's control of information . . .").

3. See Jessica Litman, "Information Privacy/Information Property," 52 Stan. L. Rev. 1283, 1287 (2000) ("The proposal that has been generating the most buzz, recently, is the idea that privacy can be cast as a property right."); Pamela Samuelson, "Privacy as Intellectual Property," 52 Stan. L. Rev. 1125, 1132 (2000) ("In recent years, a number of economists and legal commentators have argued that the law ought now to grant individuals property rights in their personal data").

4. See Litman, "Information Privacy," 1295 ("The raison d'etre of property is alienability").

5. Westin, *Privacy and Freedom*, 324.

6. See McCormick v. England, 494 S.E.2d 431 (S.C. Ct. App. 1997); Simonsen v. Swenson, 177 N.W. 831 (Neb. 1920).

7. See Peterson v. Idaho First National Bank, 367 P.2d 284 (Idaho 1961); Milohnich v. First National Bank, 224 So.2d 759 (Fla. Dist. Ct. App. 1969). For a discussion of the breach of confidence tort, see Note, "Breach of Confidence: An Emerging Tort," 82 Colum. L. Rev. 1426 (1982).

8. Ian Ayres & Robert Gertner, "Filling Gaps in Incomplete Contracts: An Economic Theory of Default Rules," 99 Yale L.J. 87, 87 (1989).

9. See Scott Shorr, "Personal Information Contracts: How to Protect Privacy without Violating the First Amendment," 80 Cornell L. Rev. 1756, 1775 (1995); Steven A. Bibas, "A Contractual Approach to Data Privacy," 17 Harv. J.L. & Pub. Pol'y 591, 592 (1994); Kalinda Basho, "The Licensing of Our Personal Information: Is It a Solution to Internet Privacy?" 88 Cal. L. Rev. 1507, 1509 (2000); Patricia Mell, "Seeking Shade in a Land of Perpetual Sunlight: Privacy as Property in the Electronic Wilderness," 11 Berkeley Tech. L.J. 1, 79 (1996).

10. See, e.g., John Hagel III & Marc Singer, *Net Worth: Shaping Markets When Consumers Make the Rules* 19–20 (1999) (advocating for an "infomediary" between consumers and vendors who would broker information to companies in exchange for money and goods to the consumer); Paul Farhi, "Me Inc.: Getting the Goods on Consumers," Wash. Post, Feb. 14, 1999, at H1.

11. Richard A. Posner, *The Economics of Justice*, 233–35 (1981).

12. Richard A. Posner, "The Right of Privacy," 12 Ga. L. Rev. 393, 398 (1978).

13. Richard S. Murphy, "Property Rights in Personal Information: An Economic Defense of Privacy," 84 Geo. L.J. 2381, 2416 (1996).

14. Id., 2416, 2398.

15. Jerry Kang, "Information Privacy in Cyberspace Transactions," 50 Stan. L. Rev. 1193, 1260, 1256–57, 1268, 1266 (1998). To be fair, Kang recognizes that in some limited circumstances (emergency room data), inalienability rules are preferable.

16. Lawrence Lessig, *Code and Other Laws of Cyberspace* 160–61 (1999).

17. See Privacy in Commercial World, 106th Cong. (2001) (statement of Paul H. Rubin), at http://www.house.gov/commerce/hearings/0301200143/Rubin66 .htm.; Direct Marketing Ass'n, Inc., Consumer Privacy Comments concerning the Direct Marketing Association before the Federal Trade Commission (July 16, 1997).

18. For a justification of this practice, see Justin Matlick, "Don't Restrain Trade in Information," Wall St. J., Dec. 2, 1998, at A22.

19. Susan E. Gindin, "Lost and Found in Cyberspace: Informational Privacy in the Age of the Internet," 34 San Diego L. Rev. 1153, 1160 (1997).

20. Erik Larson, *The Naked Consumer: How Our Private Lives Become Public Commodities* 9–10 (1992).

21. See Laura J. Gurak, *Persuasion and Privacy in Cyberspace: The Online Protests over Lotus Marketplace and the Clipper Chip* (1997).

22. Charles J. Sykes, *The End of Privacy* 31–32 (1999).

23. Fred H. Cate, *Privacy in Perspective* 10–12 (2001).

24. Id., 26, 22–23; see also Fred H. Cate, *Privacy in the Information Age* 103–08 (1997).

25. Eric Goldman, "The Privacy Hoax," Forbes (Oct. 14, 2002), at http://eric_goldman.tripod.com/articles/privacyhoax.htm.

26. Samuel D. Warren & Louis D. Brandeis, "The Right to Privacy," 4 Harv. L. Rev. 193, 211 (1890).

27. Lawrence O. Gostin, "Health Information Privacy," 80 Cornell L. Rev. 451 (1995).

28. Oscar H. Gandy, Jr., *The Panoptic Sort: A Political Economy of Personal Information* 9 (1993). See also Julie E. Cohen, "Examined Lives: Informational Privacy and the Subject as Object," 52 Stan. L. Rev. 1373, 1396–99 (2000); Paul M. Schwartz, "Internet Privacy and the State," 32 Conn. L. Rev. 815, 820–27 (2000); Anita L. Allen, "Privacy-as-Data-Control: Conceptual, Practical, and Moral Limits of the Paradigm," 32 Conn. L. Rev. 861 (2000).

29. Schwartz, "Internet Privacy," 822–23.

30. Paul M. Schwartz, "Privacy and the Economics of Personal Health Care Information," 76 Tex. L. Rev. 1, 50–51 (1997).

31. Jeff Sovern, "Opting In, Opting Out, or No Options at All: The Fight for Control of Personal Information," 74 Wash. L. Rev. 1033, 1085–87 (1999); Edward Janger & Paul M. Schwartz, "The Gramm-Leach-Bliley Act, Information Privacy, and the Limits of Default Rules," 86 Minn. L. Rev. 1219, 1230–31 (2002); John Schwartz, "Privacy Policy Notices Are Called Too Common and Too Confusing," N.Y. Times, May 7, 2001.

32. Yahoo!, Privacy Policy, available at http://docs.yahoo.com/info/privacy/us.

33. Doug Brown, "AOL to Users: Opt Out Again," Yahoo! News at http://dailynews.yahoo.com/h/zd/19991129/tc/1991129031.html.

34. See Stephanie Stoughton, "FTC Sues Toysmart.com to Halt Data Sale, Bankrupt E Retailer Made Privacy Vow to Customers," Boston Globe, July 11, 2000, at E2. For an extensive discussion of privacy and dot-com bankruptcies, see Edward J. Janger, "Muddy Property: Generating and Protecting Information Privacy Norms in Bankruptcy," 44 Wm. & Mary L. Rev. 1801 (2003).

35. See Susan Stellin, "Dot-Com Liquidations Put Consumer Data in Limbo," N.Y. Times, Dec. 4, 2000, at C4.

36. William J. Fenrich, Note, "Common Law Protection of Individuals' Rights in Personal Information," 65 Fordham L. Rev. 951, 962–63 (1996).

37. See Beth Givens, *The Privacy Rights Handbook* 19 (1997).

38. Sovern, "Opting In," 1082.

39. See id., 1101.

40. See Peter P. Swire, "Markets, Self-Regulation, and Government Enforcement in the Protection of Personal Information," at http://www.osu.edu/units/law/swire1/psntia6.htm, at 10 (containing the draft submitted to NTIA on Dec. 12, 1996).

41. Joel R. Reidenberg, "Privacy in the Information Economy: A Fortress or Frontier for Individual Rights?" 44 Fed. Comm. L.J. 195, 212 n.87 (1992).

42. Cohen, "Information Privacy," 1396.

43. Paul M. Schwartz, "Privacy and Democracy in Cyberspace," 52 Vand. L. Rev. 1609, 1661–64 (1999).

44. Id., 1662.

45. Russell Korobkin, "Inertia and Preference in Contract Negotiation: The Psychological Power of Default Rules and Form Terms," 51 Vand. L. Rev. 1583 (1998) (noting that most people accept default terms rather than bargain).

46. Pamela Samuelson, "Privacy as Intellectual Property," 52 Stan. L. Rev. 1125, 1132 (2000).

47. Katrin Schatz Byford, "Privacy in Cyberspace: Constructing a Model of Privacy for the Electronic Communications Environment," 24 Rutgers Computer & Tech. L.J. 1, 56 (1998).

48. Cohen, "Information Privacy," 1398.

49. Of course, not all attempts to translate privacy into property rights will threaten the protection of privacy. For an example of a helpful use of property rights to protect privacy, see Janger, "Muddy Property."

50. 652 N.E.2d 1351, 1354, 1356 (Ill. App. Ct. 1995).

51. Cohen, "Information Privacy," 1391.

52. Paul M. Schwartz & Joel R. Reidenberg, *Data Privacy Law* 309 (1996).

53. H. Jeff Smith, *Managing Privacy: Information Technology and Corporate America* 80 (1994).

54. See Richard Hunter, *World without Secrets: Business, Crime, and Privacy in the Age of Ubiquitous Computing* 7 (2002); "Amazon Draws Fire for DVD-Pricing Test, Privacy-Policy Change," Wall St. J., Sept. 14, 2000 at B4.

Notes to Chapter 6

1. Samuel D. Warren & Louis D. Brandeis, "The Right to Privacy," 4 Harv. L. Rev. 193, 219 (1890).

2. Smith v. City of Artesia, 772 P.2d 373, 376 (N.M. Ct. App. 1989).

3. Restatement (Second) of Torts § 652(I) comment (a).

4. 182 F.3d 1224, 1234–35 (10th Cir. 1999).

5. Eugene Volokh, "Freedom of Speech and Information Privacy: The Troubling Implications of a Right to Stop People from Speaking about You," 52 Stan. L. Rev. 1049, 1117 (2000).

6. Fred Cate, *Privacy in the Information Age* 196 (1997).

7. Id., 131.

8. Id.

9. See Paul M. Schwartz, "Privacy and Democracy in Cyberspace," 52 Vand. L. Rev. 1609, 1660–64 (1999).

10. Paul M. Schwartz, "Internet Privacy and the State," 32 Conn. L. Rev. 815, 834 (2000).

11. Spiros Simitis, "Reviewing Privacy in an Information Society," 135 U. Pa. L. Rev. 707, 709 (1987).

12. See Lawrence Lessig, *Code and Other Laws of Cyberspace* 5–6, 236 (1999); Joel R. Reidenberg, "Rules of the Road for Global Electronic Highways: Merging Trade and Technical Paradigms," 6 Harv. J. L. & Tech. 287, 296 (1993); see also Joel R. Reidenberg, "Lex Informatica: The Formulation of Information Policy Rules through Technology," 76 Tex. L. Rev. 553 (1998).

13. Yi-Fu Tuan, *Space and Place: The Perspective of Experience* 107, 116 (1977).

14. Neal Kumar Katyal, "Architecture as Crime Control," 111 Yale L.J. 1039 (2002).

15. Id., 1064; see also Thomas A. Markus, *Buildings and Power: Freedom and Control in the Origin of Modern Building Types* 25 (1993).

16. Quoted in John Nivala, "The Architecture of a Lawyer's Operation: Learning from Frank Lloyd Wright," 20 J. Legal Prof. 99, 111 (1998).

17. Michel Foucault, *Discipline and Punish: The Birth of the Prison* 206 (Alan Sheridan trans., 1977).

18. Id., 200.

19. Id., 207.

20. Clive Norris & Gary Armstrong, *The Maximum Surveillance Society: The Rise of CCTV* (1999); Jeffrey Rosen, "A Cautionary Tale for a New Age of Surveillance," N.Y. Times Magazine (Oct. 7, 2001).

21. Lessig, *Code,* 30.

22. Id., 58.

23. Katyal, "Architecture," 1073–74.

24. Hammonds v. Aetna Casualty & Surety Co., 243 F. Supp. 793 (D. Ohio 1965); McCormick v. England, 494 S.E. 2d 431 (S.C. Ct. App. 1997).

25. As one court has aptly explained the relationship: "A fiduciary relationship is one founded on trust or confidence reposed by one person in the integrity and fidelity of another. Out of such a relation, the laws raise the rule that neither party may exert influence or pressure upon the other, take selfish advantage of his trust[,] or deal with the subject matter of the trust in such a way as to benefit himself or prejudice the other except in the exercise of utmost good faith." Mobile Oil Corp. v. Rubenfeld, 339 N.Y.S.2d 623, 632 (1972).

26. Meinhard v. Salmon, 164 N.E. 545, 546 (N.Y. 1928).

27. Swerhun v. General Motors Corp., 812 F. Supp. 1218, 1222 (M.D. Fla. 1993).

28. Stephen P. Groves, Sr., "Fiduciary Duties in Common Commercial Relationships: The Plaintiff's Perspective," 29 Brief 47, 48 (2000).

29. *Moore v. Regents of the University of California,* 793 P.2d 479 (Cal. 1990) (doctor has a fiduciary duty to disclose personal interests that could affect the doctor's professional judgment).

30. Hammonds v. Aetna Casualty & Surety Co., 243 F. Supp. 793 (D. Ohio 1965); McCormick v. England, 494 S.E. 2d 431 (S.C. Ct. App. 1997). In a very interesting proposal, Jessica Litman proposes that the breach of confidentiality tort remedy apply to companies that misuse information. See Jessica Litman, "Information Privacy/Information Property," 52 Stan. L. Rev. 1283, 1304–13 (2000).

31. Peterson v. Idaho First National Bank, 367 P.2d 284 (Idaho 1961) (bank); Blair v. Union Free School District, 324 N.Y.S.2d 222 (N.Y. Dist. Ct. 1971) (school).

32. Pottinger v. Pottinger, 605 N.E.2d 1130, 1137 (Ill. App. 1992).

33. See generally, Marc Rotenberg, "Fair Information Practices and the Architecture of Privacy (What Larry Doesn't Get)," 2001 Stan. Tech. L. Rev. 1.

34. U.S. Dep't of Health, Education, and Welfare (HEW), Report of the Secretary's Advisory Committee on Automated Personal Data Systems: Records, Computers, and the Rights of Citizens 41–42 (1973).

35. Organisation for Economic Cooperation and Development, *OECD Recommendation Concerning and Guidelines Governing the Protection of Privacy and Transborder Flows of Personal Data* (1980). For a comparison of U.S. Privacy law to the OECD Guidelines, see Joel R. Reidenberg, "Restoring Americans' Privacy in Electronic Commerce," 14 Berkeley J. L. & Tech. 771 (1999).

36. See Schwartz, "Privacy and Democracy," 1667–1703; Rotenberg, "Fair Information Practices," 36–50; see generally, Joel Reidenberg, "Setting Standards for Fair Information Practices in the U.S. Private Sector," 80 Iowa L. Rev. 497 (1995).

37. Jeff Sovern, "Opting In, Opting Out, or No Options at All: The Fight for Control of Personal Information," 74 Wash. L. Rev. 1033, 1118 (1999).

38. Rotenberg, "Fair Information Practices," 32.

39. OECD Guidelines.

40. See Reidenberg, "Setting Standards," 501–11.

41. Directive of the European Parliament and the Council of Europe on the Protection of Individuals with Regard to the Processing of Personal Data and on the Free Movement of Such Data (1996).

42. Id.

43. For a compelling discussion of the need for a federal privacy agency, see Robert Gellman, "A Better Way to Approach Privacy Policy in the United States: Establish a Non-Regulatory Privacy Protection Board," 54 Hastings L.J. 1183 (2003).

44. No. 022-3260 (July 30, 2003).

45. 15 U.S.C. §§ 6801(b); 6805(b)(2).

46. U.S. General Accounting Office (GAO), Report to the Honorable Sam Johnson House of Representatives, Identity Theft: Greater Awareness and Use of Existing Data Are Needed 23 (June 2002).

47. Id.

48. See Albert B. Crenshaw, "Victims of Identity Theft Battle Creditors as Well as Crooks," Wash. Post, July 21, 2002, at H4.

49. Id.

50. GAO Identity Theft Report, 23. For more background, see generally Beth Givens, *The Privacy Rights Handbook* 227–48 (1997).

51. See Beth Givens, "Identity Theft: How It Happens, Its Impact on Victims, and Legislative Solutions," Testimony for U.S. Senate Judiciary Committee on Technology, Terrorism, and Government Information 3–4 (July 12, 2000), at http://www.privacyrights.org/ar/id_theft.htm; see also John R. Vacca, *Identity Theft* 8–9 (2003).

52. See Jennifer 8. Lee, "Fighting Back When Someone Steals Your Name," N.Y. Times, April 8, 2001.

53. Federal Trade Commission, *Identity Theft Survey Report* 4 (Sept. 2003).

54. See Janine Benner, Beth Givens, & Ed Mierzwinski, "Nowhere to Turn: Victims Speak Out on Identity Theft: A CALPIRG/Privacy Rights Clearinghouse Report," (May 2000), at http://www.privacyrights.org/ar/idtheft2000.htm; see also Lee, "Fighting Back"; Brandon McKelvey, "Financial Institutions' Duty of Confidentiality to Keep Personal Information Secure from the Threat of Identity Theft," 34 U.C. Davis L. Rev. 1077, 1086–87 (2001).

55. Christopher P. Couch, Commentary, "Forcing the Choice between Commerce and Consumers: Application of the FCRA to Identity Theft," 53 Ala. L. Rev. 583, 586 (2002).

56. McKelvey, "Financial Institutions," 1087.

57. Lynn M. LoPucki, "Human Identification Theory and the Identity Theft Problem," 80 Tex. L. Rev. 89, 90 (2001); see also Privacy Rights Clearinghouse & Identity Theft Resource Center, "Criminal Identity Theft" (May 2002), at http://www.privacyrights.org/fs/fs11g-CrimIdTheft.htm.

58. 18 U.S.C. § 1028.

59. GAO Identity Theft Report, 1.

60. Id., 17–18.

61. Stephen Mihm, "Dumpster Diving for Your Identity," N.Y. Times Magazine, Dec. 21, 2003.

62. Benner, Givens, & Mierzwinski, "Nowhere to Turn," 3.

63. Jane Black, "Who's Policing the Credit Cops?" Bus. Week Online (Aug. 29, 2002), http://www.businessweek.com/print/technology/content/aug2002/tc20020829_8532.htm.

64. 15 U.S.C. § 1681.

65. See 15 U.S.C. § 1681i.

66. 15 U.S.C. § 1681n.

67. LoPucki, "Human Identification," 92, 107.

68. 15 U.S.C. § 1681h(e), § 1681o, § 1681p.

69. 122 S. Ct. 441 (2001).

70. H.R. 2622 (108th Cong, 1st Sess.) (2003).

71. Fred H. Cate, *Privacy in Perspective* 22 (2001).

72. Federal Deposit Insurance Corporation, "ID Theft: When Bad Things Happen to Your Good Name," 3–4 (2002), at http://www.ftc.gov/bcp/conline/pubs/credit/idtheft.htm.

73. Lee, "Fighting Back."

74. GAO Identity Theft Report, 7.

75. Robert Ellis Smith, *Ben Franklin's Web Site* 288 (2000).

76. See, e.g., U.S. General Accounting Office, Report to the Chairman, Subcomm. on Social Security, Comm. on Ways and Means, House of Representatives: Social Security: Government and Commercial Use of the SSN Is Widespread (Feb. 1999); Simson Garfinkel, *Database Nation* 33–34 (2000).

77. HEW, "Records, Computers, and the Rights of Citizens," xxxii.

78. Flavio L. Komuves, "We've Got Your Number: An Overview of Legislation and Decisions to Control the Use of SSNs as Personal Identifiers," 16 J. Marshall J. Computer & Info. L. 529, 569 (1998).

79. For example, an identity thief purchased the SSNs of several top corporate executives from Internet database companies. The thief then used the SSNs to obtain more personal information about the victims. Benjamin Weiser, "Identity Theft, and These Were Big Identities," N.Y. Times, May 29, 2002.

80. See Robert O'Harrow Jr., "Identity Thieves Thrive in Information Age: Rise of Online Data Brokers Makes Criminal Impersonation Easier," Wash. Post, May 31, 2001, at A1.

81. See 11 U.S.C. § 107(a) (Any "paper filed . . . and the dockets of a bankruptcy court are public records and open to examination by an entity at a reasonable time without charge").

82. Jennifer 8. Lee, "Dirty Laundry for All to See: By Posting Court Records, Cincinnati Opens a Pandora's Box of Privacy Issues," N.Y. Times, Sept. 5, 2002, at G1.

83. Robert O'Harrow, Jr., "Identity Thieves Thrive in the Information Age," Wash. Post, May 31, 2001, at A1.

84. Robert O'Harrow, Jr., "Concerns for ID Theft Often Are Unheeded," Wash. Post, July 23, 2001, at A1.

85. LoPucki, "Human Identification," 94.

86. Id., 108–14.

87. Bruce Mohl, "Large-Scale Identity Theft Is Painful Reminder of Risk," Boston Globe, May 12, 2002, at C3.

88. See Yochi J. Dreazen, "Citibank's Email Data Offer Raises Online-Privacy Concerns," Wall St. J., Sept. 3, 2002, at D3.

89. See id.

90. Elise Jordan & Arielle Levin Becker, "Princeton Officials Broke Into Yale Online Admissions Decisions," Yale Daily News, Jul. 25, 2002; Susan Cheever, "A Tale of Ivy Rivalry Gone Awry," Newsday, Jul. 31, 2002.

91. Jordan & Becker, "Princeton Officials."

92. Tom Bell, "Princeton Punishes Hacker of Yale Site," Chi. Sun-Times, Aug. 14, 2002, at 7.

93. Patrick Healy, "Princeton Says Curiosity Led to Yale Files, Admissions Official Will Be Reassigned," Boston Globe, Aug. 14, 2002, at A2.

94. Cheever, "Ivy Rivalry."

95. Vacca, *Identity Theft,* 54.

96. Benner, Givens, & Mierzwinski, "Nowhere to Turn," 6–7.

97. Katyal, "Architecture," 1066.

98. In her testimony before Congress, Beth Givens recommended that "[a]ll consumers should be able to receive one free copy of their credit report annually," and noted that six states have enacted this measure into law. See Givens, "Identity Theft," U.S. Senate Testimony.

99. See Lynn LoPucki, "Did Privacy Cause Identity Theft?" 54 Hastings L.J. 1277 (2003).

100. See Linda Foley, "Fact Sheet 17(L): Should I Change My SSN?" (May 2002), at http://www.privacyrights.org/fs/fs171-ssn.htm.

101. Billions of pre-approved credit offers are made to consumers each year, and there is vigorous competition among creditors to find new customers. See Beth Givens, "Identity Theft," U.S. Senate Testimony.

102. See LoPucki, "Privacy," 13.

Notes to Chapter 7

1. For an excellent discussion of public records, see Robert Gellman, "Public Records: Access, Privacy, and Public Policy," http://www.cdt.org/privacy/pubrecs/pubrec.html.

2. See, e.g., Cal. Health & Safety Code § 102425(a)(1)–(11).

3. See, e.g., Cal. Health & Safety Code § 103150.

4. See, e.g., id. § 103175.

5. See Cal. Elec. Code §§ 2102, 2150(a)(1)–(10); Carole A. Lane, *Naked in Cyberspace: How to Find Personal Information Online* 274 (1997).

6. Edmund J. Pankau, *Check It Out!* 16 (1998).

7. See Lane, *Naked*, 275. Seven states make workers' compensation records publicly accessible. See *Public Records Online* 21 (Michael L. Sankey et al. eds., 3d ed. 2001).

8. See, e.g., Ind. Code Ann. § 5-14-3-4(b)(8)(A)–(C) (requiring disclosure of particular information in public employees' personnel records including salary, education, prior work experience, and any disciplinary troubles); Braun v. City of Taft, 201 Cal. Rptr. 654, 660–61 (Cal. Ct. App. 1984) (permitting disclosure of an employee's SSN, home address, and birth date); Eskaton Monterey Hosp. v. Myers, 184 Cal. Rptr. 840, 843 (Cal. Ct. App. 1982) (permitting disclosure of a state employee's personnel file); Moak v. Phila. Newspapers, Inc., 336 A.2d 920, 921, 924 (Pa. Commw. Ct. 1975) (permitting disclosure of payroll records that contained employees' names, gender, date of birth, annual salary, and other personal data). But see Idaho Code §9-340C(1) (exempting personnel records from public disclosure).

9. See Mass. Ann. Laws ch. 51, §§ 4, 6; see also Pottle v. Sch Comm. of Braintree, 482 N.E.2d 813, 817 (Mass. 1985).

10. See Lane, *Naked*, 274–75.

11. See, e.g., Cal. Gov't Code § 6254(f)(1).

12. See, e.g., Cal. R. 243.1(c) ("Unless confidentiality is required by law, court records are presumed to be open"). Not all court records are public; in most states, adoption records, grand jury records, and juvenile criminal court records are not public. See, e.g., David S. Jackson, "Privacy and Ohio's Public Records Act," 26 Cap. U. L. Rev. 107, 120 (1997). Beyond pleadings and motions (which are, for the most part, always contained in the court file), other documents (such as exhibits) and transcripts may or may not be contained in the file. For example, typically a trial transcript will only be contained in the court file if an appeal is taken. The availability of other documents in the court file is controlled by local practice. Local practices vary greatly depending on limited storage capacities in clerks' offices. Often, exhibits are kept by the parties.

13. Lane, *Naked*, 246.

14. See, e.g., Unabom Trial Media Coalition v. United States Dist. Court, 183 F.3d 949, 950 (9th Cir. 1999); United States v. Antar, 38 F.3d 1348, 1358–59 (3d Cir. 1994).

15. Lesher Communications, Inc. v. Superior Court, 274 Cal. Rptr. 154, 156–57 (Cal. Ct. App. 1990).

16. In practice, juror information is rarely sought out except in high-profile cases.

17. If Social Security information is disclosed in court filings, confidentiality is lost. 20 C.F.R. § 401.180.

18. 11 U.S.C. § 107(a).

19. Mary Jo Obee & William C. Plouffe, Jr., "Privacy in the Federal Bankruptcy Courts," 14 Notre Dame J.L. Ethics & Pub. Pol'y 1011, 1020 (2000).

20. See Jerry Markon, "Curbs Debated as Court Records Go Public on Net," Wall St. J., Feb. 27, 2001, at B1.

21. In re Keene Sentinel, 612 A.2d 911, 915–16 (N.H. 1992); see also Barron v. Fla. Freedom Newspapers, Inc., 531 So. 2d 113, 119 (Fla. 1988).

22. See Lane, *Naked*, 213.

23. See, e.g., Cal. Penal Code § 1203.10; Cal. Ct. R. 4.411.5(a)(6).

24. See, e.g., Cal. Penal Code § 1203d.

25. Jane A. Small, "Who Are the People in Your Neighborhood? Due Process, Public Protection, and Sex Offender Notification Laws," 74 N.Y.U. L. Rev. 1451, 1459 (1999).

26. See, e.g., Paul P. v. Verniero, 170 F.3d 396, 398 (3d. Cir. 1999); Russell v. Gregoire, 124 F.3d 1079, 1092 (9th Cir. 1997).

27. Edward Walsh, "Kansas City Tunes In as New Program Aims at Sex Trade: 'John TV,'" Wash. Post, July 8, 1997, at A3.

28. D. Ian Hopper, "Database, Protection, or a Kind of Prison? Web Registries of Inmates, Parolees Prompt a Debate," Wash. Post, Dec. 29, 2000, at A31.

29. See Obee & Plouffe, "Bankruptcy Courts," 1012.

30. See Susan E. Gindin, "Lost and Found in Cyberspace: Informational Privacy in the Age of the Internet," 34 San Diego L. Rev. 1153, 1156–57 (1997).

31. See *Public Records Online*, 8.

32. For example, KnowX.com states that it has amassed millions of public records, which are updated regularly. See http://www.knowx.com. Search Systems contains over 6,000 searchable public record databases. See http://www.pac-info.com. Locateme.com permits its users to search public records such as driver registrations, voter registrations, and credit headers. See http://www.locateme.com.

33. See Joanna Glasner, "Courts Face Privacy Conundrum," Wired News, Feb. 26, 2001, at http://www.wired.com/news/politics/0,1283,41967,00.html.

34. U.S. Bankruptcy Court for the Dist. of N.J., "Case Information," at http://www.njb.uscourts.gov/caseinfo/.

35. See http://www.courthousedirect.com.

36. The system under development, called Case Management/Electronic Case Files ("CM/ECF"), is designed to be in place by 2005. See Administrative Office of the U.S. Courts, "News Release," at http://privacy.uscourts.gov/Press.htm (Feb. 16, 2001).

37. See Harold L. Cross, *The People's Right to Know* 25 (1953).

38. See, e.g., Nowack v. Fuller, 219 N.W. 749, 750–51 (Mich. 1928).

39. See Cross, *Right to Know*, 135; William Ollie Key, Jr., "The Common Law Right to Inspect and Copy Judicial Records: In Camera or On Camera," 16 Ga. L. Rev. 659, 666 (1982).

40. See Cross, *Right to Know*, 26.

41. See Nowack v. Fuller, 219 N.W. 749, 751 (Mich. 1928); Comment, "Public Inspection of State and Municipal Documents: 'Everybody, Practically Everything, Anytime, Except . . . ,'" 45 Fordham L. Rev. 1105, 1108 (1977).

42. See Cross, *Right to Know*, 27; "Public Inspection," 1108.

43. See Cross, *Right to Know*, 29.

44. City of St. Matthews v. Voice of St. Matthews, Inc., 519 S.W.2d 811, 815 (Ky. Ct. App. 1974); Husband, C. v. Wife, C., 320 A.2d 717, 723 (Del. 1974) (characterizing the common law approach as permitting access to judicial records if a person "has an interest therein for some useful purpose and not for mere curiosity"); Matthew D. Bunker et al., "Access to Government-Held Information in the Computer Age: Applying Legal Doctrine to Emerging Technology," 20 Fla. St. U. L. Rev. 543, 556 (1993) ("The common law had varied among states, with most courts requiring a person requesting a record to have a legitimate interest in, and a useful purpose for, the requested record").

45. See Key, "Common Law," 668.

46. See Cross, *Right to Know*, 135–36.

47. 435 U.S. 589, 597 (1978).

48. Id., 598–99.

49. Fed. R. Civ. P. 26(c).

50. Seattle Times Co. v. Rhinehart, 467 U.S. 20, 29 (1984).

51. FTC v. Standard Fin. Mgmt. Corp., 830 F.2d 404, 408–10 (1st Cir. 1987).

52. See, e.g., Nixon, v. Warner Communications, Inc., 435 U.S. 589, 602 (1978).

53. See, e.g., United States v. Beckham, 789 F.2d 401, 413 (6th Cir. 1986).

54. See, e.g., Unabom Trial Media Coalition v. United States Dist. Court for E. Dist. of Cal., 183 F.3d 949, 951 (9th Cir. 1999).

55. See, e.g., Doe v. Frank, 951 F.2d 320, 323 (11th Cir. 1992) ("It is the exceptional case in which a plaintiff may proceed under a fictitious name").

56. See Doe v. Nat'l R.R. Passenger Corp., No. CIU.A. 94-5064, 1997 WL 116979, at *1 (E.D. Pa. Mar. 11, 1997).

57. Doe v. Shakur, 164 F.R.D. 359, 361 (S.D.N.Y. 1996); see also Bell Atl. Bus. Sys. Servs., 162 F.R.D. at 422 (D. Mass. 1995) (rejecting use of pseudonym for plaintiff alleging a sexual assault by her supervisor at work and that she might have been infected with HIV).

58. See, e.g., United States v. McVeigh, 119 F.3d 806, 811–15 (10th Cir. 1997).

59. See Jason Lawrence Cagle, Note, "Protecting Privacy on the Front Page: Why Restrictions on Commercial Use of Law Enforcement Records Violate the First Amendment," 52 Vand. L. Rev. 1421, 1422 n.2 (1999). While some states' FOIAs replaced the common law, courts in some states have held that the state's FOIA operates as an additional right of access to the common law. See id.

60. See Note, "Public Inspection," 1107.

61. 2 *Public Papers of the Presidents of the United States: Lyndon B. Johnson* 699 (1967), quoted in H.R. Rep. No. 104-795, at 8 (1996), reprinted in 1996 U.S.C.C.A.N. 3448, 3451.

62. 5 U.S.C. § 552(a)(3)(A).

63. See, e.g., United States Dep't of Justice v. Reporters Comm. for Freedom of the Press, 489 U.S. 749, 771 (1989).

64. 5 U.S.C. § 552(f).

65. Jackson, "Ohio's Public Records," 111.

66. See, e.g., Del. Code Ann. tit. 29, § 10001 (stating that "it is vital that citizens have easy access to public records in order that the society remain free and democratic"); 5 Ill. Comp. Stat. Ann. 140/1 (1) (stating that the right to inspect public records "is necessary to enable the people to fulfill their duties of discussing public issues fully and freely").

67. Roger A. Nowadzky, "A Comparative Analysis of Public Records Statutes," 28 Urb. Law. 65, 66 & n.6 (1996) (conducting a comprehensive survey of all state FOIAs as to the presumption of disclosure).

68. 5 U.S.C. §§ 552(b)(6); 552(b)(7)(C).

69. In contrast, companies seeking to protect trade secrets can initiate actions on their own to protect their information in what is known as a "reverse-FOIA" lawsuit. See Heather Harrison, Note, "Protecting Personal Information from Unauthorized Government Disclosures," 22 Memphis St. U. L. Rev. 775, 783 (1992).

70. See, e.g., D.C. Code Ann. § 2-534(a)(2); Mich. Comp. Laws Ann. § 15.243(1)(a).

71. Pa. Cons. Stat. Ann. § 66.1(2).

72. Kanzelmeyer v. Eger, 329 A.2d 307, 310 (Pa. Commw. Ct. 1974).

73. See 1 Ohio Rev. Code Ann. § 149.43(A)(1); see also State ex rel. Plain Dealer Pub. Co. v. Cleveland, 661 N.E.2d 187, 193–95 (Ohio 1996) (Resnick, J., concurring) (criticizing the lack of a privacy exception in Ohio's Public Records Act).

74. Nowadzky, "Comparative Analysis," 79.

75. 5 U.S.C. § 552a.

76. Warth v. Dep't of Justice, 595 F.2d 521, 522–23 (9th Cir. 1979).

77. 5 U.S.C. §§ 552a(b)(3).

78. See Paul M. Schwartz, "Privacy and Participation: Personal Information and Public Sector Regulation in the United States," 80 Iowa L. Rev. 553, 595–97 (1995).

79. Robert Gellman, "Does Privacy Law Work?" in *Technology and Privacy: The New Landscape* 193, 198 (Philip E. Agre & Marc Rotenberg, eds., 1997).

80. See id.; Harrison, "Protecting Personal Information," 787.

81. 5 U.S.C. § 552a(g)(4).

82. Schwartz, "Privacy and Participation," 596 ("[I]ndividuals who seek to enforce their rights under the Privacy Act face numerous statutory hurdles, limited damages, and scant chance to effect an agency's overall behavior."); Todd Robert Coles, Comment, "Does the Privacy Act of 1974 Protect Your Right to Privacy? An Examination of the Routine Use Exemption," 40 Am. U. L. Rev. 957, 975 n.118 (1991).

83. 838 F.2d 418, 425 (10th Cir. 1988).

84. See Schwartz, "Privacy and Participation," 605. For a compilation of state privacy laws, see Robert Ellis Smith, *Compilation of State and Federal Privacy Laws* (2003).

85. Schwartz, "Privacy and Participation," 605.

86. Ga. Code Ann. § 35-1-9.

87. La. Rev. Stat. Ann. § 32:398(H).

88. Amelkin v. McClure, 168 F.3d 893, 896 (6th Cir. 1999).

89. Ky. Rev. Stat. Ann. § 189.635.

90. Fla. Stat. Ann. § 316.650(11).

91. Colo. Rev. Stat. § 24-72-305.5.

92. Cal. Gov't Code § 6254(f)(3).

93. See Rajiv Chandrasekaran, "Government Finds Information Pays," Wash. Post, Mar. 9, 1998, at A1.

94. 2 U.S.C. § 438(a)(4). Although the FEC occasionally uses decoy names to check to see if candidates are engaging in improper uses of the records, the FEC has not, according to critics, done much to investigate reports of abuse. See Chandrasekaran, "Information Pays."

95. Pub. L. No. 103-322, 108 Stat. 2099 (codified as amended at 18 U.S.C. §§ 2721-25).

96. 528 U.S. 141, 148, 151 (2000).

97. Schwartz, "Privacy and Participation," 604.

Notes to Chapter 8

1. *Dateline* (NBC television broadcast, Oct. 30, 1998).

2. Louis D. Brandeis, *Other People's Money* 92 (1932).

3. Engrav v. Cragun, 769 P.2d 1224, 1228 (Mont. 1989); Houston Chronicle Publ'g Co. v. City of Houston, 531 S.W.2d 177, 186 (Tex. App. 1975); United States v. Hickey, 767 F.2d 705, 708 (10th Cir. 1985).

4. In re Cont'l Ill. Sec. Litig., 732 F.2d 1302, 1308 (7th Cir. 1984).

5. Letter from James Madison to W.T. Barry (Aug. 4, 1822), in 9 *The Writings of James Madison* 103 (Gaillard Hunt ed., 1910).

6. Cowley v. Pulsifer, 137 Mass. 392, 394 (1884).

7. United States v. Chagra, 701 F.2d 354, 363 n.25 (5th Cir. 1983); G. Michael Fenner & James L. Koley, "Access to Judicial Proceedings: To Richmond Newspapers and Beyond," 16 Harv. C.R.-C.L. L. Rev. 415, 436 n.109 (1981).

8. 489 U.S. 749, 763–64 (1989).

9. 297 P. 91 (Cal. Dist. Ct. App. 1931).

10. 483 P.2d 34 (Cal. 1971).

11. Westphal v. Lakeland Register, 2 Media L. Rep. (BNA) 2262, 2263 (Fla. Cir. Ct. 1977); Roshto v. Hebert, 439 So. 2d 428, 431 (La. 1983); Montesano v. Donrey Media Group, 668 P.2d 1081, 1088 (Nev. 1983); Jenkins v. Bolla, 600 A.2d 1293, 1296–97 (Pa. Super. Ct. 1992).

12. 608 P.2d 716 (Cal. 1980).

13. Id. (quoting William L. Prosser, "Privacy," 48 Cal. L. Rev. 383, 418 [1960]).

14. Restatement (Second) of Torts § 652D cmt. b (1977).

15. Id. § 652B cmt. c.

16. 420 U.S. 469, 495 (1975).

17. 946 F.2d 202, 207 (3d Cir. 1991).

18. 87 F.3d 176, 179 (6th Cir. 1996); see also Doe v. City of New York, 15 F.3d 264, 268 (2d Cir. 1994) ("[A]n individual cannot expect to have a constitutionally protected privacy interest in matters of public record").

19. 895 F.2d 188, 190–95 (4th Cir. 1990).

20. 124 F.3d 1079, 1094 (9th Cir. 1997).

21. 170 F.3d 396, 400–01, 405 (3d Cir. 1999). But see Doe v. Portiz, 662 A.2d 367, 411 (N.J. 1995) (following the conception from *Reporters Committee* when examining the constitutionality of Megan's Law and noting that "a privacy interest is implicated when the government assembles . . . diverse pieces of information into a single package and disseminates that package to the public, thereby ensuring that a person cannot assume anonymity").

22. State Employees Ass'n v. Dep't of Mgmt. & Budget, 404 N.W.2d 606, 615 (Mich. 1987) (quoting Tobin v. Mich. Civil Serv. Comm'n, 331 N.W.2d 184, 189 [Mich. 1982]).

23. Moak v. Phila. Newspapers, Inc., 336 A.2d 920, 924 (Pa. Commw. Ct. 1975).

24. Mans v. Lebanon Sch. Bd., 290 A.2d 866, 868 (N.H. 1972) (quoting H.R. Rep. No. 1497, at 11 [1966]) (discussing federal FOIA); see also Pottle v. Sch. Comm. of Braintree, 482 N.E.2d 813, 816–17 (Mass. 1985) (holding that payroll records containing names, salaries, overtime pay, and addresses of policemen and school employees were not private within the meaning of Massachusetts's FOIA privacy exception because the information was not intimate).

25. Jayson Blair & William K. Rashbaum, "Man Broke Into Accounts of Celebrities, Police Say," N.Y. Times, Mar. 21, 2001, at B3.

26. Robert O'Harrow, Jr., "Identity Thieves Thrive in Information Age: Rise of On-line Data Brokers Makes Criminal Impersonation Easier," Wash. Post, May 31, 2001, at A1.

27. See Priscilla M. Regan, *Legislating Privacy: Technology, Social Values, and Public Policy* 102 (1995).

28. Sykes, *End of Privacy*, 42–44.

29. Planned Parenthood v. Am. Coalition of Life Activists, 290 F.3d 1058 (9th Cir. 2002) (en banc).

30. Arthur Miller, *The Assault on Privacy* 39 (1971).

31. See, e.g., Charles J. Sykes, *The End of Privacy: Personal Rights in the Surveillance Society* 44 (1999); see also Note, "Privacy and Efficient Government: Proposals for a National Data Center," 82 Harv. L. Rev. 400, 404 (1968).

32. Robert Ellis Smith, *Ben Franklin's Web Site: Privacy and Curiosity from Plymouth Rock to the Internet* 31 (2000).

33. See Richard Sobel, "The Degradation of Political Identity under a National Identification System," 8 B.U. J. Sci. & Tech. L. 37, 39 (2002). See generally Amitai Etzioni, *The Limits of Privacy* (1999).

34. Immigration Reform and Control Act of 1986, Pub. L. No. 99-603, 100 Stat. 3359 (codified as amended at 8 U.S.C. §§ 1324a–1365).

35. See Personal Responsibility and Work Opportunity Reconciliation Act of 1996, Pub. L. No. 104-193, 110 Stat. 2105. See generally Robert O' Harrow, Jr., "Uncle Sam Has All Your Numbers," Wash. Post, June 27,1999 at A1.

36. Sobel, "Degradation," 48.

37. See id., 50–53.

38. U.S. Dep't of Health, Education, and Welfare (HEW), "Report of the Secretary's Advisory Committee on Automated Personal Data Systems: Records, Computers, and the Rights of Citizens," 112 (1973).

39. See Erik Larson, *The Naked Consumer: How Our Private Lives Become Public Commodities* 53–54 (1992).

40. See Fred H. Cate et al., "The Right to Privacy and the Public's Right to Know: The 'Central Purpose' of the Freedom of Information Act," 46 Admin. L. Rev. 41, 50–51 (1994) (citing studies by the General Accounting Office, Department of Health and Human Services, and the Department of Defense).

41. Patricia M. Wald, "The Freedom of Information Act: A Short Case Study in the Perils and Paybacks of Legislating Democratic Values," 33 Emory L.J. 649, 667 (1984).

42. See, e.g., U.S. Dep't of Justice v. Reporters Comm. for Freedom of the Press, 489 U.S. 749, 772 (1989); see also Halloran v. Veterans Admin., 874 F.2d 315, 323 (5th Cir. 1989) ("[I]f disclosure of the requested information does not serve the purpose of informing the citizenry about the activities of their government, disclosure will not be warranted even though the public may nonetheless prefer, albeit for other reasons, that the information be released").

43. 416 A.2d 244, 247–48 (D.C. 1980).

44. 194 F.3d 954, 960 (9th Cir. 1999).

45. J.M. Balkin, "Ideological Drift and the Struggle over Meaning," 25 Conn. L. Rev. 869, 871 (1993).

46. See HEW, "Records, Computers, and the Rights of Citizens," viii.

47. Judicial Conference, Request for Comment on Privacy and Public Access to Electronic Case Files (Sept. 26, 2001), available at http:// www.privacy.uscourts .gov/ RFC.htm.

48. See Grayson Barber, "Too Easy an Answer: Beware of Simplifying the Impact of Posting Court Records Online," 170 N.J.L.J. 99 (2002).

49. 448 U.S. 555, 575–78 (1980).

50. 457 U.S. 596 (1982).

51. Press-Enterprise Co. v. Superior Court, 464 U.S. 501 (1984) (jury selection); Press-Enterprise Co. v. Superior Court, 478 U.S. 1 (1986) (pretrial proceedings).

52. See United States v. Criden, 675 F.2d 550, 557 (3d Cir. 1982); United States v. Chagra, 701 F.2d 354, 363 (5th Cir. 1983).

53. 733 F.2d 1059, 1070 (3d Cir. 1984) (internal quotations and citation omitted).

54. United States v. McVeigh, 119 F.3d 806, 811 (10th Cir. 1997); see also Littlejohn v. BIC Corp., 851 F.2d 673, 678 (3d Cir. 1988) ("Access means more than the ability to attend open court proceedings; it encompasses the right of the public to inspect and to copy judicial records."); Associated Press v. United States Dist. Court, 705 F.2d 1143, 1145 (4th Cir. 1984) ("There is no reason to distinguish between pretrial proceedings and the documents filed in regard to them"). But see Lanphere & Urbaniak v. Colorado, 21 F.3d 1508, 1512 (10th Cir. 1994) ("[T]here is no general First Amendment right in the public to access criminal justice records").

55. 357 U.S. 449, 462 (1958).

56. 988 F.2d 1344, 1354 (4th Cir. 1993).

57. 429 U.S. 589, 605 (1977).

58. After *Whalen* and *Nixon*, the Supreme Court has done little to develop the right of information privacy. A majority of the circuit courts have accepted the constitutional right to information privacy. See, e.g., In re Crawford, 194 F.3d 954, 958 (9th Cir. 1999); Walls v. City of Petersburg, 895 F.2d 188, 192 (4th Cir. 1990); Barry v. City of New York, 712 F.2d 1554, 1559 (2d Cir. 1983); United States v. Westinghouse Elec. Corp., 638 F.2d 570, 577 (3d Cir. 1980); Plante v. Gonzalez, 575 F.2d 1119, 1132, 1134 (5th Cir. 1978). One circuit court has expressed "grave doubts" as to the existence of the right, stopping short of confronting the issue of whether the right existed. Am. Fed'n of Gov't Employees v. Dep't of Housing & Urban Dev., 118 F.3d 786, 788, 791–92 (D.C. Cir. 1997). For more background about the constitutional right to information privacy, see Elbert Lin, "Prioritizing Privacy: A Constitutional Response to the Internet," 17 Berkeley Tech. L.J. 1085, 1124–28 (2002).

59. 420 U.S. 469, 494–95, 496–97 (1975).

60. 443 U.S. 97, 103 (1979).

61. 491 U.S. 524, 541 (1989).

62. 528 U.S. 32 (1999).

63. The Florida Star v. B.J.F., 491 U.S. 524, 538, 535 (1989).

64. L.A. Police Dep't v. United Reporting Publ'g Corp., 528 U.S. 32, 45 (1999) (Stevens, J., dissenting).

65. See, e.g., Chaplinsky v. New Hampshire, 315 U.S. 568, 573 (1942); N.Y. Times Co. v. Sullivan, 376 U.S. 254, 296 (1964) (public figures must prove actual malice to prevail in defamation suits).

66. See Central Hudson Gas v. Public Service Commission, 447 U.S. 557 (1980).

Notes to Chapter 9

1. See Dana Hawkins, "Gospel of a Privacy Guru: Be Wary; Assume the Worst," U.S. News & World Rep., June 25, 2001, http://www.usnews.com/usnews/nycu/tech/articles/010625/tech/privacy.htm (describing hotel chain sharing lists of the movies, including pornographic ones, customers pay to watch in their hotel rooms).

2. Julia Scheeres, "No Thumbprint, No Rental Car," Wired News, Nov. 21, 2001, at http://wired.com/news/print/0,1294,48552,00.html.

3. See, e.g., Paul M. Schwartz, "Beyond Lessig's Code for Internet Privacy: Cyberspace Filters, Privacy-Control, and the Fair Information Practices," 2000 Wisc. L. Rev. 743, 770–71 (describing lack of employee privacy).

4. See Dana Hawkins, "Digital Skulduggery," U.S. News & World Rep., Oct. 2, 2000 at 64.

5. J.C. Conklin, "Under the Radar: Content Advisor Snoops as Workers Surf Web," Wall St. J., Oct. 15, 1998, at B8.

6. This information was requested in employer questionnaires in American Federation of Government Employees v. HUD, 118 F.3d 786 (D.C. Cir. 1997) and Walls v. City of Petersburg, 895 F.2d 188 (4th Cir. 1990).

7. See Sarah Schafer, "Searching for a Workable Fit; Employers Try Psychological Tests to Help with More than the Right Hire," Wash. Post, Jan. 14, 1999, at V5.

8. See 18 U.S.C. § 2703(c), as amended by the USA-PATRIOT Act §§ 210–11.

9. See John Markoff, "Pentagon Plans a Computer System That Would Peek at Personal Data of Americans," N.Y. Times, Nov. 9, 2002.

10. http://www.darpa.mil/iao/index.htm.

11. William Safire, "You Are a Suspect," N.Y. Times, Nov. 14, 2002, at A35.

12. See Cheryl Bolen, "Senate Withholds Data-Mining Funds until DOD Addresses Privacy, Rights Issues," Privacy Law Watch, Jan. 27, 2003.

13. See Glenn R. Simpson, "Big Brother-in-Law: If the FBI Hopes to Get the Goods on You, It May Ask ChoicePoint," Wall St. J., Apr. 13, 2001, at A1.

14. See id.

15. See id.

16. See Gregory Palast, "Florida's Flawed 'Voter-Cleansing' Program," Salon.com, at http://www.salonmag.com/politics/feature/2000/12/04/voter_file/index.html (Dec. 4, 2000).

17. See Robert O'Harrow, Jr., "U.S. Backs Florida's New Counterterrorism Databases: 'Matrix' Offers Law Agencies Faster Access to Americans' Personal Records," Wash. Post, Aug. 6, 2003, at A1; Brief of Amici Curiae Electronic Privacy Information Center (EPIC) and Legal Scholars and Technical Experts, in Hiibel v. Sixth Judicial District Court of Nevada, No. 03-5554 (U.S. Supreme Court, Dec. 13, 2003).

18. Daniela Deane, "Legal Niceties Aside . . . ; Federal Agents without Subpoenas Asking Firms for Records," Wash. Post, Nov. 7, 2001, at E1.

19. The Attorney General's Guidelines on General Crimes, Racketeering Enterprise and Domestic Security/Terrorism Investigations § II.C.1 (March 21, 1989).

20. The Attorney General's Guidelines on General Crimes, Racketeering Enterprise and Terrorism Enterprise Investigations § VI (May 30, 2002).

21. Id., § VI.B.1.

22. Lisa Guernsey, "What Did You Do before the War?" N.Y. Times, Nov. 22, 2001, at G1.

23. See Paul Beckett, "Big Banks, U.S. Weigh Pooling Data on Terror," Wall St. J., Nov. 26, 2001, at A2; Robert O'Harrow, Jr., "Financial Database to Screen Accounts: Joint Effort Targets Suspicious Activities," Wash. Post, May 30, 2002, at E1.

24. Dan Eggen, "FBI Seeks Data on Foreign Students," Wash. Post, Dec. 25, 2002, at A1.

25. Don Phillips, "JetBlue Apologizes for Use of Passenger Records," Wash. Post, Sept. 20, 2003, at E1.

26. Sara Kehaulani Goo, "Northwest Gave U.S. Data on Passengers," Wash. Post, Jan. 18, 2004, at A1.

27. John Schwartz, "Some Companies Will Release Customer Records on Request," N.Y. Times, Dec. 18, 2002, at A16.

28. See Mike Snider, "Privacy Advocates Fear Trade-Off for Security; FBI Sends Warrants to Service Providers," USA Today, Sept. 13, 2001, at D8.

29. See Robert Lemos, "FBI Taps ISPs in Hunt for Attackers," ZD Net Sept. 12, 2001, at http://zdnet.com/filters/printerfriendly/0,6061,5096919-2,00.html.

30. E. Judson Jennings, "Carnivore: U.S. Government Surveillance of Internet Transmissions," 6 Va. J. L. & Tech. 10, 49, 96 (2001).

31. MSN Statement of Privacy, at http://privacy.msn.com.

32. Amazon.com Privacy Notice, at http://www.amazon.com.

33. Privacy Policy, at http://pages.ebay.com/help/community/png-priv.html.

34. Model Privacy Statement, at http://truste.com/bus/pub_sample.html.

35. For example, Larry Ellison, the CEO of Oracle Corporation, proposed a system of national identification involving biometrics. See Larry Ellison, "Digital IDs Can Help Prevent Terrorism," Wall St. J., Oct. 8, 2001, at A26.

36. See Greg Schneider & Robert O'Harrow, Jr., "Pentagon Makes Rush Order for Anti-Terror Technology," Wash. Post, Oct. 26, 2001, at A10.

37. Robert O'Harrow, Jr., "Drivers Angered over Firm's Purchase of Photos," Wash. Post, Jan. 28, 1999, at E1; Robert O'Harrow, Jr. & Liz Leyden, "U.S. Helped Fund Photo Database of Driver IDs: Firm's Plan Seen as Way to Fight Identity Crime," Wash. Post, Feb. 18, 1999, at A1.

38. 31 U.S.C. § 1081.

39. See 31 C.F.R. § 103.22(1).

40. See Personal Responsibility and Work Opportunity Reconciliation Act of 1996, Pub. L. No. 104-193, 110 Stat. 2105. See also Robert O' Harrow, Jr., "Uncle Sam Has All Your Numbers," Wash. Post, June 27, 1999, at A1.

41. Pub. L. 103-414, 108 Stat. 4279.

42. USA-PATRIOT Act of 2001, § 215 (amending 50 U.S.C. § 501).

43. See Eric Lichtblau, "Justice Dept. Lists Use of New Power to Fight Terror," N.Y. Times, May 21, 2003, at A1.

44. California Bankers Ass'n v. Shultz, 416 U.S. 21, 85 (1974) (Douglas, J. dissenting).

45. See Margaret Raymond, "Rejecting Totalitarianism: Translating the Guarantees of Constitutional Criminal Procedure," 76 N.C. L. Rev. 1193, 1198 (1998).

46. Olmstead v. United States, 277 U.S. 438, 479 (1928) (Brandeis, J., dissenting).

47. See Paul M. Schwartz, "Privacy and Democracy in Cyberspace," 52 Vand. L. Rev. 1609, 1658–65 (1999).

48. Julie E. Cohen, "Examined Lives: Informational Privacy and the Subject as Object," 52 Stan. L. Rev. 1373, 1425 (2000).

49. NAACP v. Alabama, 357 U.S. 449, 462 (1958).

50. See, e.g., Shelton v. Tucker, 364 U.S. 479, 489 (1960) (holding unconstitutional a law requiring teachers to disclose membership in organizations); NAACP v. Alabama, 357 U.S. 449, 466 (1958) (restricting compelled disclosure of membership lists of NAACP).

51. 401 U.S. 1 (1971).

52. Id., 6.

53. It is unclear how receptive the Court will be to this argument. The Court has held that mere information gathering about a group's public activities did not harm First Amendment interests enough to give rise to standing. See Laird v. Tatum, 408 U.S. 1, 12–15 (1972).

54. 362 U.S. 60, 63–65 (1960).

55. McIntyre v. Ohio Elections Commission, 514 U.S. 334 (1995); Watchtower Bible & Tract Society v. Village of Stratton, 122 S. Ct. 2080 (2002).

56. See, e.g., Doe v. 2TheMart.com, Inc., 140 F.Supp.2d 1088, 1093–95 (W.D. Wash. 2001); Columbia Insurance Co. v. Seescandy.com, 185 F.R.D. 573, 578–80 (N.D. Cal. 1999).

57. Julie E. Cohen, "The Right to Read Anonymously: A Closer Look at 'Copyright Management' in Cyberspace," 28 Conn. L. Rev. 981, 1012 (1996).

58. See Silas J. Wasserstrom & Louis Michael Seidman, "The Fourth Amendment as Constitutional Theory," 77 Geo. L.J. 19, 82 (1988).

59. Lawrence M. Friedman, *Crime and Punishment in American History* 27 (1993).

60. Carol S. Steiker, "Second Thoughts about First Principles," 107 Harv. L. Rev. 820, 830–31 (1994).

61. See William J. Stuntz, "The Substantive Origins of Criminal Procedure," 105 Yale L.J. 393, 401 (1995).

62. See, e.g., Friedman, *Crime and Punishment*, 67.

63. Curt Gentry, *J. Edgar Hoover: The Man and the Secrets* 112 (1991). The organization created in 1908 was called the Bureau of Investigation (BI); it became the FBI in 1935. See id., 113.

64. Id., 111–12.

65. See, e.g., Albert J. Reiss, Jr., "Police Organization in the Twentieth Century, in Modern Policing," 51, 74 (Michael Tonry & Norval Morris eds., 1992).

66. For a discussion of the harms of a national identification system, see Richard Sobel, "The Degradation of Political Identity under a National Identification System," 8 B.U. J. Sci. & Tech. L. 37 (2002).

67. Whitfield Diffie & Susan Landau, *Privacy on the Line: The Politics of Wiretapping and Encryption* 138, 143–46 (1998).

68. Philadelphia Yearly Meeting of the Religious Society of Friends v. Tate, 519 F.2d 1335 (3d Cir. 1975).

69. See Priscilla M. Regan, *Legislating Privacy: Technology, Social Values, and Public Policy* 96 (1995).

70. See Gary T. Marx, *Under Cover: Police Surveillance in America* 209–10 (1988).

71. See Regan, *Legislating Privacy*, 87.

72. See Computer Matching and Privacy Protection Act (CMPPA) of 1988, Pub. L. No. 100-503, 102 Stat. 2507.

73. See Gen. Accounting Office, "Computer Matching: Quality of Decisions and Supporting Analyses Little Affected by 1988 Act" (1993); Paul M. Schwartz, "Privacy and Participation: Personal Information and Public Sector Regulation in the United States," 80 Iowa L. Rev. 553, 588 (1995) (noting that CMPPA "creates no substantive guidelines to determine when matching is acceptable").

74. See Regan, *Legislating Privacy*, 90.

75. Oscar H. Gandy, Jr., "Exploring Identity and Identification in Cyberspace," 14 Notre Dame J.L. Ethics & Pub. Pol'y 1085, 1100 (2000).

76. Spiros Simitis, "Reviewing Privacy in an Information Society," 135 U. Pa. L. Rev. 707, 719 (1987).

77. Joe Sharkey, "A Safer Sky or Welcome to Flight 1984?" N.Y. Times (March 11, 2003).

78. Ira Berkow, "Rower with Muslim Name Is an All-American Suspect," N.Y. Times, Feb. 21, 2003, at D1.

79. Pamela Samuelson, "Privacy as Intellectual Property?" 52 Stan. L. Rev. 1125, 1143 (2000). See also David H. Flaherty, *Protecting Privacy in Surveillance Societies* 373–74 (1989).

80. Eric. K. Yamamoto, Margaret Chon, Carol I. Izumi, Jerry Kang, & Frank H. Wu, *Race, Rights, and Reparations: Law and the Japanese American Internment* 38–39, 94 (2001).

81. Frank J. Donner, *The Age of Surveillance: The Aims and Methods of America's Political Intelligence System* 33 (1980).

82. See Gentry, *Hoover*, 76.

83. See Charles H. McCormick, *Seeing Reds: Federal Surveillance of Radicals in the Pittsburgh Mill District*, 1917–1921, at 120, 103 (1997); Richard Gid Powers, *Secrecy and Power: The Life of J. Edgar Hoover* 69 (1987).

84. See Donner, *Surveillance*, 34; Gentry, *Hoover*, 79; Powers, *Hoover*, 68.

85. See Gentry, *Hoover*, 93.

86. See Powers, *Hoover*, 79–80.

87. See Gentry, *Hoover*, 98–99.

88. See Ellen Schrecker, *The Age of McCarthyism: A Brief History with Documents* 92–94 (1994).

89. Id., 10.

90. Gentry, *Hoover*, 378–80, 402; Powers, *Hoover*, 320–21.

91. See Schrecker, *McCarthyism*, 76–84.

92. Powers, *Hoover*, 321.

93. See Schrecker, *McCarthyism*, 77.

94. See Seth I. Kreimer, "Sunlight, Secrets, and Scarlet Letters: The Tension between Privacy and Disclosure in Constitutional Law," 140 U. Pa. L. Rev. 1, 13–71 (1991).

95. Schrecker, *McCarthyism*, 76–84.

96. Charles J. Sykes, *The End of Privacy: Personal Rights in the Surveillance Society* 160 (1999). See Diffie & Landau, *Privacy on the Line*, 163 (wiretapping of members of Congress and Supreme Court Justices); Gentry, *Hoover*, 51–52 (providing detailed description of Hoover's collection of files).

97. See David J. Garrow, *The FBI and Martin Luther King, Jr.* 165 (1980).

98. See Ronald Kessler, *The Bureau: The Secret History of the FBI* 164–65 (2002); Gentry, *Hoover*, 616.

99. See, e.g., Diffie & Landau, *Privacy on the Line*, 140–42. It was not until 1975, nearly a decade after the wiretapping and three years after Hoover's death, that Congress conducted an inquiry into the wiretapping of King through the famous Church Committee. See id., 178.

100. Garrow, *Martin Luther King*, 100–01.

101. Id., 126.

102. Id., 26.

103. See id., 78. Hoover's dislike of King may have also stemmed from racism. It is well-documented that Hoover was racist. See id., 153.

104. See id., 79–83.

105. See id., 151.

106. Id., 209.

Notes to Chapter 10

1. U.S. Const. amend. IV.
2. Akhil Reed Amar, *The Constitution and Criminal Procedure* 9 (1997).
3. See, e.g., Harris v. United States, 390 U.S. 234, 236 (1968).
4. See Katz v. United States, 389 U.S. 347, 347 (1967).
5. Brinegar v. United States, 338 U.S. 160, 175–76 (1949).
6. See Amar, *Criminal Procedure*, 3–4.
7. See id.; Sherry F. Colb, "The Qualitative Dimension of Fourth Amendment 'Reasonableness,'" 98 Colum. L. Rev. 1642, 1648 (1998).
8. See Amar, *Criminal Procedure*, 3–4; Christopher Slobogin, "The World without a Fourth Amendment," 39 UCLA L. Rev. 1, 18 (1991).
9. 392 U.S. 1, 1 (1968). See also Camara v. Municipal Court, 387 U.S. 523 (1967). For a critique of *Terry* and *Camara*, see Scott E. Sundby, "A Return to Fourth Amendment Basics: Undoing the Mischief of *Camara* and *Terry*," 72 Minn. L. Rev. 383 (1988).
10. See, e.g., Vernonia Sch. Dist. v. Acton, 515 U.S. 646 (1995) (drug testing by school officials); Nat'l Treasury Employees Union v. Von Rabb, 489 U.S. 656 (1989) (drug testing of Customs officials); Skinner v. Ry Labor Executives Ass'n, 489 U.S. 602 (1989) (drug testing of railroad employees); O'Connor v. Ortega, 480 U.S. 709 (1987) (search by government employer); New Jersey v. TLO, 469 U.S. 325 (1985) (search by school officials).
11. Silas J. Wasserstrom & Louis Michael Seidman, "The Fourth Amendment as Constitutional Theory," 77 Geo. L.J. 19, 43 (1988).
12. Mapp v. Ohio 367 U.S. 643, 643 (1961). For more background about the development of the exclusionary rule, see Potter Stewart, "The Road to *Mapp v. Ohio* and Beyond: The Origins, Development and Future of the Exclusionary Rule in Search and Seizure Cases," 83 Colum. L. Rev. 1365 (1983).
13. Silverthorne Lumber Co. v. United States, 251 U.S. 385, 392 (1920).
14. Arnold H. Loewy, "The Fourth Amendment as a Device for Protecting the Innocent," 81 Mich. L. Rev. 1229, 1266 (1983).
15. Several commentators have criticized the exclusionary rule, advocating a system of civil damages rather than the exclusion of inculpatory evidence. See Amar, *Criminal Procedure*, 20–21, 28; Christopher Slobogin, "Why Liberals Should Chuck the Exclusionary Rule," 1999 U. Ill. L. Rev. 363, 400–01 (1999). Other commentators argue that civil damages will prove to be much less successful than the exclusionary rule. See Loewy, "Fourth Amendment," 1266; Tracey Maclin, "When the Cure for the Fourth Amendment Is Worse than the Disease," 68 S. Cal. L. Rev. 1, 62 (1994).
16. See William J. Stuntz, "Privacy's Problem and the Law of Criminal Procedure," 93 Mich. L. Rev. 1016, 1019 (1995).
17. William J. Stuntz, "The Substantive Origins of Criminal Procedure," 105 Yale L.J. 393, 442 (1995).
18. See Stuntz, "Privacy's Problem," 1019.
19. Stuntz, "Substantive Origins," 446.
20. Stuntz, "Privacy's Problem," 1077.
21. Scott E. Sundby, "'Everyman's' Fourth Amendment: Privacy or Mutual Trust between Government and Citizen?" 94 Colum. L. Rev. 1751, 1757–58 (1994).
22. Id., 1771.

23. See Daniel J. Solove, "Conceptualizing Privacy," 90 Cal. L. Rev. 1087, 1146–47 (2002).

24. Raymond Shih-Ray Ku, "The Founders' Privacy: The Fourth Amendment and the Power of Technological Surveillance," 86 Minn. L. Rev. 1325, 1340 (2002) (examining connection between the Fourth Amendment and separation of powers).

25. See Daniel Yeager, "Does Privacy Really Have a Problem in the Law of Criminal Procedure?" 49 Rutgers L. Rev. 1283, 1309–10 (1997) (agreeing with Stuntz that regulatory inspections can be more invasive of privacy than regular searches, but disagreeing that "encounterless police investigations should be more loosely controlled"). Louis Seidman disputes Stuntz's view that the Fourth Amendment places privacy above coercion. See Louis Michael Seidman, "The Problems with Privacy's Problem," 93 Mich. L. Rev. 1079 (1995).

26. Although corporations are deemed "persons" under the Fourteenth Amendment, see Santa Clara County v. S. Pac. R.R., 118 U.S. 394, 394–95 (1886), they are not afforded Fourth Amendment rights. See California Bankers Ass'n v. Shultz, 416 U.S. 21, 65 (1974) (stating that "corporations can claim no equality with individuals in the enjoyment of a right to privacy").

27. Stuntz, "Privacy's Problem," 1037.

28. Id.

29. Amar, *Criminal Procedure*, 11.

30. See id.

31. Id., 31.

32. Leonard W. Levy, *Origins of the Bill of Rights* 154 (1999).

33. Sundby, "Everyman," 1804.

34. Louis Fisher, "Congress and the Fourth Amendment," 21 Ga. L. Rev. 107, 115 (1986) ("The spirit and letter of the fourth amendment counseled against the belief that Congress intended to authorize a 'fishing expedition' into private papers on the possibility that they might disclose a crime").

35. U.S. Const. amend. IV.

36. Maclin, "Fourth Amendment Principles," 8. Indeed, as Maclin notes: "Everyone, including Amar, agrees that the Framers opposed general warrants." Id., 9. See also Levy, *Origins*, 158.

37. Ku, "Founder's Privacy," 1334–35.

38. Wasserstrom & Seidman, "Fourth Amendment," 82.

39. David M. O'Brien, *Privacy, Law, and Public Policy* 38 (1979). See also Levy, *Origins*, 150; Stuntz, "Substantive Origins," 406.

40. *The Debates in Several Conventions on the Adoption of the Federal Constitution* Vol. 3, 448–49 (Jonathan Elliot ed., 1974).

41. James Madison, "The Federalist, No. 51," in *The Federalist* 347, 349 (Jacob E. Cooke ed., 1961).

42. Ku, "Founders' Privacy," 1333–40.

43. Madison, "The Federalist, No. 48," in *The Federalist*, 333.

44. Madison, "The Federalist, No. 51," 349.

45. Gordon S. Wood, *The Creation of the American Republic 1776–1787*, at 605 (1969).

46. Madison drafted the language of the Fourth Amendment. See Fisher, "Congress," 111–12. As Levy observes, "Madison chose the maximum protection conceivable at the time." Levy, *Origins*, 176.

47. Slobogin, "World without a Fourth Amendment," 17.

48. William J. Stuntz, "O.J. Simpson, Bill Clinton, and the Transsubstantive Fourth Amendment," 114 Harv. L. Rev. 842, 848 (2001).

49. See id., 848.

50. McDonald v. United States, 335 U.S. 451, 455–56 (1948). See also Steagald v. United States, 451 U.S. 204, 212 (1981) (warrants are necessary because law enforcement officials "may lack sufficient objectivity"); Coolidge v. New Hampshire, 403 U.S. 443, 450 (1971) (stating that "prosecutors and policemen simply cannot be asked to maintain the requisite neutrality with regard to their own investigations"); Johnson v. United States, 333 U.S. 10, 13–14 (1948) (stating that the Fourth Amendment ensures that inferences of potential culpability "be drawn by a neutral and detached magistrate instead of being judged by the officer engaged in the often competitive enterprise of ferreting out crime").

51. Amar, *Criminal Procedure*, 39.

52. See Carol S. Steiker, "Second Thoughts about First Principles," 107 Harv. L. Rev. 820, 853 (1994).

53. 116 U.S. 616 (1886).

54. Id., 630.

55. See, e.g., Amar, *Criminal Procedure*, 22 (explaining that *Boyd* was part of the Lochner Court's staunch protection of property); Alan Westin, *Privacy and Freedom* 339–41 (1967) (describing the conception of privacy in *Boyd* as "propertied privacy").

56. 198 U.S. 45 (1905).

57. See generally Daniel J. Solove, "The Darkest Domain: Deference, Judicial Review, and the Bill of Rights," 84 Iowa L. Rev. 941, 949–51 (1999).

58. 96 U.S. 727, 733 (1877).

59. 141 U.S. 250, 252 (1891).

60. See Samuel Warren & Louis Brandeis, "The Right to Privacy," 4 Harv. L. Rev. 193, 193–95 (1890).

61. 277 U.S. 438 (1928).

62. Id., 464.

63. Id., 473 (Brandeis, J., dissenting) (internal quotations omitted).

64. Id.

65. Id., 473 (internal quotations omitted).

66. 316 U.S. 129, 134 (1942).

67. 389 U.S. 347, 351–52 (1967).

68. Id., 361 (Harlan, J., concurring).

69. Olmstead, 277 U.S. 438, 470 (1928) (Holmes, J., dissenting). See also Richard F. Hixson, *Privacy in a Public Society: Human Rights in Conflict* 49 (1987). For a history of the early days of wiretapping, see Note, "The Right to Privacy in Nineteenth Century America," 94 Harv. L. Rev. 1892 (1981).

70. Fisher, "Congress," 127.

71. See Nardone v. United States, 302 U.S. 379 (1937) (evidence directly obtained by wiretapping excluded from evidence); Nardone v. United States, 308 U.S. 338 (1939) (evidence obtained as the fruit of illegal wiretapping could not be used in court).

72. Robert Ellis Smith, *Ben Franklin's Web Site: Privacy and Curiosity from Plymouth Rock to the Internet* 160 (2000).

73. See Diffie & Landau, *Privacy on the Line*, 155–65.

74. See id., 161–62.

75. See id., 144.
76. Id., 173.
77. Samuel Dash, Richard Schwartz, & Robert Knowlton, *The Eavesdroppers* (1959).
78. 488 U.S. 445, 451–52 (1989).
79. 486 U.S. 35, 40 (1988).
80. Id.
81. 425 U.S. 435, 443 (1976).
82. Id., 442.
83. 442 U.S. 735, 743 (1979).
84. See Orin S. Kerr, U.S. Dep't of Justice, *Searching and Seizing Computers and Obtaining Electronic Evidence in Criminal Investigations*, § I.B.3 (Jan. 2001). Kerr, who wrote the DOJ's manual, is now a law professor and a leading expert in electronic surveillance law.
85. Id., § I.C.1(b)(iv).
86. Olmstead, 277 U.S. 438, 474 (1928) (Brandeis, J., dissenting).
87. See Jerry Berman & Deirdre Mulligan, "Privacy in the Digital Age: Work in Progress," 23 Nova L. Rev. 551, 563–64 (1999).
88. Fisher, "Congress," 152.
89. Stuntz, "O.J. Simpson," 857–58.
90. Ronan E. Degnan, "Obtaining Witnesses and Documents (or Things)," 108 F.R.D. 223, 232 (1986).
91. Stuntz, "O.J. Simpson," 864.
92. Grand juries are still used in some states as well as in the federal system. See Degnan, "Obtaining Witnesses," 229.
93. United States v. R. Enter., Inc., 498 U.S. 292, 301 (1991).
94. Stuntz, "Privacy's Problem," 1038.
95. Oklahoma Press Pub. Co. v. Walling Wage, and Hour Admin., 327 U.S. 186, 208–09 (1946).
96. Stuntz, "O.J. Simpson," 867.
97. Omnibus Crime and Control and Safe Streets Act of 1968, 18 U.S.C. §§ 2510–22 (2001).
98. 18 U.S.C. §§ 2510–22 (Wiretap Act); 18 U.S.C. §§ 2701–11 (Stored Communications Act); 18 U.S.C. §§ 3121–27 (Pen Register Act).
99. Id. § 2518.
100. See Orin S. Kerr, "Internet Surveillance Law after the USA-Patriot Act: The Big Brother That Isn't," 97 Nw. U. L. Rev. 607, 621 (2003).
101. 18 U.S.C. § 2518 (10)(a).
102. This conclusion is debatable, however, because telephone companies can also store telephone communications, and it is unlikely that the Court would go so far as to say that this fact eliminates any reasonable expectation of privacy in such communications.
103. 18 U.S.C. § 2510(17) (emphasis added).
104. Kerr, *Searching and Seizing*, § III.B.
105. Id., § III.D.1.
106. 18 U.S.C. § 2703(c)(1)(C).
107. 18 U.S.C. § 2703(d).
108. See, e.g., United States v. Hambrick, 55 F. Supp.2d 504 (W.D. Va. 1999). For a compelling argument for why electronic surveillance statutes should have an

exclusionary rule, see Orin S. Kerr, "Lifting the 'Fog' of Internet Surveillance: How a Suppression Remedy Would Change Computer Law," 54 Hastings L.J. 805 (2003).

109. 18 U.S.C. § 3121(a).

110. 18 U.S.C. § 3123(a).

111. "Upon application made under section 3122(a)(1), the court shall enter an ex parte order authorizing the installation and use of a pen register or trap and trace device. . . ." Id. §3123 (a)(1).

112. United States v. Fregoso, 60 F.3d 1314, 1320 (8th Cir. 1995). See also Kerr, *Searching and Seizing,* §IV.B.

113. See 29 U.S.C. §§ 3401–22.

114. 29 U.S.C. § 3407.

115. 29 U.S.C. § 3408.

116. 15 U.S.C. § 1681f.

117. 15 U.S.C. § 1681b(a)(1).

118. 47 U.S.C. § 551.

119. 47 U.S.C. § 551(h)(1).

120. 47 U.S.C. § 551(h)(2).

121. 18 U.S.C. § 2710(b)(2)(C).

122. Protection of patient-physician confidentiality extends back to the Hippocratic Oath, circa 400 BC. For a discussion of the extensive legal protection accorded to the patient-physician relationship, see Daniel J. Solove & Marc Rotenberg, *Information Privacy Law* 217–44 (2003).

123. Under the breach of confidentiality tort, doctors and banks can be liable for breaching confidentiality. See McCormick v. England, 494 S.E.2d 431 (S.C. Ct. App. 1997) (patient-physician confidentiality); Peterson v. Idaho First National Bank, 367 P.2d 284 (Idaho 1961) (bank-customer confidentiality).

124. 45 C.F.R. § 164.512(f)(1)(ii).

125. Id. § 164.512(f)(2).

126. 45 C.F.R. § 160.102.

127. Pew Internet & American Life Project, "Exposed Online: Why the New Federal Health Privacy Regulation Doesn't Offer Much Protection to Internet Users" 6–8 (Nov. 2001).

Notes to Chapter 11

1. For an extensive discussion about the complexity of defining privacy, see Daniel J. Solove, "Conceptualizing Privacy," 90 Cal. L. Rev. 1087 (2002).

2. Julie. C. Inness, *Privacy, Intimacy, and Isolation* 56 (1992) ("[P]rivacy's content covers *intimate* information, access, and decisions."); Tom Gerety, "Redefining Privacy," 12 Harv. C.R.-C.L. L. Rev. 233, 263 (1977) ("Intimacy is the chief restricting concept in the definition of privacy").

3. See Inness, *Intimacy,* 78 (intimate matters draw "their value and meaning from the agent's love, care, or liking").

4. See Smith v. Maryland, 442 U.S. 735, 740–41 n.5 (1979) (noting that "where an individual's subjective expectations had been 'conditioned' by influences alien to well-recognized Fourth Amendment freedoms, those subjective expectations obviously could play no meaningful role in ascertaining what the scope of Fourth Amendment protection was").

5. See Current Opinions of the Judicial Council of the American Medical Ass'n Canon 5.05 (1984) (observing that "the information disclosed to a physician during the course of the relationship between the physician and patient is confidential to the greatest possible degree").

6. See, e.g., Jaffee v. Redmond, 518 U.S. 1, 6–7 (1996) (recognizing psychotherapist-patient privilege and social worker-patient privilege under the Federal Rules of Evidence); Glen Weissenberger, *Federal Rules of Evidence: Rules, Legislative History, Commentary and Authority* § 501.8.

7. See, e.g., Hammonds v. AETNA Casualty and Surety Co., 243 F. Supp. 793, 799 (D. Ohio 1965).

8. See, e.g., Cal. Health & Safety Code § 199.21 (prohibiting disclosure of HIV test results); N.Y. Pub. Health L. § 17 (prohibiting disclosure of minors' medical records pertaining to sexually transmitted diseases and abortion).

9. See Weissenberger, *Evidence*, 190.

10. Christopher Slobogin, "Technologically-Assisted Physical Surveillance: The American Bar Association's Tentative Draft Standards," 10 Harv. J.L. & Tech. 383, 400 (1997).

11. 5 U.S.C. § 552(a)(5).

12. Anthony G. Amsterdam, "Perspectives on the Fourth Amendment," 58 Minn. L. Rev. 349, 404 (1974).

13. Edward J. Janger & Paul M. Schwartz, "The Gramm-Leach-Bliley Act, Information Privacy, and the Limits of Default Rules," 86 Minn. L. Rev. 1219, 1241–42 (2002).

14. Mechanisms of restriction are also embodied in evidentiary privileges. These privileges protect particular relationships, such as those between attorney and client, physicians and patients, and others. Privileges are needed to ensure that our conversations with our lawyers and doctors remain candid.

15. U.S. Const. amend V.

16. 116 U.S. 616, 638 (1886).

17. 255 U.S. 298, 309 (1921).

18. Warden v. Hayden, 387 U.S. 294, 309–10 (1967).

19. William J. Stuntz, "Privacy's Problem and the Law of Criminal Procedure," 93 Mich. L. Rev. 1016, 1050 (1995).

20. Louis Fisher, "Congress and the Fourth Amendment," 21 Ga. L. Rev. 107, 151 (1986).

21. 436 U.S. 547 (1978).

22. Id., 571.

23. Pub. L. No. 96-440, 94 Stat. 1879, codified at 42 U.S.C. § 2000aa.

24. William J. Stuntz, "O.J. Simpson, Bill Clinton, and the Transsubstantive Fourth Amendment," 114 Harv. L. Rev. 842, 857 (2001).

25. Carol S. Steiker, "Second Thoughts about First Principles," 107 Harv. L. Rev. 820, 834 (1994).

26. Robert Gellman, "Does Privacy Law Work?" in *Technology and Privacy: The New Landscape* 193, 198 (Philip E. Agre & Marc Rotenberg eds., 1997).

Notes to Chapter 12

1. Quoted in Daniel J. Solove & Marc Rotenberg, *Information Privacy Law* 507 (2003).

2. Amitai Etzioni, *The Limits of Privacy* 131 (1999).

3. Id.

4. See Shaun B. Spencer, "Reasonable Expectations and the Erosion of Privacy," 39 San Diego L. Rev. 843, 846–68 (2002) (discussing how courts, legislatures, and other government entities shape expectations of privacy).

5. Robert Ellis Smith, *Ben Franklin's Web Site* 23–25 (2000).

6. Id., 49; Priscilla M. Regan, *Legislating Privacy: Technology, Social Values, and Public Policy* 46–49 (1995).

7. Id., 50–51; see also David H. Flaherty, *Privacy in Colonial New England* 115–27 (1972).

8. Thomas Jefferson in 1798, quoted in David J. Seipp, *The Right to Privacy in American History* 1 (1978).

9. Quoted in Smith, *Franklin's Web Site,* 56–57.

10. Id., at 50–51. This law, which protects against prying into another's mail, is still valid today. See 42 U.S.C. § 1702.

11. 96 U.S. 727, 733 (1877).

12. See Regan, *Legislating Privacy,* 47; see also David J. Seipp, *Right to Privacy,* 43–50 (1978).

13. Samuel D. Warren & Louis D. Brandeis, "The Right to Privacy," 4 Harv. L. Rev. 193 (1890).

Index

About the Author

Daniel J. Solove is Associate Professor of Law at the George Washington University Law School. Previously, he taught at Seton Hall Law School. He is the author (with Marc Rotenbeg) of *Information Privacy Law.* Professor Solove received his J.D. from Yale Law School.